bars &
squares

more than **200** recipes

Jill Snider

Robert ROSE

Bars & Squares
Text copyright © 2006 Jill Snider
Photographs copyright © 2006 Robert Rose Inc.
Cover and text design copyright © 2006 Robert Rose Inc.

For complete cataloguing information, see page 252.

Disclaimer
The recipes in this book have been carefully tested by our kitchen and our tasters. To the best of our
knowledge, they are safe and nutritious for ordinary use and users. For those people with food or
other allergies, or who have special food requirements or health issues, please read the suggested
contents of each recipe carefully and determine whether or not they may create a problem for you.
All recipes are used at the risk of the consumer.

We cannot be responsible for any hazards, loss or damage which may occur as a result of any
recipe use.

For those with special needs, allergies, requirements or health problems, in the event of any
doubt, please contact your medical adviser prior to the use of any recipe.

Design & Production: PageWave Graphics Inc.
Editor: Judith Finlayson
Copy Editor: Julia Armstrong
Recipe Editor & Tester: Jennifer MacKenzie
Index: Belle Wong
Photography: Colin Erricson
Food Stylists: Kathryn Robertson & Kate Bush
Prop Stylist: Charlene Erricson

Cover: Caramel Honey Pecan Bars (see recipe, page 156) and Praline Bars (see recipe, page 70)

We acknowledge the financial support of the Government of Canada through the Book Publishing
Industry Development Program (BPIDP) for our publishing activities.

Published by: Robert Rose Inc.
120 Eglinton Ave. E., Suite 800, Toronto, Ontario, Canada M4P 1E2
Tel: (416) 322-6552   Fax: (416) 322-6936

Printed in Canada

1 2 3 4 5 6 7 8 9   TCP   14 13 12 11 10 09 08 07 06

Contents

Acknowledgments

I'd like to thank the many talented people who helped make the idea of a cookbook on bars and squares a reality: my publisher, Bob Dees, who firmly believes that bars are not only easy to make but delicious; Andrew Smith, Joseph Gisini, Kevin Cockburn and Daniella Zanchetta of PageWave Graphics, who work through editorial, design, layouts and production to put it all together; Brenda Venedam and Laurie Andrechuk, who accurately input the recipes; Judith Finlayson, Jennifer MacKenzie and Julia Armstrong for their editorial support; Kate Bush and Kathryn Robertson for their amazing food styling; Charlene Erricson for her prop styling; and Colin Erricson for his outstanding photographs, which make everything jump off the page.

I'd also like to thank my wonderful mother, Teddy. Although she is no longer with me, I know she would have loved the chapter on nuts. Her only comment would have been, "I think these could use a few more nuts."

Thanks also to my sister, Judie, and nieces, Jennie and Susie, for serving the recipes from my previous books at every possible occasion and showing my books to everyone they know. And to all my friends and neighbors who tasted and commented on the recipes and generously offered to take excess bars off my hands after the testing was done.

Introduction

The enticing aroma of home baking wafting from the kitchen usually brings back pleasant memories of everyday events as well as special occasions. As the ultimate comfort food, homemade cookies are probably remembered most warmly, but bar cookies, such as brownies and other kinds of squares, are simply an expedient way to produce similar results. If you're in the mood for cookies, think about bars. Nothing is easier to make; you just spread the batter in the pan, bake and cut. Bars usually contain relatively few ingredients, and the ones with multiple layers are likely to be simpler than they appear. The short baking time means you don't need to spend a lot of time in the kitchen. And since it's usually just as easy to make a big batch as a small one, one recipe can produce a large number, which is great for potlucks and bake sales.

Another advantage to bars is that they keep well when properly packed. They can be stored at room temperature, sometimes for as long as a week. They also freeze well, which means you can bake when it's convenient, getting a head start on special occasions and holiday baking. And they're extremely versatile. A luscious bar is just the thing for coffee breaks and snacks, school lunches and cookie swaps. With the addition of ice cream, a sundae sauce or fruit purée, they're easily transformed into a delicious dessert. Sometimes an addition as simple as a chocolate drizzle or a dusting of confectioner's (icing) sugar is all it takes to dress them up for a special occasion. You can also cut them into diamonds or triangles to vary the look.

Whatever your tastes, whatever the occasion and whatever your time frame, I'm sure you'll find a recipe in this book to meet your needs. Some recipes will seem familiar because they qualify as old favorites. Others will seem new and, I hope, will inspire you to experiment. Whether you're baking for everyday or for a special occasion, I sincerely hope you have fun and enjoy the experience.

Happy baking and happy eating!

— *Jill Snider*

Baking for Success

Baking bars and squares is relatively quick and easy compared with other types of baking. To achieve success, you need only the basics: reliable, easy-to-follow recipes, good equipment, quality ingredients and attention to detail. The following information will help you achieve the best results every time you bake.

Know Your Oven

Oven temperature plays a critical role in baking. If your oven is too hot, your baked goods will be overly brown on the surface and may not be completely cooked through. If it is not hot enough, you'll end up overcooking the interior to achieve the desirable degree of browning.

Ideally, the temperature you set determines how hot the oven will be once it's finished preheating. The problem is, most ovens are 25°F (10°C) hotter or cooler than their setting. Using your oven and observing how quickly or slowly it cooks in relation to the recipes you use will give you a general sense of whether it's hotter or cooler than the setting. A more accurate solution, which I recommend, is to purchase a reliable oven thermometer. This simple, inexpensive device will tell you the exact temperature your oven cooks at, allowing you to adjust the setting accordingly.

Convection Ovens

Convection ovens cook differently than traditional ones. If using a convection oven to bake the recipes in this book, check your manual and follow the instructions. Because convection ovens are more energy efficient than traditional models, you can either reduce the baking time by about 25 percent or lower the oven temperature by 25°F (10°C). As a rule of thumb, when baking anything for less than 15 minutes, reduce the oven temperature rather than the baking time. Convection ovens, like traditional ones, need to be preheated to the desired temperature when baking.

Use the Right Equipment

Having good-quality equipment makes a big difference when baking. You don't need to invest a lot of money — often the most expensive pans and utensils aren't the best. But take time to ensure you have what you need and that it works best for you.

Baking Pans

The quality of your pan can make a big difference to the end result, so it's worth doing research before buying. Ask for advice at a good kitchen supply store or read cooking magazines that test and rate equipment, such as *Cook's Illustrated.*

Good-quality, shiny metal pans are a great investment because they bake evenly and do not rust. The recipes in this book have been tested using metal pans; however, glass baking dishes also work well. Some pans cook more quickly than others. If using glass baking dishes or nonstick pans, especially dark ones, lower the oven temperature by 25°F (10°C).

Every recipe in this book calls for one of five pan sizes: an 8-inch (2 L) square; a 9-inch (2.5 L) square; a 13- by 9-inch (3 L) rectangle; a 15- by 10- by 1-inch (2 L) jelly roll pan; or a 17- by 11- by 1-inch (3 L) jelly roll pan.

For optimum results, use the pan size recommended in the recipe. A different size will affect the baking time and likely change the final result. If your pan is too small, it may overflow or produce underbaked, sunken, doughy bars. If too large, you'll end up with dry, overdone bars.

Bowls

Every kitchen needs a variety of bowls in different sizes for combining and mixing ingredients. Metal or glass bowls are preferable. Plastic does not work well for beating egg whites, as it retains oils, which can hamper results. Invest in a few bowls of each size: small, medium and large.

Wooden Spoons

These are great for mixing (although many bars can be done by hand) because the handles are sturdy and comfortable to hold.

Electric Mixer

An electric mixer is advantageous for mixing dense ingredients such as cream cheese or for beating egg whites to stiff peaks. It's also useful for achieving a smooth, creamy texture when making frostings. You can use either an electric countertop (stand) mixer or a good-quality hand mixer. If you do a lot of baking, the countertop model is much more efficient and easier to use.

TIP
Protecting Nonstick Surfaces
I prefer regular metal pans over nonstick ones because I like to cut my bars right in the pan. It wouldn't take long to ruin a nonstick surface that way. If your pans are nonstick, consider lining them with parchment paper or greased aluminum foil.

TIP
Beating Ingredients
Although many recipes call for an electric mixer, when beating ingredients such as butter and sugar, you can also use a wooden spoon as long as the butter is soft. Beat until smoothly blended, about 3 minutes.

Wire Whisks

Even if you use an electric mixer, you should have a couple of all-purpose wire whisks, in particular small and medium. These are useful for beating eggs before adding them to batters and for blending eggs and sugar and other mixtures that don't require much beating.

Pastry Blender

For layered bars that have a shortbread or cookie crust, I like to use a pastry blender to cut cold butter into the flour-sugar mixture. You can also use two knives, your fingers, a food processor or a mixer to achieve the desired crumble mixture. The butter should be cold and cubed, except when mixing by hand or using a mixer to prepare crusts, in which case it should be soft.

Spatulas

A couple of rubber spatulas are useful for folding in ingredients and scraping down the side of a mixing bowl. Offset spatulas, which have a bend in the metal spreader, are also useful for spreading mixtures evenly into the pan and for applying frostings. I like to have both a small and medium one in my kitchen. They're also handy for removing cut bars from the pan.

Racks

Wire racks are essential for cooling baked goods. Setting the pan on a wire rack allows circulating air to cool the bottom. It's a good idea to have a variety of sizes and shapes (square, rectangular) to suit whatever you're making. I recommend stainless-steel racks since they last a long time and won't rust.

Cooling and Cutting Bars and Squares

Most bar cookies should be cooled completely in the pan on a rack before cutting them. There are two exceptions: plain shortbreads and crisp bars are often given a preliminary cut while warm, then cut again after cooling completely. If they're not precut, they tend to shatter. If the bar has a sticky filling, it's a good idea to loosen the edge from the pan by running a knife around the edge while still warm. All the recipes indicate when to cut the bars.

Most bar cookies are best cut with a sharp knife. For optimum results, use a sturdy plastic knife to cut brownies and sticky or particularly moist bars or those baked in a nonstick pan. Use a wet knife to cut meringue-topped or cheesecake bars, wiping the crumbs and filling off after each cut. To keep the pan stationary while cutting, place a damp paper towel, dishcloth or computer mouse pad under it.

To prevent the pan from scratching and to make it easy to remove bars, line it with parchment paper or greased aluminum foil. Leave a substantial overhang to serve as a handle. Once cooled, you can lift the entire piece out of the pan and transfer it to a cutting board for easy cutting. Sometimes chilling firms up the bar, making it easier to remove in one piece.

Freezing Bars and Squares

Almost all bars and squares can be frozen with excellent results, even those with a glaze or frosting on top. However, if they have fresh fruit in the topping, like the Raspberry Truffle Brownies (see recipe, page 26), and you plan to freeze them, do not add the fruit before baking. Instead, it can be added as a garnish when the bars are served.

There are several ways to freeze bars, depending on how you plan to use them. If you want to serve the whole pan at once, then freeze it in a single piece. In this case, line the pan with parchment paper or greased aluminum foil and let it cool completely after baking. Once cool, lift the bar out of the pan, remove the paper, wrap the entire piece tightly in plastic wrap and freeze. If you prefer to use just a few pieces at a time, cut the cooled bars into pieces and freeze them individually wrapped or in small groups (up to a dozen). If they have a frosting or a glaze that's a bit soft, freeze them unwrapped for about one hour to firm up the frosting, then wrap tightly. Frozen bars and squares will keep fresh for about three months.

Bars and Squares Cutting Guide

Bar cookies can be cut in a variety of shapes and sizes. Whether you cut them into bars or squares is usually a matter of choice. We have specified cutting into bars or squares in the recipes, but in most cases either is fine. Bar cookies can also be cut into slender sticks, diamonds and triangles to add interest to any cookie platter.

Cutting Bars and Squares

See chart, next page.

Simplify Cutting

Use a ruler to mark the lines evenly. It's easier to keep the lines straight if you start from the middle of the pan or the middle of the side with an even number of rows. This works for all yields except when cutting 77 squares in a 17- by 11- by 1-inch jelly roll pan. In this case, cut parallel lines approximately $1\frac{1}{2}$ inches (4 cm) apart. When cutting squares in a rectangular pan, they won't be perfectly square, but close enough to fool most eyes.

TIP

A 9-inch (2.5 L) square pan will yield the same number of pieces as an 8-inch (2 L) square pan, but the pieces will be slightly larger.

Here's a guide to make cutting bars and squares easier:

SIZE OF PAN	DESIRED NUMBER OF BARS	NUMBER OF ROWS
8- by 8-inch (2 L) or 9- by 9-inch (2.5 L) pan	16 squares	4 rows by 4 rows
8- by 8-inch (2 L) or 9- by 9-inch (2.5 L) pan	18 bars	6 rows by 3 rows
8- by 8-inch (2 L) or 9- by 9-inch (2.5 L) pan	20 bars	4 rows by 5 rows
8- by 8-inch (2 L) or 9- by 9-inch (2.5 L) pan	24 bars	6 rows by 4 rows
8- by 8-inch (2 L) or 9- by 9-inch (2.5 L) pan	25 squares	5 rows by 5 rows
8- by 8-inch (2 L) or 9- by 9-inch (2.5 L) pan	32 bars	4 rows by 8 rows
8- by 8-inch (2 L) or 9- by 9-inch (2.5 L) pan	36 squares	6 rows by 6 rows
8- by 8-inch (2 L) or 9- by 9-inch (2.5 L) pan	48 bars	8 rows by 6 rows
13- by 9-inch (3 L) pan	20 bars	4 rows by 5 rows
13- by 9-inch (3 L) pan	24 squares	6 rows by 4 rows
13- by 9-inch (3 L) pan	32 bars	8 rows by 4 rows
13- by 9-inch (3 L) pan	36 bars	6 rows by 6 rows
13- by 9-inch (3 L) pan	48 bars	8 rows by 6 rows
13- by 9-inch (3 L) pan	54 bars	6 rows by 9 rows
15- by 10- by 1-inch (2 L) jelly roll pan	24 squares	6 rows by 4 rows
15- by 10- by 1-inch (2 L) jelly roll pan	36 squares	6 rows by 6 rows
15- by 10- by 1-inch (2 L) jelly roll pan	40 bars	10 rows by 4 rows
15- by 10- by 1-inch (2 L) jelly roll pan	48 squares	8 rows by 6 rows
15- by 10- by 1-inch (2 L) jelly roll pan	48 bars	12 rows by 4 rows
15- by 10- by 1-inch (2 L) jelly roll pan	54 squares	9 rows by 6 rows
15- by 10- by 1-inch (2 L) jelly roll pan	60 squares	10 rows by 6 rows
17- by 11- by 1-inch (3 L) jelly roll pan	24 squares	6 rows by 4 rows
17- by 11- by 1-inch (3 L) jelly roll pan	36 bars	6 rows by 6 rows
17- by 11- by 1-inch (3 L) jelly roll pan	40 bars	10 rows by 4 rows
17- by 11- by 1-inch (3 L) jelly roll pan	48 bars	12 rows by 4 rows
17- by 11- by 1-inch (3 L) jelly roll pan	54 squares	9 rows by 6 rows
17- by 11- by 1-inch (3 L) jelly roll pan	60 bars	12 rows by 5 rows
17- by 11- by 1-inch (3 L) jelly roll pan	66 bars	11 rows by 6 rows
17- by 11- by 1-inch (3 L) jelly roll pan	77 squares	11 rows by 7 rows

Cutting Triangles

To cut triangle shapes, cut squares in half diagonally.

Cutting Diamond Shapes

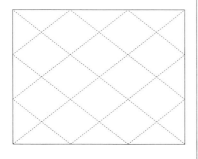

Diamond shapes work best in rectangular pans. To cut diamond shapes, cut 2 diagonal lines from corner to corner to meet in the middle. Then cut a series of parallel lines 1 or $1\frac{1}{2}$ inches (2.5 or 4 cm) apart. The odd-shaped pieces in the corners and at the ends of the pan are samples for the cook. They're also great to mix into or crumble on top of ice cream.

Storing Bars and Squares

To store bars and squares, layer them in a tightly covered cookie tin or container, with sheets of waxed paper between the layers. Or, if you prefer, wrap them individually in plastic wrap, then stack them in a container. Fragile or frosted bars are better stored in a single layer. They'll keep nicely at room temperature, unless the recipe specifies otherwise, for a few days.

Freezing

Most bars freeze very well, which is ideal for make-ahead baking. I've indicated on the recipe if freezing is not recommended or if it is excellent. Wrap cut bars in plastic wrap in small packages of 1 to 2 dozen and store in plastic freezer bags or freezer-safe containers with airtight lids for up to 3 months. The advantage of precutting is that you can take out what you need without having to thaw the whole package. Write the date on the package so you know when it was frozen. Defrost bars at room temperature in their wrappings. Some bars are even delicious eaten directly from the freezer or semi-frozen.

Fresh Fruit Yields

Often recipes call for a quantity of fruit such as 1 tsp (5 mL) lemon zest or 1 cup (250 mL) mashed banana. To make your baking easier, here are some measured yields for fresh fruits commonly used in making bars and squares.

Lemons: One medium lemon yields about 3 tbsp (45 mL) juice and 1 tbsp (15 mL) grated zest.

Limes: One lime yields about 3 tbsp (45 mL) juice and 1 tsp (5 mL) grated zest.

Oranges: One orange yields about $\frac{1}{3}$ cup (75 mL) juice and 4 tsp (20 mL) grated zest.

Apples: One pound (500 g), or 3 medium, yields about 2 cups (500 mL) sliced apples.

Bananas: One pound (500 g), or 2 or 3 large, yields about 1 cup (250 mL) mashed banana.

Strawberries: One pound (500 g) contains about $2\frac{2}{3}$ cups (650 mL) whole; 2 to $2\frac{1}{3}$ cups (500 to 575 mL) sliced; or $1\frac{2}{3}$ cups (400 mL) crushed.

Raspberries: One pound (500 g) contains about 4 cups (1 L) whole; or $1\frac{3}{4}$ to 2 cups (425 to 500 mL) crushed.

TIP

Don't store crisp and soft, moist bars together in the same container. The moisture in the soft bars will make the crisp ones soft.

Ingredient Equivalents

INGREDIENT	WEIGHT OR QUANTITY	QUANTITY
Apricots (dried)	1 lb (500 g)	3 cups (750 mL)
Butter, margarine	1 lb (500 g)	2 cups (500 mL)
Cherries, maraschino	about 33	10-oz (300 mL) jar
Chocolate, baking	8-oz (225 g) pkg	8 squares
Chocolate chips	6-oz (175 g) bag	1 cup (250 mL)
Cocoa powder, unsweetened	8-oz (250 g) container	about 3 cups (750 mL)
Coconut, shredded or flaked	7-oz (225 g) bag	2⅔ cups (650 mL)
Cranberries, dried	8-oz (250 g) bag	about 2⅔ cups (650 mL)
Cranberries, fresh or frozen	12-oz (340 g) bag	3 cups (750 mL)
Cream cheese	8-oz (250 g) pkg	1 cup (250 mL)
Dates (pitted), chopped	1 lb (500 g)	2½ cups (625 mL)
Egg product substitute	¼ cup (50 mL)	1 whole large egg
Figs (dried), chopped	1 lb (500 g)	2⅔ cups (650 mL)
Flour, all-purpose	1 lb (500 g)	3⅓ cups (825 mL)
Flour, whole wheat	1 lb (500 g)	3½ cups (875 mL)
Honey	16-oz (500 g) jar	about 1¼ cups (300 mL)
Marshmallows, large	10-oz (300 g) bag	40 marshmallows
	5 marshmallows	½ cup (125 mL)
	1 large marshmallow	10 miniature
Marshmallows, miniature	10½-oz (320 g) bag	5 cups (1.25 L)
	½ cup (125 mL)	45 marshmallows
	10 miniature	1 large marshmallow
Milk, evaporated	14-oz (388 mL) can	1½ cups (375 mL)
Nuts, shelled		
Almonds (whole)	1 lb (500 g)	3½ cups (875 mL)
Peanuts (whole)	1 lb (500 g)	3 cups (750 mL)
Pecans (halves)	1 lb (500 g)	4 cups (1 L)
Walnuts (halves)	1 lb (500 g)	6¼ cups (1.55 L)
Peanut butter	18-oz (550 g) jar	2 cups (500 mL)
Raisins	1 lb (500 g)	2¾ cups (675 mL)
Sour cream	8-oz (250 g) container	1 cup (250 mL)
Sugar, brown	2 lb (1 kg)	about 5 cups (1.25 L) packed
Sugar, granulated	1 lb (500 g)	2¼ cups (550 mL)
Sugar, confectioner's (icing)	2 lb (1 kg)	about 7½ cups (1.875 L)

Emergency Substitutions

It's always best to use ingredients the recipe calls for as that reflects how they were tested. But in a pinch, here are some substitutions you can use to avoid a last-minute trip to the store.

Leavenings

1 tsp (5 mL) baking powder =
¼ tsp (1 mL) baking soda plus
½ tsp (2 mL) cream of tartar

Flour

1 cup (250 mL) all-purpose flour, unsifted =
1 cup (250 mL) plus 2 tbsp (25 mL) cake and pastry flour, unsifted

1 cup (250 mL) cake and pastry flour, unsifted =
1 cup (250 mL) minus 2 tbsp (25 mL) all-purpose flour, unsifted

1 cup (250 mL) whole wheat flour =
1 cup (250 mL) all-purpose flour

Unbleached all-purpose flour and all-purpose flour can be used interchangeably.

Sweeteners

1 cup (250 mL) granulated sugar =
1 cup (250 mL) packed brown sugar

1 cup (250 mL) packed brown sugar =
1 cup (250 mL) granulated sugar mixed with 2 tbsp (25 mL) molasses

Corn syrup =
Equal amount of maple syrup

1 cup (250 mL) honey =
1¼ cups (300 mL) granulated sugar plus ¼ cup (50 mL) liquid

Chocolate

1 square (1oz/28 g) unsweetened chocolate =
3 tbsp (45 mL) cocoa powder plus 1 tbsp (15 mL) shortening, butter or margarine

1 cup (250 mL) semi-sweet chocolate chips =
6 squares (1oz/28 g each) semi-sweet chocolate, chopped

Dairy Products

1 cup (250 mL) butter =
1 cup (250 mL) hard margarine
OR IN A PINCH
1 cup (250 mL) shortening plus 2 tbsp (25 mL) water

1 cup (250 mL) buttermilk or soured milk =
1 tbsp (15 mL) lemon juice or vinegar plus milk to make 1 cup (250 mL) (let stand for 5 minutes, then stir before using)

1 cup (250 mL) whole milk =
1 cup (250 mL) 2% milk
OR
½ cup (125 mL) evaporated milk plus ½ cup (125 mL) water
OR
1 cup (250 mL) skim milk plus 2 tbsp (25 mL) butter

1 cup (250 mL) sour cream =
⅞ cup (225 mL) buttermilk or plain yogurt plus 3 tbsp (45 mL) butter

1 cup (250 mL) whipping (35%) cream (for use in cooking, not for whipping) =
¾ cup (175 mL) whole milk plus ⅓ cup (75 mL) butter

Egg

1 whole egg =
2 egg whites, 2 egg yolks plus 1 tbsp (15 mL) water
OR
¼ cup (50 mL) egg substitute product

Spices

1 tsp (5 mL) ground cinnamon =
1 tsp (5 mL) pumpkin pie spice

1 tsp (5 mL) ground allspice =
½ tsp (2 mL) ground cinnamon plus pinch ground cloves

1 tbsp (15 mL) chopped gingerroot =
1 tsp (5 mL) ground dried ginger
OR
1 tbsp (15 mL) minced candied ginger with sugar washed off

Miscellaneous

½ cup (125 mL) raisins =
½ cup (125 mL) dried cranberries, dried cherries, dried blueberries, chopped pitted prunes, apricots or dates

Nuts (any amount)

Almonds, hazelnuts, pecans, walnuts and peanuts are interchangeable in any of the recipes in this book.

Brownies

In my opinion, brownies are the ultimate square. Brownie lovers are divided into two camps: those who like a brownie that is rich, chewy, moist and fudge-like and those who prefer a tender, lighter version that resembles a cake in texture. You'll find plenty of both kinds here. You will also find blonde brownies, or blondies, which have the same dense, moist, chewy texture as their chocolate cousins but are a golden color and taste of butterscotch rather than chocolate.

Brownies are ultra-easy to make and very forgiving. Often they're a one-bowl recipe, mixed with a whisk or wooden spoon rather than an electric mixer. Depending on your mood and the availability of ingredients, you can make them plain and simple or load them up with all the trappings to add flavors and texture. Better still, any brownie or blondie can quickly become a sundae. Just add ice cream and sundae sauce.

Brownies keep well at room temperature for approximately a week and can be frozen for up to 3 months. When freezing, I prefer to cut them into individual pieces, wrap well in plastic wrap and store them in airtight freezer bags. If you plan to serve the entire bar at once, line the baking pan with parchment paper or greased aluminum foil, which overhangs the sides. After baking, allow the bar to cool completely in the pan. Using the overhanging paper or foil as a handle, lift it out in one big piece, remove the paper and wrap tightly in plastic wrap for freezing.

Double Fudge Brownies

This brownie looks like a relatively plain two-layer one, but it's actually an intensely flavored chocolate base topped with a rich creamy filling.

MAKES 20 TO 54 BARS OR SQUARES
(see Cutting Guide, page 10)

- **Preparation: 35 minutes**
- **Baking: 30 minutes**
- **Cooling: 4 hours**
- **Freezing: excellent**

TIPS

Rather than combine the dry ingredients in a bowl (Step 2), place a large piece of waxed paper on the counter. Spread the flour on the paper. Fill a fine sieve with the cocoa powder, baking powder and salt and tap until all have sifted through to the flour. Using the paper as a funnel, transfer the dry ingredients to the chocolate mixture.

If you don't have a mixer, you can make the frosting using a large wooden spoon. You may need a bit more cream to achieve a spreadable consistency. This frosting, like most, freezes well.

- **Preheat oven to 325°F (160°C)**
- **13- by 9-inch (3 L) cake pan, greased**

BROWNIE

1 cup	butter	250 mL
4	squares (1 oz/28 g each) unsweetened chocolate, chopped	4
2	eggs	2
2 cups	granulated sugar	500 mL
2 tsp	vanilla	10 mL
1¼ cups	all-purpose flour	300 mL
3 tbsp	unsweetened cocoa powder, sifted	45 mL
¼ tsp	baking powder	1 mL
¼ tsp	salt	1 mL

CHOCOLATE FROSTING

½ cup	butter	125 mL
2	squares (1 oz/28 g each) unsweetened chocolate, chopped	2
4 cups	confectioner's (icing) sugar, sifted	1 L
5 to 6 tbsp	half-and-half (10%) cream	75 to 90 mL
1 tsp	vanilla	5 mL

1. *Brownie:* In a saucepan over low heat, melt butter and chocolate, stirring constantly, until smooth. Remove from heat and let cool slightly.

2. In a bowl, whisk eggs until blended. Whisk in sugar and vanilla until combined. Whisk in chocolate mixture. Combine flour, cocoa, baking powder and salt. Add to chocolate mixture and mix well. Spread evenly in prepared pan.

3. Bake in preheated oven until set, 25 to 30 minutes. Let cool for 5 minutes in pan on rack.

4. *Chocolate Frosting:* Meanwhile, in a small saucepan over low heat, melt butter and chocolate, stirring until smooth. Remove from heat and let cool slightly. In a bowl, combine confectioner's sugar, melted chocolate mixture, 5 tbsp (75 mL) of the cream and vanilla. Using a mixer, beat on low speed until smooth, adding a little more cream, if necessary, to make a spreadable consistency.

5. Drop frosting by spoonfuls onto the hot base, then spread gently to cover. Let cool for 4 hours in pan on rack to completely set. Cut into bars or squares.

Moist 'n' Chewy Chocolate Brownies

These brownies contain a little less chocolate than some of the more luscious ones, but they still have rich chocolate flavor. Their texture is pleasantly moist and chewy.

MAKES 16 TO 48 BARS OR SQUARES
(see Cutting Guide, page 10)

- **Preparation: 15 minutes**
- **Baking: 30 minutes**
- **Freezing: excellent**

TIPS

These brownies are quite dense and chewy. If you prefer them more cake-like, add an egg.

Instead of greasing pans, line them with parchment paper, which extends up the sides and over the edges so you can lift out the brownies in a block. Spraying the pan lightly with cooking spray or greasing it lightly before adding the parchment helps the paper to stick, preventing it from shifting.

- **Preheat oven to 375°F (190°C)**
- **9-inch (2.5 L) square cake pan, greased**

½ cup	butter	125 mL
3	squares (1 oz/28 g each) unsweetened chocolate, chopped	3
1¼ cups	granulated sugar	300 mL
1½ tsp	vanilla	7 mL
3	eggs	3
⅔ cup	all-purpose flour	150 mL
½ tsp	baking powder	2 mL
¼ tsp	salt	1 mL

1. In a saucepan over low heat, melt butter and chocolate, stirring constantly, until smooth. Remove from heat. Stir in sugar and vanilla, mixing well. Whisk in eggs, one at a time, beating lightly after each addition.

2. Combine flour, baking powder and salt. Stir into chocolate mixture until well blended. Spread evenly in prepared pan.

3. Bake in preheated oven just until set, 25 to 30 minutes. Let cool completely in pan on rack. Cut into bars or squares.

Variations

Add ½ cup (125 mL) chopped nuts after the chocolate and dry mixtures have been combined.

Frost with a chocolate frosting. Chocolate Frosting (see recipe, page 16) and Cocoa Frosting (see recipe, page 18) both work well with this brownie.

Chunky Chocolate Walnut Brownies

You can't go wrong with this — a great plain chocolate brownie with lots of nuts. If you're feeling in the mood for a little excess, add the yummy Cocoa Frosting. Either way, these are a winner.

MAKES 16 TO 48 BARS OR SQUARES
(see Cutting Guide, page 10)

- **Preparation: 15 minutes**
- **Baking: 35 minutes**
- **Freezing: excellent without frosting**

TIPS

If you're using a stand mixer with a large bowl to mix this brownie, whisk the eggs until frothy before adding them. There is not enough volume in the eggs to achieve this result with the mixer. Then continue with Step 2.

In this recipe, beating the eggs and sugar thoroughly produces brownies with a soft, light texture. If you beat the mixture less, or by hand using a wooden spoon, you'll have a firmer brownie.

- **Preheat oven to 350°F (180°C)**
- **9-inch (2.5 L) square cake pan, greased**

BROWNIE

5	squares (1 oz/28 g each) unsweetened chocolate, chopped	5
2/3 cup	butter	150 mL
3	eggs	3
1 2/3 cups	granulated sugar	400 mL
1 1/2 tsp	vanilla	7 mL
1 cup	all-purpose flour	250 mL
1 cup	coarsely chopped walnuts	250 mL

COCOA FROSTING, OPTIONAL

3 1/2 cups	confectioner's (icing) sugar	875 mL
1/2 cup	unsweetened cocoa powder	125 mL
1/2 cup	butter, softened	125 mL
5 to 6 tbsp	half-and-half (10%) cream	75 to 90 mL

1. *Brownie:* In a saucepan over low heat, melt chocolate and butter, stirring constantly, until smooth. Remove from heat. Set aside.

2. In a large bowl, using an electric mixer on high speed, beat eggs until frothy. Gradually add sugar, beating until thick and creamy, about 5 minutes. Stir in chocolate mixture and vanilla. Stir in flour, mixing well. Stir in walnuts. Spread evenly in prepared pan.

3. Bake in preheated oven just until set, 30 to 35 minutes. Let cool completely in pan on rack. Frost, if desired. Cut into bars or squares.

4. *Cocoa Frosting (if using):* Sift together confectioner's sugar and cocoa powder. In a bowl, using an electric mixer on medium speed, beat butter and half of the sugar mixture. Add 5 tbsp (75 mL) of the cream, beating until smooth. Gradually add remaining confectioner's sugar and cocoa mixture, beating until smooth and adding more cream, as necessary, to make a spreadable consistency.

Variation
Replace walnuts with pecans.

Decadent Mocha Brownies

With these delicious brownies you can have your coffee and eat it, too. The espresso adds amazing flavor.

MAKES 16 TO 48 BARS OR SQUARES
(see Cutting Guide, page 10)

- **Preparation: 15 minutes**
- **Baking: 30 minutes**
- **Freezing: excellent**

TIPS

If you prefer a more intense chocolate flavor, use bittersweet chocolate in place of semi-sweet.

Instant espresso coffee powder is usually sold in specialty coffee stores, such as Starbucks. If you don't have it, substitute 2 tbsp (25 mL) instant coffee powder in this recipe.

These brownies have a wonderful texture. The key is to not overbeat the batter and to not overbake them. They should still be a little soft in the center when you remove them from the oven. They'll firm up when cooling.

For a fabulous dessert, try these with a scoop of ice cream and warm chocolate sauce.

- **Preheat oven to 350°F (180°C)**
- **8-inch (2 L) square cake pan, greased**

8	squares (1 oz/28 g each) semi-sweet chocolate, chopped	8
¼ cup	butter	50 mL
2	eggs	2
¾ cup	packed brown sugar	175 mL
1½ tsp	vanilla	7 mL
¾ cup	all-purpose flour	175 mL
1 tbsp	instant espresso coffee powder (see Tips, left)	15 mL
1 tsp	baking powder	5 mL
⅔ cup	semi-sweet chocolate chips	150 mL

1. In a saucepan over low heat, melt chocolate and butter, stirring constantly, until smooth. Remove from heat. Set aside.

2. In a large bowl, whisk eggs, brown sugar and vanilla just until blended. Stir in chocolate mixture. Stir in flour, coffee powder and baking powder, mixing well. Stir in chocolate chips. Spread evenly in prepared pan.

3. Bake in preheated oven until almost set and still a little soft in the center, 25 to 30 minutes. Let cool completely in pan on rack. Cut into bars or squares.

Variations

Reduce the chocolate chips to ⅓ cup (75 mL) and add ⅓ cup (75 mL) chopped pecans or walnuts.

Omit the coffee powder. You'll still have a wonderful plain brownie.

Brownie Overload

This is the ultimate brownie. It's a real hit at bake sales. You couldn't stir any more ingredients into the batter if you tried.

MAKES 20 TO 54 BARS OR SQUARES
(see **Cutting Guide, page 10**)

- **Preparation: 20 minutes**
- **Baking: 35 minutes**
- **Freezing: excellent**

TIPS

To ease cleanup, rather than combining the dry ingredients in a bowl, place a large piece of waxed paper on the counter. Spread the flour on the paper. Fill a fine sieve with the cocoa powder, baking soda and salt and tap until all have sifted through to the flour. Using the paper as a funnel, transfer the dry ingredients to the chocolate mixture. That way, there's one less bowl to wash.

When baking, always have eggs at room temperature to obtain the best volume.

This method differs from some brownies in that the eggs are beaten thoroughly, resulting in a beautiful, shiny top.

- **Preheat oven to 350°F (180°C)**
- **13- by 9-inch (3 L) cake pan, greased**

1 cup	butter	250 mL
2½ cups	coarsely chopped bittersweet chocolate, divided	625 mL
2 cups	all-purpose flour	500 mL
½ cup	unsweetened cocoa powder, sifted (see Tips, page 28)	125 mL
1 tsp	baking soda	5 mL
½ tsp	salt	2 mL
4	eggs	4
1 cup	granulated sugar	250 mL
1 cup	packed brown sugar	250 mL
2 tsp	vanilla	10 mL
2 cups	coarsely chopped deluxe mixed nuts (no peanuts, about 8 oz/250 g)	500 mL
1 cup	dried cranberries	250 mL

1. In a saucepan over low heat, melt butter and 1½ cups (375 mL) of the chocolate, stirring constantly, until smooth. Remove from heat. Let cool for 10 minutes.

2. Combine flour, cocoa, baking soda and salt. Mix well.

3. In a bowl, using an electric mixer on medium speed, beat eggs, granulated and brown sugars and vanilla until thick and creamy, about 2 minutes. Add melted chocolate mixture and mix on low speed until blended. Stir in flour mixture, mixing just to combine. Stir in nuts, remaining 1 cup (250 mL) chocolate and cranberries and mix well (the batter will be very thick). Spread evenly in prepared pan.

4. Bake in preheated oven until set, 30 to 35 minutes. Let cool completely in pan on rack. Cut into bars or squares.

Variations

Replace dried cranberries with dried cherries or raisins.

Substitute an equal quantity of good-quality chocolate chips for the chopped chocolate.

Toffee Brownies

◆

Keep this recipe in mind for those days when you want to bake but don't have much time. It's extra easy to make, with no sacrifice on taste.

MAKES 16 TO 48 BARS OR SQUARES (see Cutting Guide, page 10)

- **Preparation: 15 minutes**
- **Baking: 30 minutes**
- **Freezing: excellent**

TIPS

For best results, always have your ingredients at room temperature before you start to bake. This is especially important if you're adding eggs to a warm mixture.

Don't overbeat brownie batter or it will rise too high and then collapse.

My favorite brand of toffee bits is Skor, and I buy them in bulk. Others, such as Heath bits, are also available in bulk, but I don't recommend being over-inventoried on this product. If toffee bits become stale, they take longer to soften.

- **Preheat oven to 350°F (180°C)**
- **8-inch (2 L) square cake pan, greased**

2	squares (1 oz/28 g each) unsweetened chocolate, chopped	2
½ cup	butter	125 mL
1 cup	granulated sugar	250 mL
2	eggs	2
1 tsp	vanilla	5 mL
¾ cup	all-purpose flour	175 mL
¾ cup	toffee bits	175 mL
⅔ cup	miniature semi-sweet chocolate chips	150 mL

1. In a saucepan over low heat, melt chocolate and butter, stirring constantly, until smooth. Remove from heat. Stir in sugar, mixing until smooth. Whisk in eggs, one at a time, mixing lightly after each addition. Stir in vanilla and flour, mixing well.

2. Combine toffee bits and chocolate chips. Set aside ⅓ cup (75 mL) for topping. Stir remainder into batter. Spread evenly in prepared pan. Sprinkle reserved toffee-chocolate mixture evenly on top.

3. Bake in preheated oven until set, 25 to 30 minutes. Let cool completely in pan on rack. Cut into bars or squares.

Variations

Replace toffee bits and chocolate chips with 1¼ cups (300 mL) chopped chocolate toffee bar. Reserve ⅓ cup (75 mL) for topping.

Add ⅓ cup (75 mL) chopped almonds to the batter along with the chocolate chips.

Chocolate Toffee Bar Brownies

◆

Crunchy toffee bars add flourish to this fabulous version.

MAKES 20 TO 54 BARS OR SQUARES
(see **Cutting Guide**, **page 10**)

- **Preparation: 20 minutes**
- **Cooling: 30 minutes**
- **Baking: 30 minutes**
- **Freezing: excellent**

TIPS

If you prefer a brownie with a lighter texture, beat eggs, sugar and flavorings, such as almond extract, separately until thick and creamy. Stir chocolate mixture then dry ingredients into egg mixture.

Rather than dirty a bowl when combining the dry ingredients (Step 2), place a large piece of waxed paper on the counter. Spread the flour on the paper. Sprinkle with the baking soda and salt. Using the paper as a funnel, transfer the dry ingredients to the chocolate mixture.

- **Preheat oven to 350°F (180°C)**
- **13- by 9-inch (3 L) cake pan, greased**

3½	squares (1 oz/28 g each) unsweetened chocolate, chopped	3½
¾ cup	butter	175 mL
1⅔ cups	granulated sugar	400 mL
3	eggs	3
½ tsp	almond extract	2 mL
¾ cup	all-purpose flour	175 mL
¼ tsp	baking soda	1 mL
¼ tsp	salt	1 mL
1 cup	coarsely chopped almonds	250 mL
4	crunchy chocolate-covered toffee bars (1.4 oz/39 g each), chopped	4

1. In a saucepan over low heat, melt chocolate and butter, stirring constantly, until smooth. Remove from heat. Let cool to lukewarm, about 30 minutes.

2. Whisk in sugar until well blended. Add eggs, one at a time, whisking lightly after each addition. Stir in almond extract. Combine flour, baking soda and salt. Stir into chocolate mixture, mixing until smooth. Stir in almonds. Spread evenly in prepared pan.

3. Bake in preheated oven until set, 25 to 30 minutes. Immediately sprinkle chopped chocolate bars on top. Let cool completely in pan on rack. Cut into bars or squares.

Variation
Replace almonds with hazelnuts and almond extract with 1 tsp (5 mL) vanilla.

Caramel Brownies

The name doesn't capture the amount of flavor packed in just one square. Rich, chewy and loaded with gooey caramel, chocolate chips and crunchy pecans, these brownies are sensational.

MAKES 20 TO 54 BARS OR SQUARES
(see Cutting Guide, page 10)

- Preparation: 25 minutes
- Baking: 42 minutes
- Freezing: excellent

TIPS

A reliable kitchen scale is a good investment. Having a scale allows you to purchase ingredients in bulk, then weigh out exactly what you need.

Because oven temperatures vary, I recommend that you treat all recipe times as guidelines and begin checking what you're baking well before the minimum recommended time.

- Preheat oven to 350°F (180°C)
- 13- by 9-inch (3 L) cake pan, greased

2 cups	granulated sugar	500 mL
²/₃ cup	unsweetened cocoa powder, sifted	150 mL
1 cup	vegetable oil	250 mL
4	eggs	4
¼ cup	milk	50 mL
1½ cups	all-purpose flour	375 mL
1 tsp	baking powder	5 mL
½ tsp	salt	2 mL
1 cup	semi-sweet chocolate chips	250 mL
1 cup	chopped pecans, divided	250 mL
14 oz	soft caramels, unwrapped (about 50)	400 g
1	can (10 oz/300 mL) sweetened condensed milk	1

1. In a large bowl, whisk sugar, cocoa, oil, eggs and milk until smooth. Combine flour, baking powder and salt. Stir into cocoa mixture, mixing well. Stir in chocolate chips and ½ cup (125 mL) of the pecans. Spread two-thirds of the batter evenly in prepared pan. Bake in preheated oven for 12 minutes.

2. Meanwhile, in a heavy saucepan over low heat, heat caramels and sweetened condensed milk, stirring constantly, until caramels are melted and mixture is smooth. Pour over partially baked brownie layer. Sprinkle remaining pecans on top. Drop remaining chocolate batter by spoonfuls over caramel layer. Spread gently, then swirl with the tip of a knife to marbleize the uncooked chocolate batter and caramel layers.

3. Bake in preheated oven just until set, 25 to 30 minutes. Let cool completely in pan on rack. Cut into bars or squares.

Variation
Replace pecans with peanuts or walnuts.

Raspberry Truffle Brownies

Make these luscious brownies for any occasion — I guarantee success.

MAKES 16 TO 48 BARS OR SQUARES
(see Cutting Guide, page 10)

- **Preparation: 20 minutes**
- **Baking: 30 minutes**
- **Freezing: excellent without berries**

TIPS

You can use regular raspberry jam, with seeds, in place of the seedless, but it will have less raspberry flavor.

If you prefer more raspberry flavor and a hint of pink, add 2 tbsp (25 mL) regular raspberry jam to the topping. The seedless version doesn't work as well because the red color isn't as intense.

If you plan to freeze these brownies, don't add the raspberries until serving.

White chocolate has become a popular ingredient in baking. However, it's not really chocolate at all but rather a blend of sugar, cocoa butter, milk solids and vanilla. Because it doesn't melt as easily as regular chocolate, it's particularly important to use low heat and stir it constantly.

- **Preheat oven to 350°F (180°C)**
- **8-inch (2 L) square cake pan, greased**

BROWNIE

3	squares (1 oz/28 g each) unsweetened chocolate	3
1/3 cup	butter	75 mL
1/4 cup	seedless raspberry jam (see Tips, left)	50 mL
2	eggs	2
1 cup	granulated sugar	250 mL
1/2 cup	all-purpose flour	125 mL

TOPPING

2 tbsp	whipping (35%) cream	25 mL
2 tbsp	butter	25 mL
4	squares (1 oz/28 g each) white chocolate, chopped	4
1 1/4 cups	fresh raspberries	300 mL

1. *Brownie:* In a saucepan over low heat, melt unsweetened chocolate, butter and jam, stirring constantly, until smooth. Remove from heat.

2. In a bowl, whisk eggs and sugar until frothy. Whisk in chocolate mixture, then flour, mixing until smooth. Spread evenly in prepared pan.

3. Bake in preheated oven until set, 25 to 30 minutes. Let cool completely in pan on rack.

4. *Topping:* In a small saucepan over low heat, heat cream, butter and white chocolate, stirring until smooth. Let cool for 30 minutes. Spread evenly over brownie. Top with raspberries and chill until cold. Cut into bars or squares.

Variation
If you prefer an intensely chocolate brownie, replace the white chocolate in the topping with semi-sweet chocolate.

Raspberry Cheesecake Brownies

The slightly tart taste of raspberries in a creamy cheesecake topping, coupled with a dense, moist chocolate base, is a sensational combination.

MAKES 16 TO 48 BARS OR SQUARES
(see Cutting Guide, page 10)

- **Preparation: 25 minutes**
- **Baking: 45 minutes**
- **Chilling: overnight**
- **Freezing: excellent without raspberries on top (see Tips, below)**

TIPS

When beating this topping, and others with comparable small volumes, use a hand mixer and a small bowl, or beat with a wooden spoon. The volume is insufficient to work in a stand mixer with a large bowl.

If you plan to freeze these brownies, omit the raspberries before baking and add them as a garnish when serving.

If using frozen raspberries, scatter them over the topping in their frozen state so they'll hold their shape better.

- **Preheat oven to 350°F (180°C)**
- **9-inch (2.5 L) square cake pan, greased**

BROWNIE

4	squares (1 oz/28 g each) unsweetened chocolate, chopped	4
½ cup	butter	125 mL
2 tbsp	unsweetened cocoa powder, sifted (see Tips, page 28)	25 mL
1 tbsp	instant coffee granules	15 mL
1⅓ cups	granulated sugar	325 mL
1 tsp	vanilla	5 mL
¼ tsp	salt	1 mL
3	eggs	3
1 cup	all-purpose flour	250 mL

TOPPING

4 oz	cream cheese, softened	125 g
¼ cup	granulated sugar	50 mL
1	egg	1
1 tbsp	grated lemon zest	15 mL
1 tbsp	freshly squeezed lemon juice	15 mL
1¼ cups	fresh or individually frozen raspberries (see Tips, left)	300 mL

1. *Brownie:* In a saucepan over low heat, combine chocolate, butter, cocoa and coffee granules, stirring constantly, until chocolate is melted and mixture is smooth. Remove from heat. Stir in sugar, vanilla and salt. Whisk in eggs, one at a time, mixing well after each addition. Stir in flour, mixing until smooth. Spread evenly in prepared pan. Set aside.

2. *Topping:* In a bowl, using an electric mixer on medium speed, beat cream cheese, sugar, egg, lemon zest and juice until smooth. Spread evenly over unbaked base. Scatter raspberries over top.

3. Bake in preheated oven just until set, 40 to 45 minutes. Let cool completely in pan on rack. Chill overnight. Cut into bars or squares.

Chocolate Chunk Banana Brownies

This very chocolaty brownie is flavored with mashed bananas and filled with chunks of chocolate and walnuts.

MAKES 20 TO 54 BARS OR SQUARES
(see Cutting Guide, page 10)

- **Preparation: 20 minutes**
- **Baking: 30 minutes**
- **Freezing: excellent**

TIPS

These brownies are nice plain, dusted with confectioner's (icing) sugar or topped with a chocolate frosting (see recipes, pages 16 and 18).

For recipes calling for chopped chocolate, I like to buy large bittersweet chocolate bars and chop them to the size of chips.

Always sift cocoa before using to get rid of any lumps that have formed during storage.

- **Preheat oven to 350°F (180°C)**
- **13- by 9-inch (3 L) cake pan, greased**

1 cup	granulated sugar	250 mL
⅓ cup	vegetable oil	75 mL
2	eggs	2
1 cup	mashed ripe banana (2 large bananas)	250 mL
¾ cup	unsweetened cocoa powder, sifted (see Tips, left)	175 mL
1 cup	all-purpose flour	250 mL
1 tsp	baking powder	5 mL
½ tsp	baking soda	2 mL
¼ tsp	salt	1 mL
1½ cups	chopped semi-sweet chocolate	375 mL
1⅓ cups	coarsely chopped walnuts	325 mL

1. In a large bowl, using an electric mixer on medium speed, beat sugar, oil and eggs until thick and light, about 2 minutes. Add banana and cocoa and beat on low speed.

2. Combine flour, baking powder, baking soda and salt. Add to cocoa mixture, beating on low speed just to blend. Stir in chopped chocolate and walnuts. Spread evenly in prepared pan.

3. Bake in preheated oven just until set, 25 to 30 minutes. Let cool completely in pan on rack. Cut into bars or squares.

Variations

Replace chocolate chunks with chocolate chips.

Substitute peanut butter chips for the chopped chocolate and coarsely chopped peanuts for the walnuts.

Amazing Amaretto Brownies

Slightly chewy and a little sweet, these have a delicious almond flavor.

MAKES 20 TO 54 BARS OR SQUARES (see Cutting Guide, page 10)

- **Preparation: 25 minutes**
- **Baking: 25 minutes**
- **Freezing: excellent**

TIPS

To ease cleanup, rather than combining the dry ingredients in a bowl, place a large piece of waxed paper on the counter. After measuring, combine the flour, baking powder, salt and ground almonds on the paper. Use the paper as a funnel to transfer the dry ingredients to the chocolate mixture.

Amaretto is the most common almond liqueur. If you prefer, substitute a mixture of almond extract and water for the liqueur. When making the frosting, replace the 1 tbsp (15 mL) almond liqueur with ¼ tsp (1 mL) almond extract mixed with 1 tbsp (15 mL) water. Use ½ tsp (2 mL) almond extract mixed with 2 tbsp (25 mL) water in the batter.

- **Preheat oven to 350°F (180°C)**
- **13- by 9-inch (3 L) cake pan, greased**

BROWNIE

1 cup	sliced almonds, toasted, divided	250 mL
8	squares (1 oz/28 g each) semi-sweet chocolate, chopped	8
⅓ cup	butter	75 mL
1 cup	granulated sugar	250 mL
2	eggs	2
2 tbsp	almond liqueur	25 mL
1¼ cups	all-purpose flour	300 mL
1 tsp	baking powder	5 mL
¼ tsp	salt	1 mL

FROSTING

¼ cup	butter, softened	50 mL
3 cups	confectioner's (icing) sugar, sifted	750 mL
2 tbsp	milk	25 mL
1 tbsp	almond liqueur	15 mL

1. *Brownie:* In a food processor, process ⅓ cup (75 mL) of the almonds until ground. Chop remaining almonds. Set aside.

2. In a saucepan over low heat, melt chocolate and butter, stirring constantly, until smooth. Remove from heat. Stir in sugar, mixing until smooth. Add eggs, one at a time, whisking lightly after each addition. Stir in liqueur.

3. Combine flour, baking powder, salt and ground almonds. Stir into chocolate mixture, mixing until smooth. Spread evenly in prepared pan.

4. Bake in preheated oven just until set, 20 to 25 minutes. Let cool completely in pan on rack.

5. *Frosting:* In a bowl, using an electric mixer on medium speed, beat butter, confectioner's sugar, milk and liqueur until smooth and creamy. Spread over brownie. Sprinkle with reserved chopped almonds. Cut into bars or squares.

Variation

Fold the chopped almonds into the batter after the chocolate mixture has been blended in, instead of sprinkling them on top.

Cappuccino Brownies

I love to pair these flavorful brownies with a steaming mug of cappuccino.

MAKES 16 TO 48 BARS OR SQUARES
(see Cutting Guide, page 10)

- **Preparation: 25 minutes**
- **Baking: 35 minutes**
- **Chilling: 1 hour**
- **Freezing: excellent**

TIPS

Instant espresso powder is usually sold in specialty coffee stores, such as Starbucks. If you don't have it, substitute 2 tbsp (25 mL) instant coffee granules in the Brownie and 1 tbsp (15 mL) in the Frosting. Crush the granules with the back of a spoon before adding to the recipe.

When freezing brownies, I recommend cutting and wrapping individual squares. They thaw quickly, and you can take out only as many as you need.

Brownies usually rise during baking then collapse slightly on cooling. This is what creates that dense, moist, chewy texture.

- **Preheat oven to 350°F (180°C)**
- **8-inch (2 L) square cake pan, greased**

BROWNIE

1 cup	semi-sweet chocolate chips	250 mL
½ cup	butter	125 mL
1 cup	granulated sugar	250 mL
1 tsp	vanilla	5 mL
2	eggs	2
1 cup	all-purpose flour	250 mL
1 tbsp	instant espresso coffee powder	15 mL
½ tsp	baking powder	2 mL
¼ tsp	salt	1 mL

FROSTING

1½ tsp	instant espresso coffee powder	7 mL
1 to 2 tbsp	milk or cream	15 to 25 mL
2 cups	confectioner's (icing) sugar, sifted	500 mL
¼ cup	butter, softened	50 mL

GLAZE

1 cup	semi-sweet chocolate chips	250 mL
⅓ cup	whipping (35%) cream	75 mL

1. *Brownie:* In a saucepan over low heat, melt chocolate chips and butter, stirring constantly, until smooth. Whisk in sugar and vanilla, mixing well. Add eggs, one at a time, whisking lightly after each addition.

2. Combine flour, espresso powder, baking powder and salt. Stir into chocolate mixture, mixing well. Spread evenly in prepared pan.

3. Bake in preheated oven just until set, 30 to 35 minutes. Let cool completely in pan on rack.

4. *Frosting:* In a bowl, combine espresso powder and 1 tbsp (15 mL) milk, stirring to dissolve. Add confectioner's sugar and butter. Using an electric mixer, beat on low speed to blend then on medium speed until creamy, adding more milk, if necessary, to make a smooth, spreadable consistency. Spread evenly over brownie. Chill to harden, about 1 hour.

5. *Glaze:* In a saucepan over low heat, combine chocolate chips and whipping cream, stirring constantly, until melted and smooth. Let cool to lukewarm. Spread over frosting. Chill until chocolate is set, about 1 hour. Cut into bars or squares.

Coconut Marshmallow Brownies

A line of white marshmallows between two layers of dark chocolate makes this attractive and tasty.

MAKES 16 TO 48 BARS OR SQUARES
(see Cutting Guide, page 10)

- **Preparation: 25 minutes**
- **Baking: 32 minutes**
- **Freezing: excellent**

TIPS

Make sure your marshmallows are fresh and soft. Stale ones don't soften properly.

I have specified sweetened coconut because it seems to be more readily available than the unsweetened variety. But sweetened and unsweetened coconut can be used interchangeably in any recipe to suit your preference.

- **Preheat oven to 375°F (190°C)**
- **8-inch (2 L) square cake pan, greased**

BROWNIE

1	square (1 oz/28 g) unsweetened chocolate, chopped	1
2 tbsp	butter	25 mL
¾ cup	all-purpose flour	175 mL
1 tsp	baking powder	5 mL
¼ tsp	salt	1 mL
2	eggs	2
1¼ cups	packed brown sugar	300 mL
½ cup	flaked sweetened coconut (see Tips, left)	125 mL
⅓ cup	chopped walnuts	75 mL
20	marshmallows	20

TOPPING

2	squares (1 oz/28 g each) unsweetened chocolate, chopped	2
2 tbsp	butter	25 mL
1 cup	confectioner's (icing) sugar, sifted	250 mL
1 tsp	vanilla	5 mL
1 to 2 tbsp	whipping (35%) cream	15 to 25 mL

1. *Brownie:* In a saucepan over low heat, melt chocolate and butter, stirring constantly, until smooth. Remove from heat. Set aside.

2. Combine flour, baking powder and salt. In a bowl, using an electric mixer on high speed, beat eggs and brown sugar until light and creamy. Stir in flour mixture, mixing well. Divide batter in half. Stir coconut into one half of the batter. Stir chocolate mixture and walnuts into the other half. Spread coconut batter in prepared pan. Drop chocolate batter by spoonfuls over top. Spread evenly.

3. Bake in preheated oven just until set, 25 to 30 minutes. Cut marshmallows in half. Place on hot brownie. Bake for 2 minutes longer to soften. Let cool completely in pan on rack.

4. *Topping:* In a small saucepan over low heat, melt chocolate and butter, stirring constantly, until smooth. Remove from heat and let cool for 10 minutes. Whisk in confectioner's sugar, vanilla and just enough cream to make a smooth, spreadable consistency. Spread quickly over marshmallows. Let cool. Cut into bars or squares.

Rocky Road Brownies

◆

Any chapter on brownies should include some form of this classic chewy version. In this recipe, the marshmallows disappear during baking; in other versions, you can actually see a marshmallow layer.

MAKES 16 TO 48 BARS OR SQUARES
(see Cutting Guide, page 10)

- **Preparation: 20 minutes**
- **Baking: 40 minutes**
- **Freezing: excellent**

TIPS

I recommend that you use pure vanilla extract in all your baking. Nothing else will give you the same burst of flavor.

You will always get the best results when you use the pan size recommended in a recipe. But if you need to substitute an 8-inch (2 L) square cake pan when baking these rocky roads, add 5 to 10 minutes to the baking time.

Not only do brownies freeze well, but it's also hard to resist them right from the freezer.

- **Preheat oven to 325°F (160°C)**
- **9-inch (2.5 L) square cake pan, greased (see Tips, left)**

BROWNIE

3	squares (1 oz/28 g each) unsweetened chocolate, chopped	3
¾ cup	butter	175 mL
1½ cups	granulated sugar	375 mL
1 tsp	vanilla	5 mL
3	eggs	3
1 cup	all-purpose flour	250 mL
¾ tsp	baking powder	3 mL
1½ cups	miniature marshmallows	375 mL
1½ cups	peanuts	375 mL

CHOCOLATE GLAZE, OPTIONAL

4	squares (1 oz/28 g each) semi-sweet chocolate, chopped	4
2 tbsp	whipping (35%) cream	25 mL

1. *Brownie:* In a saucepan over low heat, melt chocolate and butter, stirring constantly, until smooth. Remove from heat. Add sugar and vanilla and mix well. Add eggs, one at a time, whisking lightly after each addition.

2. Combine flour and baking powder. Stir into chocolate mixture, mixing well. Stir in marshmallows and peanuts. Spread evenly in prepared pan.

3. Bake in preheated oven just until set, 35 to 40 minutes. Let cool completely in pan on rack.

4. *Chocolate Glaze (if using):* In a small saucepan over low heat, combine chocolate and whipping cream, stirring until chocolate is melted and mixture is smooth. Let cool for 20 minutes. Spread over brownie. Chill until chocolate is set. Cut into bars or squares.

Variation

Although your brownies won't qualify as rocky road, you can substitute an equal quantity of any other nut for the peanuts.

Chocolate Peanut Butter Brownies

This triple layer bar is a delicious combination of flavors. The mild chocolate complements the creamy peanut butter.

MAKES 16 TO 48 BARS OR SQUARES (see **Cutting Guide**, page 10)

- **Preparation: 30 minutes**
- **Baking: 30 minutes**
- **Freezing: excellent**

TIPS

Dry roasted peanuts have great taste and a crunchy texture that works well in brownies.

Peanuts, like all nuts, tend to go rancid quickly because of their high fat content. Store them in the freezer to retain freshness.

Most ovens have "hot spots," which result in unevenly baked goods. Prevent uneven baking by placing the pans in the center of the oven and rotating them halfway through the baking time if necessary. Use just one oven rack — don't stack.

- **Preheat oven to 350°F (180°C)**
- **9-inch (2.5 L) square cake pan, greased**

CRUST

1 1/4 cups	graham wafer crumbs	300 mL
1/4 cup	granulated sugar	50 mL
1/3 cup	finely chopped peanuts	75 mL
1/2 cup	butter, melted	125 mL

BROWNIE FILLING

2	squares (1 oz/28 g each) unsweetened chocolate, chopped	2
1/2 cup	butter	125 mL
1 cup	granulated sugar	250 mL
2	eggs	2
1 tsp	vanilla	5 mL
2/3 cup	all-purpose flour	150 mL
2/3 cup	chopped peanuts	150 mL

PEANUT BUTTER FROSTING

1/4 cup	butter, softened	50 mL
2 tbsp	creamy peanut butter	25 mL
2 cups	confectioner's (icing) sugar, sifted	500 mL
1 to 3 tbsp	milk	15 to 45 mL

1. *Crust:* In a bowl, combine graham wafer crumbs, sugar, peanuts and butter. Mix until crumbs are thoroughly moistened. Press evenly in prepared pan. Set aside.

2. *Brownie Filling:* In a saucepan over low heat, melt chocolate and butter, stirring constantly, until smooth. Remove from heat. Stir in sugar and mix until smooth. Add eggs, one at a time, whisking lightly after each addition. Stir in vanilla. Stir in flour and peanuts, mixing well. Spread evenly in prepared pan.

3. Bake in preheated oven just until set, 25 to 30 minutes. Let cool completely in pan on rack.

4. *Peanut Butter Frosting:* In a bowl, using an electric mixer on low speed, beat butter and peanut butter until blended. Alternately add confectioner's sugar and milk, using just enough milk to make a smooth, spreadable consistency. Spread evenly over brownie. Cut into bars or squares.

Milk Chocolate Pecan Brownies

◆

This pairing of chunks of milk chocolate and pecans in a dark chocolate brownie is one of my favorites.

MAKES 20 TO 54 BARS OR SQUARES (see Cutting Guide, page 10)

- **Preparation: 20 minutes**
- **Baking: 30 minutes**
- **Freezing: excellent**

TIPS

To ease cleanup, rather than combining the dry ingredients (Step 2), in a bowl, place a large piece of waxed paper on the counter. After measuring, combine the flour, baking powder and salt on the paper. Using the paper as a funnel, transfer the dry ingredients to the chocolate mixture.

If you like the pairing of coffee and chocolate, try adding 1 tbsp (15 mL) instant espresso coffee powder to the flour mixture. Instant espresso coffee is usually sold in specialty coffee stores.

- **Preheat oven to 350°F (180°C)**
- **13- by 9-inch (3 L) cake pan, greased**

7	squares (1 oz/28 g each) unsweetened chocolate, chopped	7
3	squares (1 oz/28 g each) semi-sweet chocolate, chopped	3
1 cup	butter	250 mL
2 cups	packed brown sugar	500 mL
4	eggs	4
1 cup	all-purpose flour	250 mL
¾ tsp	baking powder	3 mL
½ tsp	salt	2 mL
1 cup	milk chocolate chips	250 mL
1¼ cups	coarsely chopped pecans	300 mL

1. In a saucepan over low heat, melt unsweetened and semi-sweet chocolate and butter, stirring constantly, until smooth. Remove from heat. Whisk in brown sugar until smooth. Add eggs, one at a time, whisking lightly after each addition.

2. Combine flour, baking powder and salt. Stir into chocolate mixture, mixing well. Stir in milk chocolate chips and pecans. Spread evenly in prepared pan.

3. Bake in preheated oven just until set, 25 to 30 minutes. Let cool completely in pan on rack. Cut into bars or squares.

Variations

Use whatever nuts your family likes.

If you prefer a stronger chocolate flavor, replace the milk chocolate chips with chopped bittersweet chocolate or semi-sweet chocolate chips.

White Chocolate Cranberry Hazelnut Brownies

◆

I'm sure this creamy white chocolate brownie, loaded with hazelnuts and cranberries, will become one of your favorites.

MAKES 16 TO 48 BARS OR SQUARES (see Cutting Guide, page 10)

- **Preparation: 20 minutes**
- **Baking: 30 minutes**
- **Freezing: excellent**

TIPS

These make a nice holiday gift. Pack them in a decorative airtight cookie tin or box, tie with a festive ribbon and add the recipe with your gift tag.

If you can find orange-flavored dried cranberries, try them in this recipe. They taste particularly delicious in this brownie.

- **Preheat oven to 375°F (190°C)**
- **8-inch (2 L) square cake pan, greased**

6	squares (1 oz/28 g each) white chocolate, chopped	6
¾ cup	granulated sugar	175 mL
2	eggs	2
⅓ cup	butter, melted	75 mL
1 tsp	vanilla	5 mL
1¼ cups	all-purpose flour	300 mL
¾ tsp	baking powder	3 mL
¾ cup	coarsely chopped hazelnuts	175 mL
⅓ cup	dried cranberries	75 mL

1. In a small saucepan over low heat, melt white chocolate, stirring constantly, until smooth. Remove from heat and set aside.

2. In a bowl, whisk sugar and eggs until blended. Whisk in melted butter and vanilla. Combine flour and baking powder. Stir into egg mixture alternately with melted chocolate, making 2 additions of each and mixing until smooth. Stir in hazelnuts and cranberries. Spread evenly in prepared pan.

3. Bake in preheated oven just until set and golden, 25 to 30 minutes. Let cool completely in pan on rack. Cut into bars or squares.

White Chocolate Apricot Brownies

Here's a golden brownie that's moist and chewy yet cake-like. I love the flavor of apricots and almonds.

MAKES 16 TO 48 BARS OR SQUARES (see Cutting Guide, page 10)

- Preparation: 20 minutes
- Baking: 30 minutes
- Freezing: excellent

TIPS

To ease cleanup, rather than combining the dry ingredients in a bowl (Step 2), place a large piece of waxed paper on the counter. After measuring, combine the flour, baking powder and salt on the paper. Using the paper as a funnel, transfer the dry ingredients to the chocolate mixture.

The easiest way to chop dried apricots is with a pair of kitchen shears. Spray the blades with cooking spray or brush them lightly with oil to prevent sticking.

If you prefer a sweeter taste, dust the brownie with confectioner's (icing) sugar after it's cooled.

- **Preheat oven to 350°F (180°C)**
- **9-inch (2.5 L) square cake pan, greased**

4	squares (1 oz/28 g each) white chocolate, chopped	4
1/3 cup	butter	75 mL
1/2 cup	granulated sugar	125 mL
2	eggs	2
2 tsp	grated orange zest	10 mL
3/4 cup	all-purpose flour	175 mL
1/2 tsp	baking powder	2 mL
1/4 tsp	salt	1 mL
1 cup	chopped dried apricots (see Tips, left)	250 mL
2/3 cup	slivered almonds	150 mL

1. In a large saucepan over low heat, melt white chocolate and butter, stirring constantly, until smooth. Remove from heat. Add eggs, one at a time, whisking lightly after each addition. Stir in orange zest.

2. Combine flour, baking powder and salt. Stir into chocolate mixture, mixing well. Stir in apricots and almonds. Spread evenly in prepared pan.

3. Bake in preheated oven just until set, 25 to 30 minutes. Let cool completely in pan on rack. Cut into bars or squares.

Variations

Omit orange zest. Add 1/2 tsp (2 mL) almond extract or 1 tsp (5 mL) vanilla.

Replace apricots with dried cranberries.

White Chocolate Macadamia Brownies

This rich, buttery brownie has a chewy texture and lots of crunchy macadamia nuts.

MAKES 20 TO 54 BARS OR SQUARES (see Cutting Guide, page 10)

- **Preparation: 20 minutes**
- **Baking: 25 minutes**
- **Freezing: excellent**

TIPS

I prefer to use butter in baking because it has the best flavor of all the fats.

For a great dessert, cut these brownies into larger squares and serve them slightly warm with a generous drizzle of hot fudge sauce and a sprinkling of chopped macadamia nuts.

For the best taste, store and serve these bars at room temperature. If you're keeping them for longer than 3 days, freeze them.

- **Preheat oven to 350°F (180°C)**
- **13- by 9-inch (3 L) cake pan, greased**

12	squares (1 oz/28 g each) white chocolate, chopped and divided	12
½ cup	butter	125 mL
2	eggs	2
½ cup	granulated sugar	125 mL
1 tsp	vanilla	5 mL
1 cup	all-purpose flour	250 mL
¼ tsp	salt	1 mL
1 cup	chopped toasted macadamia nuts	250 mL

1. In a saucepan over low heat, melt 7 squares of the white chocolate with the butter, stirring constantly, until smooth. Remove from heat and set aside.

2. In a large bowl, using an electric mixer on high speed, beat eggs until frothy. Gradually add sugar, beating until thick and creamy. Stir in chocolate mixture and vanilla. Stir in flour and salt, mixing well. Stir in nuts and remaining white chocolate. Spread evenly in prepared pan.

3. Bake in preheated oven just until set, about 25 minutes. Let cool completely in pan on rack. Cut into bars or squares.

Variations

Replace the white chocolate with milk chocolate.

Replace macadamia nuts with slivered almonds or cashews.

Chocolate Macadamia Blondies

◆

Here's an all-time favorite that's very easy to make.

**MAKES 20 TO
54 BARS OR SQUARES
(see Cutting Guide,
page 10)**

- **Preparation: 20 minutes**
- **Baking: 35 minutes**
- **Freezing: excellent**

TIPS

Macadamia nuts are expensive, which makes these bars quite special. If you're making them for a kids' party, you may prefer to try them with almonds. I'm sure there'll be no complaints and no bars leftover either.

Chop macadamia nuts by hand with a sharp chef's knife. Because they're softer than most nuts, they don't chop well in a food processor.

- **Preheat oven to 325°F (160°C)**
- **13- by 9-inch (3 L) cake pan, greased**

1 cup	butter, softened	250 mL
2¼ cups	packed brown sugar	550 mL
2	eggs	2
1½ tsp	vanilla	7 mL
2 cups	all-purpose flour	500 mL
2 tsp	baking powder	10 mL
1 cup	milk chocolate chips	250 mL
1 cup	white chocolate chips	250 mL
1⅓ cups	coarsely chopped macadamia nuts, divided	325 mL

1. In a large bowl, using an electric mixer on medium speed, beat butter and brown sugar until light and creamy, about 5 minutes. Add eggs and vanilla, beating until smooth.

2. Combine flour and baking powder. Beat into butter mixture on low speed, mixing well. Stir in milk chocolate and white chocolate chips and 1 cup (250 mL) of the macadamia nuts. Spread evenly in prepared pan. Sprinkle remaining nuts on top and press lightly into batter.

3. Bake in preheated oven just until set, 30 to 35 minutes. Let cool completely in pan on rack. Cut into bars or squares.

Variations

Replace milk chocolate chips with semi-sweet chocolate chips.

Replace white chocolate chips with semi-sweet chocolate chips to make a brownie.

Substitute white chocolate chunks for both types of chips.

Cherry Almond Blondies

This moist, cake-like bar has a wonderful almond flavor and dried cherries throughout.

MAKES 20 TO 54 BARS OR SQUARES
(see Cutting Guide, page 10)

- **Preparation: 25 minutes**
- **Baking: 45 minutes**
- **Freezing: excellent**

TIPS

To ease cleanup, rather than combining the dry ingredients in a bowl (Step 2), place a large piece of waxed paper on the counter. Spread the flour on the paper. Sprinkle the ground almonds, baking powder and salt over top. Using the paper as a funnel, transfer the dry ingredients to the batter.

Serve these bars as an alternative to, or along with, fruitcake. Add some white shortbread and you have a very attractive Christmas platter or gift box.

- **Preheat oven to 350°F (180°C)**
- **13- by 9-inch (3 L) cake pan, greased**

¼ cup	almond liqueur	50 mL
1 cup	dried cherries	250 mL
2½ cups	all-purpose flour	625 mL
½ cup	ground almonds	125 mL
2 tsp	baking powder	10 mL
¼ tsp	salt	1 mL
1 cup	butter, softened	250 mL
1¾ cups	granulated sugar	425 mL
4	eggs	4
1 tbsp	grated orange zest	15 mL
1 cup	sliced almonds	250 mL
7 oz	almond paste, diced	200 g

1. In a saucepan over medium heat, bring almond liqueur and cherries to boil. Remove from heat. Let cool for 30 minutes.

2. Combine flour, ground almonds, baking powder and salt.

3. In a bowl, using an electric mixer on medium speed, beat butter and sugar until smooth and creamy, about 3 minutes. Add eggs, one at a time, beating well after each addition. Beat in orange zest. Stir in dry ingredients, mixing just until combined. Stir in sliced almonds, almond paste and cherry mixture. Spread evenly in prepared pan.

4. Bake in preheated oven until a toothpick inserted in center comes out clean, 40 to 45 minutes. Let cool completely in pan on rack. Cut into bars or squares.

Variations

Replace dried cherries with snipped dried apricots.

Replace almond liqueur with orange juice.

Apple Blondies with Brown Sugar Frosting

◆

I'm not sure whether I like the frosting or the apple blondie the best. Both components are scrumptious. You'll have to decide for yourself.

MAKES 20 TO 54 BARS OR SQUARES (see Cutting Guide, page 10)

- **Preparation: 25 minutes**
- **Baking: 30 minutes**
- **Freezing: excellent**

TIPS

This frosting is very soft when first mixed, which makes it very nice to spread. It firms up on cooling.

Choose apples that are crisp, tart and not too moist. Granny Smith, Golden Delicious and Spartans are good choices for this recipe.

- **Preheat oven to 350°F (180°C)**
- **13- by 9-inch (3 L) cake pan, greased**

BLONDIE

⅔ cup	butter, softened	150 mL
2 cups	packed brown sugar	500 mL
2	eggs	2
1 tsp	vanilla	2 mL
2 cups	all-purpose flour	500 mL
2 tsp	baking powder	10 mL
¼ tsp	salt	1 mL
1 cup	chopped peeled apples	250 mL
¾ cup	chopped walnuts	175 mL

BROWN SUGAR FROSTING

½ cup	butter	125 mL
1 cup	packed brown sugar	250 mL
¼ cup	milk or cream	50 mL
2 cups	confectioner's (icing) sugar, sifted	500 mL

1. *Blondie:* In a large bowl, using an electric mixer on medium speed, beat butter, brown sugar, eggs and vanilla until thick and smooth, about 3 minutes. Combine flour, baking powder and salt. Add to butter mixture on low speed, mixing until blended. Stir in apples and nuts, mixing well. Spread evenly in prepared pan.

2. Bake in preheated oven until set and golden, 25 to 30 minutes. Let cool completely in pan on rack.

3. *Brown Sugar Frosting:* In a small saucepan over low heat, melt butter. Stir in brown sugar and milk. Bring mixture just to a boil then remove from heat and let cool to lukewarm. Stir in confectioner's sugar, mixing until smooth. Spread evenly over bar. Let stand until frosting is firm enough to cut. Cut into bars or squares.

Variations

Omit the frosting if you prefer a plain apple walnut blondie. If you're not a fan of nuts, omit the walnuts.

Chocolate Bars and Squares

Bars that feature chocolate range from ooey, gooey, moist and chewy to crisp and crunchy. They are easy to make for spur-of-the-moment company, yet delicious enough for elegant entertaining. There is nothing like a rich chocolate dessert to impress your guests. If you have chocoholics among your relatives and friends, a gift of homemade chocolate cookie bars is so much nicer and more personal than a box of store-bought chocolates. Although the recipes in this chapter also feature fruit, nuts, coconut, caramel and other great ingredients, the ruling flavor is chocolate. Enjoy.

◄ *Two-Tone Dream Bars*

Two-Tone Dream Bars

Although these look and sound quite decadent they're actually fairly light in texture. The perfect solution for any midnight cravings.

MAKES 20 TO 54 BARS (see Cutting Guide, page 10)

- **Preparation: 25 minutes**
- **Baking: 32 minutes**
- **Freezing: excellent**

TIPS

A small offset spatula makes spreading easy, especially on small areas such as the top of bars. It's also good at getting into corners.

To store bars, refrigerate them in an airtight container or leave at room temperature, depending on the type of bar. If you plan to freeze them, wrap tightly in plastic wrap and freeze for up to 3 months. I like to cut them into bars before freezing so I can remove the required number whenever I need them rather than having to thaw or cut the entire piece.

- **Preheat oven to 350°F (180°C)**
- **13- by 9-inch (3 L) cake pan, greased**

CRUST

1 cup	all-purpose flour	250 mL
⅓ cup	granulated sugar	75 mL
⅓ cup	butter, softened	75 mL

FILLING

1 cup	graham wafer crumbs	250 mL
1 cup	semi-sweet chocolate chips	250 mL
⅔ cup	coarsely chopped walnuts	150 mL
1	can (10 oz/300 mL) sweetened condensed milk	1

TOPPING

8	squares (1 oz/28 g each) white chocolate, chopped	8
2 tbsp	butter	25 mL

1. *Crust:* In a bowl, combine flour, sugar and butter. Using an electric mixer on low speed, beat until crumbly. Press evenly into prepared pan. Bake in preheated oven until golden around the edges, 10 to 12 minutes.

2. *Filling:* In a bowl, combine graham wafer crumbs, chocolate chips, walnuts and condensed milk, mixing until well blended. Drop mixture by spoonfuls over warm base. Spread evenly. Return to oven and bake until top is lightly browned, about 20 minutes. Let cool completely in pan on rack.

3. *Topping:* In a saucepan over low heat, melt white chocolate and butter, stirring constantly, until smooth. Spread evenly over bars. Chill until chocolate sets, about 10 minutes. Cut into bars.

Variations

Use your favorite kind of chocolate chip for the filling in this recipe. White and milk chocolate chips are especially nice.

Replace the graham wafer crumbs with vanilla wafer crumbs.

One-Bite Chocolate Cheesecake Bars

♦

These bars are sumptuous. The almond crust and the creamy, not-too-rich chocolate cheesecake top are a marriage made in heaven.

MAKES 18 TO 48 BARS (see Cutting Guide, page 10)

- **Preparation: 25 minutes**
- **Baking: 47 minutes**
- **Freezing: excellent**

TIPS

There are a number of ways to melt chocolate chips. You can place them in a double boiler over hot, not boiling, water or in a small saucepan over low heat. In both cases, stir frequently until smooth. Or melt them in a microwave oven on medium power until softened (about 1 minute for ¼ cup/50 mL), then stir until smooth.

If you prefer, use a food processor rather than a mixer to prepare the base and the topping. It's actually quicker. When mixing the base in a food processor, use cold butter, cubed.

- **Preheat oven to 350°F (180°C)**
- **8-inch (2 L) square cake pan, greased**

BASE

1 cup	all-purpose flour	250 mL
¼ cup	granulated sugar	50 mL
½ cup	ground almonds	125 mL
½ cup	butter, softened	125 mL

TOPPING

1	pkg (8 oz/250 g) cream cheese, softened	1
⅔ cup	semi-sweet chocolate chips, melted (see Tips, left)	150 mL
⅔ cup	granulated sugar	150 mL
2	eggs	2
⅔ cup	table (18%) cream	150 mL
½ tsp	almond extract	2 mL

1. *Base:* In a bowl, combine flour, sugar and ground almonds. Using an electric mixer on low speed, beat in butter until crumbly. Press evenly into prepared pan. Bake in preheated oven until golden around the edges, 10 to 12 minutes.

2. *Topping:* In a large bowl, using an electric mixer on low speed, beat cream cheese until smooth. Add melted chocolate, sugar and eggs, beating on low speed until blended. Gradually add cream and almond extract, mixing until smooth. Spread over base.

3. Return to oven and bake until top is just set, 25 to 35 minutes. Let cool completely in pan on rack, then refrigerate until firm for easy cutting. Cut into bars.

Variations

Replace almond extract with 1 tbsp (15 mL) instant espresso coffee powder.

Replace the ground almonds with ¼ cup (50 mL) flaked sweetened coconut and the almond extract with an equal quantity of vanilla.

Caramel Peanut Ripple Bars

With several different layers, these bars are particularly attractive. Even so, they're surprisingly easy to make.

MAKES 20 TO 54 BARS
(see Cutting Guide, page 10)

- **Preparation: 35 minutes**
- **Baking: 30 minutes**
- **Freezing: excellent**

TIPS

When lining a pan with parchment, leave an overhang at the sides. When the bar is completely cool, you can lift it right out of the pan and transfer to a cutting board for easy slicing.

To store, place cooled bars in a single layer in a covered airtight container. Store at room temperature for 4 days or freeze for up to 4 months.

- **Preheat oven to 350°F (180°C)**
- **13- by 9-inch (3 L) cake pan, greased and lined with parchment**

½ cup + 2 tbsp	butter, softened, divided	125 mL + 25 mL
1 cup	packed brown sugar	250 mL
1	egg	1
1 tsp	vanilla	5 mL
1¼ cups	all-purpose flour	300 mL
½ tsp	baking soda	2 mL
1½ cups	quick-cooking rolled oats	375 mL
6 oz	soft caramels, unwrapped (about 20)	180 g
2 tbsp	milk	25 mL
2¾ cups	miniature marshmallows, divided	675 mL
1⅓ cups	peanuts, divided	325 mL
1½ cups	semi-sweet chocolate chips	375 mL
1	can (10 oz/300 mL) sweetened condensed milk	1

1. In a large bowl, using an electric mixer on low speed, beat ½ cup (125 mL) butter and brown sugar until creamy. Add egg and vanilla, beating until smooth. Beat in flour and baking soda, mixing well. Stir in oats until blended. Reserve ⅔ cup (150 mL) of the oat mixture for the top. Press remaining mixture firmly into prepared pan. Set aside.

2. In a saucepan over low heat, combine caramels and milk. Heat, stirring, until caramels have melted and mixture is smooth. Carefully spread over base. Sprinkle 2 cups (500 mL) of the marshmallows and 1 cup (250 mL) of the peanuts on top.

3. In a small saucepan, combine chocolate chips, sweetened condensed milk and remaining 2 tbsp (25 mL) of the butter. Heat over low heat, stirring constantly, until chocolate is melted and mixture is smooth. Pour evenly over marshmallows and peanut layer. Using your fingertips, scatter reserved oat mixture on top. Sprinkle with remaining marshmallows and peanuts.

4. Bake in preheated oven until golden, 25 to 30 minutes. Let cool completely in pan on rack. Cut into bars.

Chocolate Marshmallow Crisps

You can't go wrong with this combination of chocolate, peanut butter and crisp rice cereal. It's always a favorite.

MAKES 24 TO 60 BARS OR SQUARES
(see **Cutting Guide**, page 10)

- **Preparation: 25 minutes**
- **Baking: 23 minutes**
- **Freezing: excellent**

TIPS

Mini candy-coated chocolate pieces, such as M&M's can be purchased in bulk stores. They're nice to have on hand as an easy decorating tool for baking with kids. If you prefer a more adult look, leave them out.

So long as peanut allergies aren't a concern, these bars make a great treat for kids' lunch boxes.

- **Preheat oven to 350°F (180°C)**
- **15- by 10- by 1-inch (2 L) jelly roll pan, greased**

BASE

¾ cup	butter, softened	175 mL
1½ cups	granulated sugar	375 mL
3	eggs	3
1⅓ cups	all-purpose flour	325 mL
⅓ cup	unsweetened cocoa powder, sifted	75 mL
½ tsp	baking powder	2 mL
¼ tsp	salt	1 mL
¾ cup	chopped peanuts	175 mL
4 cups	miniature marshmallows	1 L

TOPPING

1½ cups	semi-sweet chocolate chips	375 mL
1 cup	creamy peanut butter	250 mL
3 tbsp	butter	45 mL
2 cups	crisp rice cereal	500 mL
1 cup	miniature candy-coated chocolate pieces, optional (see Tips, left)	250 mL

1. *Base:* In a large bowl, using an electric mixer on medium speed, beat butter, sugar and eggs until light and creamy.

2. Combine flour, cocoa, baking powder and salt. On low speed, beat into creamed mixture, mixing well. Stir in peanuts. Spread evenly in prepared pan.

3. Bake in preheated oven just until set, 15 to 20 minutes. Sprinkle marshmallows in single layer over top. Return to oven until marshmallows are puffed, 2 to 3 minutes. Let cool completely in pan on rack.

4. *Topping:* In a saucepan, combine chocolate chips, peanut butter and butter. Heat over low heat, stirring constantly, until chocolate is melted and mixture is smooth. Stir in cereal and candy. Spread immediately over base. Chill to set topping. Cut into bars or squares.

Variation

If you prefer a milder chocolate taste, substitute milk chocolate chips for the semi-sweet.

Chocolate Buttercrunch Bars

These bars have everything. They're moist, chewy, crunchy and delicious all in one bite. You can tell from the batter (a bit of dough holding lots of fabulous ingredients together) that they'll be amazing.

MAKES 18 TO 48 BARS (see Cutting Guide, page 10)

- **Preparation: 20 minutes**
- **Baking: 30 minutes**
- **Freezing: excellent**

TIPS

Skor or Heath bars work well in this recipe.

Chill the candy bars before chopping. Put them in a heavy plastic bag and smash with a meat mallet for easy crushing. You'll end up with a mixture of large and small pieces, which is nice.

- **Preheat oven to 350°F (180°C)**
- **9-inch (2.5 L) square cake pan, greased**

½ cup	butter, melted	125 mL
¾ cup	packed brown sugar	175 mL
¼ cup	granulated sugar	50 mL
1	egg	1
1 tsp	vanilla	5 mL
¾ tsp	almond extract	3 mL
¾ cup	all-purpose flour	175 mL
¼ tsp	baking soda	1 mL
¼ tsp	cinnamon	1 mL
4	crunchy chocolate-covered toffee bars (1.4 oz/39 g each), chopped (see Tips, left)	4
¾ cup	coarsely chopped unblanched almonds, toasted	175 mL
⅔ cup	semi-sweet chocolate chips	150 mL

1. In a bowl, whisk melted butter, brown and granulated sugars, egg, vanilla and almond extract until smoothly blended. Stir in flour, baking soda and cinnamon, mixing well. Stir in candy bars, almonds and chocolate chips. Mix well. Spread evenly in prepared pan.

2. Bake in preheated oven just until set, 25 to 30 minutes. Let cool completely in pan on rack. Cut into bars.

Variations
Omit the almond extract if it isn't a favorite flavor.

Replace the almonds with roasted peanuts.

Substitute Crispy Crunch for the toffee bars.

Chocolate Toffee Squares

It takes about as long to make these squares as it would to go to the store for a chocolate toffee bar. The big difference is you end up with about 25 times the amount of treats.

MAKES 24 TO 60 SQUARES
(see Cutting Guide, page 10)

- **Preparation: 15 minutes**
- **Baking: 15 minutes**
- **Freezing: excellent**

TIPS

Since it's quite rich, I recommend cutting this bar to yield 60 small squares.

Toffee bits are available in bags. They're broken pieces of the toffee part of Heath or Skor bars (no chocolate).

Cut these squares in half on the diagonal to make triangles for a different look. Squares or triangles — they both taste terrific.

Be sure to use fresh, pure chocolate chips. When chocolate chips get older or are made from imitation chocolate, they don't melt as easily, making spreading difficult. Store chocolate in a cool, dry place, not in the freezer or refrigerator.

- **Preheat oven to 350°F (180°C)**
- **15- by 10- by 1-inch (2 L) jelly roll pan, ungreased**

1 cup	butter, softened	250 mL
1 cup	packed brown sugar	250 mL
1	egg yolk	1
2 cups	all-purpose flour	500 mL
1¾ cups	toffee bits, divided	425 mL
2 cups	semi-sweet chocolate chips	500 mL
1 cup	milk chocolate chips	250 mL

1. In a bowl, using an electric mixer on medium speed, beat butter until creamy, about 2 minutes. Add brown sugar and egg yolk, beating until smooth. Stir in flour and ¾ cup (175 mL) of the toffee bits, mixing until crumbly and well blended. Press evenly into prepared pan. Bake in preheated oven until golden, about 15 minutes.

2. Immediately sprinkle semi-sweet chocolate chips evenly over top. Let stand for 5 minutes or until softened. Spread chocolate evenly over top. Sprinkle milk chocolate chips and remaining toffee bits over chocolate. Let cool completely in pan on rack. Cut into squares.

Variations

Replace milk chocolate chips with white chocolate or butterscotch chips.

For a nutty variation, replace the milk chocolate chips with sliced almonds or chopped pecans.

Chewy Chocolate Almond Bars

These bars are great for entertaining and make a superb addition to any potluck. They're easy to make and one of my favorites.

MAKES 18 TO 48 BARS (see Cutting Guide, page 10)

- **Preparation: 20 minutes**
- **Baking: 42 minutes**
- **Freezing: excellent**

TIPS

To measure dry ingredients, use nesting-type dry measures that are level on top. Lightly spoon ingredients into the measure, then level off with a knife or spatula.

Measure ingredients like corn syrup in liquid measuring cups that have a spout. Liquid measures are usually glass or clear plastic.

If using glass baking dishes in place of metal pans, decrease the oven temperature by 25°F (10°C).

- **Preheat oven to 350°F (180°C)**
- **9-inch (2.5 L) square cake pan, greased**

CRUST

1 cup	all-purpose flour	250 mL
½ cup	ground almonds	125 mL
¼ cup	packed brown sugar	50 mL
½ cup	cold butter, cubed	125 mL

TOPPING

2	eggs	2
½ cup	granulated sugar	125 mL
½ cup	corn syrup	125 mL
2 tbsp	butter, melted	25 mL
½ tsp	almond extract	2 mL
1 cup	milk chocolate chips	250 mL
¾ cup	slivered almonds	175 mL

1. *Crust:* In a bowl, combine flour, ground almonds and brown sugar. Using a pastry blender, 2 knives or your fingers, cut in butter until mixture resembles coarse crumbs. Press evenly into prepared pan. Bake in preheated oven until golden around the edges, 10 to 12 minutes.

2. *Topping:* In a bowl, whisk eggs, sugar, syrup, melted butter and almond extract until well blended. Stir in chocolate chips and almonds. Pour evenly over crust.

3. Return to oven and bake until set and golden, 25 to 30 minutes. Let cool completely in pan on rack. Cut into bars.

Variations

If you prefer, substitute an equal quantity of white chocolate chips for milk chocolate chips in this recipe.

Replace almonds with pecans, walnuts, cashews or peanuts.

Crunchy Toffee Chocolate Bars

These squares are crunchy, creamy and chocolaty in one delicious mouthful.

**MAKES 20 TO 54 BARS
(see Cutting Guide, page 10)**

- **Preparation: 30 minutes**
- **Baking: 42 minutes**
- **Cooking: 10 minutes**
- **Freezing: excellent**

TIPS

If you prefer, use a large wooden spoon to mix the crust instead of an electric mixer.

Toffee bits are available in bags. They're broken pieces of the toffee part of Heath or Skor bars (no chocolate).

Be sure to use fresh, pure chocolate chips. When chocolate chips get older or are made from imitation chocolate, they don't melt as easily, making spreading difficult. Store chocolate in a cool, dry place, not in the freezer or refrigerator.

- **Preheat oven to 350°F (180°C)**
- **13- by 9-inch (3 L) cake pan, greased**

CRUST

¾ cup	butter, softened	175 mL
¾ cup	packed brown sugar	175 mL
1½ cups	all-purpose flour	375 mL
½ cup	quick-cooking rolled oats	125 mL

FILLING

1	can (10 oz/300 mL) sweetened condensed milk	1
2 tbsp	butter	25 mL
½ tsp	almond extract	2 mL
2 cups	semi-sweet chocolate chips	500 mL
1 cup	toffee bits (see Tips, left)	250 mL
½ cup	finely chopped almonds	125 mL

1. *Crust:* In a bowl, combine butter, brown sugar, flour and rolled oats. Using an electric mixer on low speed, mix until well blended and mixture comes together. Press evenly into prepared pan. Bake in preheated oven until light golden, 20 to 25 minutes. Let cool in pan on rack while preparing filling.

2. *Filling:* In a small heavy saucepan over medium heat, combine sweetened condensed milk, butter and almond extract. Heat, stirring constantly, until thickened, 5 to 10 minutes. Spread over cooled base.

3. Return to oven and bake until top is golden, 12 to 15 minutes. Sprinkle chocolate chips evenly over top. Return to oven and bake until chocolate is shiny and soft, about 2 minutes. Remove from oven. Spread chocolate evenly. Sprinkle toffee bits and almonds on top, pressing lightly into the chocolate layer. Let cool completely in pan on rack. If necessary, refrigerate just to set chocolate before cutting into bars. Store at room temperature.

Double Deluxe Bars

Two layers make up one delicious bar. A tender cookie-like base holds a dense fruit and nut topping with lots of chocolate chips scattered throughout.

MAKES 20 TO 54 BARS (see Cutting Guide, page 10)

- **Preparation: 20 minutes**
- **Baking: 40 minutes**
- **Freezing: excellent**

TIPS

Dried fruits dry out during storage. To restore some of the lost moisture, plump them in boiling water for a few minutes. Drain well and pat dry before using.

Due to its high moisture content, brown sugar tends to lump during storage. It should be stored in an airtight container or heavy plastic bag in a cool, dry place. If it hardens and becomes lumpy, put it in a plastic bag with a slice of apple. Seal tightly and leave a few days to soften.

- **Preheat oven to 350°F (180°C)**
- **13- by 9-inch (3 L) cake pan, greased**

CRUST

2 cups	all-purpose flour	500 mL
½ cup	packed brown sugar	125 mL
¾ cup	cold butter, cubed	175 mL

TOPPING

¼ cup	all-purpose flour	50 mL
½ tsp	baking powder	2 mL
¼ tsp	salt	1 mL
2	eggs	2
1½ cups	packed brown sugar	375 mL
1 tsp	vanilla	5 mL
1½ cups	semi-sweet chocolate chips	375 mL
1 cup	dried cranberries	250 mL
¾ cup	flaked coconut	175 mL
¾ cup	chopped pecans	175 mL

1. *Crust:* In a bowl, combine flour and brown sugar. Using a pastry blender, 2 knives or your fingers, cut in butter until mixture resembles coarse crumbs. Press evenly into prepared pan. Bake in preheated oven until golden around the edges, 12 to 15 minutes.

2. *Topping:* Combine flour, baking powder and salt. Set aside. In a bowl, whisk eggs, brown sugar and vanilla until frothy. Whisk in flour mixture, mixing well. Stir in chocolate chips, cranberries, coconut and pecans, mixing until ingredients are moistened. Spread over crust.

3. Return to oven and bake until topping is set and golden, 20 to 25 minutes. Let cool completely in pan on rack. Cut into bars.

Variations

Replace dried cranberries with raisins.

Use your favorite nut in place of pecans.

Chocolate Pecan Squares

These squares remind me of bite-size pieces of pecan pie enhanced with chocolate. Because they are so rich, I like to cut them in small pieces. Triangles are a pretty shape.

MAKES 16 TO 36 SQUARES (see Cutting Guide, page 10)

- Preparation: 20 minutes
- Baking: 45 minutes
- Freezing: excellent

TIPS

Most recipes in this book call for butter, melted, which means you measure the butter, then melt it. If the recipe calls for melted butter, then it's melted before measuring.

If you've run out of chocolate chips, chop up a chocolate bar or chocolate squares.

- **Preheat oven to 350°F (180°C)**
- **9-inch (2.5 L) square cake pan, greased**

CRUST

1 cup	all-purpose flour	250 mL
¼ cup	granulated sugar	50 mL
⅓ cup	butter, softened	75 mL

TOPPING

2	eggs	2
½ cup	granulated sugar	125 mL
½ cup	corn syrup	125 mL
2 tbsp	butter, melted	25 mL
1 cup	semi-sweet chocolate chips	250 mL
¾ cup	chopped pecans	175 mL

1. *Crust:* In a bowl, combine flour, sugar and butter. Using an electric mixer on low speed, beat until crumbly. Press evenly into prepared pan. Bake in preheated oven until edges are lightly browned, 12 to 15 minutes.

2. *Topping:* In a bowl, whisk eggs, sugar, corn syrup and melted butter until blended. Stir in chocolate chips and pecans. Pour evenly over crust.

3. Return to oven and bake until set and golden, 25 to 30 minutes. Let cool completely in pan on rack. Cut into squares.

Variation

Try walnuts or almonds instead of the pecans for a nice flavor change.

Butterscotch Chip Bars

Make these bars and enjoy chocolate frosted butterscotch chip cookies in half the time they usually take.

MAKES 20 TO 54 BARS (see Cutting Guide, page 10)

- **Preparation: 20 minutes**
- **Baking: 37 minutes**
- **Freezing: excellent**

TIPS

If you don't have chocolate chips, substitute 4 (1 oz/ 28 g each) semi-sweet chocolate squares, chopped. They melt very nicely.

With age, chocolate gets a whitish coating. This is completely harmless and will disappear when it's heated.

Store chocolate in a cool, dry place.

Be sure to use fresh, pure chocolate chips. When chocolate chips get older or are made from imitation chocolate, they don't melt as easily, making spreading difficult. Store chocolate in a cool, dry place, not in the freezer or refrigerator.

- **Preheat oven to 350°F (180°C)**
- **13- by 9-inch (3 L) cake pan, greased**

1 cup	butter, softened	250 mL
1½ cups	packed brown sugar	375 mL
2	eggs	2
1 tsp	vanilla	5 mL
2 cups	all-purpose flour	500 mL
1 tsp	baking soda	5 mL
½ tsp	salt	2 mL
1¾ cups	butterscotch chips	425 mL
1 cup	semi-sweet chocolate chips	250 mL
½ cup	chopped pecans	125 mL

1. In a large bowl, using an electric mixer on medium speed, beat butter and brown sugar until smooth and creamy, about 3 minutes. Add eggs, one at a time, beating thoroughly after each addition. Add vanilla and mix until blended.

2. Combine flour, baking soda and salt. Add to creamed mixture, mixing on low speed until smooth, about 3 minutes. Stir in butterscotch chips. Spread evenly in prepared pan.

3. Bake in preheated oven until set and golden, about 35 minutes.

4. Sprinkle chocolate chips over hot bars. Return to oven until chocolate melts, about 2 minutes. Spread chocolate evenly over surface. Sprinkle pecans on top. Let cool completely in pan on rack. Cut into bars.

Variation

For a more chocolaty bar, replace the butterscotch chips with semi-sweet or milk chocolate chips.

Chocolate Caramel Oat Squares

A chocolate bar–like filling nestles between layers of a crumble cookie crust.

MAKES 24 TO 60 SQUARES (see Cutting Guide, page 10)

- **Preparation: 20 minutes**
- **Baking: 25 minutes**
- **Freezing: excellent**

TIPS

If you prefer, bake these squares in two 9-inch (2.5 L) square pans for the same amount of time.

Chilling caramels makes them easier to unwrap. Of course, the easiest way is to let the kids help with this job. Be sure to have a few extra caramels on hand to replace the ones that disappear.

The fresher the caramels the more easily they melt.

- **Preheat oven to 350°F (180°C)**
- **15- by 10- by 1-inch (2 L) jelly roll pan**

CRUST

2 cups	all-purpose flour	500 mL
2 cups	quick-cooking rolled oats	500 mL
1⅓ cups	packed brown sugar	325 mL
1 tsp	baking soda	5 mL
¼ tsp	salt	1 mL
1½ cups	cold butter, cubed	375 mL

FILLING

1 lb	soft caramels, unwrapped (about 60)	500 g
1 cup	evaporated milk	250 mL
2 cups	semi-sweet chocolate chips	500 mL
1 cup	chopped walnuts	250 mL

1. *Crust:* In a bowl, combine flour, oats, brown sugar, baking soda and salt. Using a pastry blender, 2 knives or your fingers, cut in butter until mixture resembles coarse crumbs. Press half of mixture evenly into prepared pan. Bake in preheated oven just until starting to brown around the edges, about 5 minutes. Set remainder aside.

2. *Filling:* In a heavy saucepan, combine caramels and evaporated milk. Heat over low heat, stirring until caramels are melted and mixture is smooth. Remove from heat and set aside.

3. Sprinkle chocolate chips and walnuts over hot crust. Pour caramel mixture evenly over top. Sprinkle with remaining crust mixture.

4. Return to oven and bake until golden, 15 to 20 minutes. Let cool completely in pan on rack. Cut into squares.

Variation
Replace semi-sweet chocolate chips with milk chocolate, white or butterscotch chips.

Good 'n' Gooey Chocolate Cashew Squares

Try serving these squares warm with a scoop of vanilla ice cream on the side.

MAKES 24 SQUARES (see Cutting Guide, page 10)

- **Preparation: 20 minutes**
- **Baking: 37 minutes**
- **Freezing: excellent**

TIPS

If you prefer, mix the crust in a food processor or cut the butter in using a pastry blender, 2 knives or your fingers. In both cases, use cold butter, cubed, rather than softened butter. Whichever method you use, the mixture should resemble coarse crumbs.

When baking bars in dark non-stick pans, reduce the baking time of the crust and topping by about 5 minutes.

- **Preheat oven to 350°F (180°C)**
- **13- by 9-inch (3 L) cake pan, greased**

CRUST

1 ½ cups	all-purpose flour	375 mL
⅓ cup	packed brown sugar	75 mL
½ cup	butter, softened	125 mL

TOPPING

3	eggs	3
¾ cup	granulated sugar	175 mL
¾ cup	corn syrup	175 mL
3 tbsp	butter, melted	45 mL
1 ½ cups	coarsely chopped cashews	375 mL
1 ½ cups	semi-sweet chocolate chips	375 mL

1. *Crust:* In a bowl, combine flour, brown sugar and butter. Using an electric mixer on low speed, beat until crumbly. Press evenly into prepared pan. Bake in preheated oven until golden around the edges, 10 to 12 minutes.

2. *Topping:* In a bowl, whisk eggs, sugar, syrup and melted butter until smooth. Stir in cashews and chocolate chips. Spread evenly over base.

3. Return to oven and bake until set and golden, about 25 minutes. Let cool completely in pan on rack. Cut into squares.

Variations

Use white or milk chocolate chips instead of semi-sweet.

Replace the cashews with walnuts.

1-2-3 Chocolate Bars

Here's a delicious treat that's quick and easy to make. If you have the ingredients on hand, it's perfect for unexpected company.

MAKES 20 TO 54 BARS (see Cutting Guide, page 10)

- **Preparation: 15 minutes**
- **Baking: 25 minutes**
- **Freezing: excellent**

TIPS

Brands of sweetened condensed milk vary in consistency. Some, usually the cheaper brands, are very thin. I recommend that you try several, choose your favorite and stick to it. Condensed milk should be pourable but not too thin. The recipes in this book were tested using whole or regular condensed milk. Lower-fat versions are available and, in most cases, make a satisfactory substitute.

These bars are very rich and chocolaty. One pan goes a long way.

- **Preheat oven to 350°F (180°C)**
- **13- by 9-inch (3 L) cake pan, greased**

CRUST

1⅓ cups	graham wafer crumbs	325 mL
¼ cup	unsweetened cocoa powder, sifted	50 mL
¼ cup	granulated sugar	50 mL
½ cup	butter, melted	125 mL

TOPPING

1	can (10 oz/300 mL) sweetened condensed milk	1
1	egg	1
¼ cup	all-purpose flour	50 mL
¼ cup	unsweetened cocoa powder, sifted	50 mL
½ tsp	baking powder	2 mL
½ tsp	vanilla	2 mL
1 cup	chopped pecans	250 mL
2 cups	semi-sweet chocolate chips, divided	500 mL

1. *Crust:* In a bowl, combine graham wafer crumbs, cocoa powder and granulated sugar. Stir well. Add melted butter and mix well. Press evenly into prepared pan. Set aside.

2. *Topping:* In a bowl, whisk sweetened condensed milk, egg, flour, cocoa powder, baking powder and vanilla until smoothly blended. Stir in pecans and 1½ cups (375 mL) of the chocolate chips. Spread evenly over base. Sprinkle remaining ½ cup (125 mL) chocolate chips evenly on top. Press in lightly.

3. Bake in preheated oven until set, 20 to 25 minutes. Let cool completely in pan on rack. Cut into bars.

Variation
Vary the type of nut or chip to suit your taste.

Chocolate Sandwich Squares

◆

This sandwich cookie is very easy to make. The filling bakes right in so no last-minute filling is required.

MAKES 24 SQUARES
(see **Cutting Guide**, page 10)

- **Preparation: 20 minutes**
- **Baking: 35 minutes**
- **Freezing: excellent**

TIPS

For easy pouring, melt the butter in a measuring cup or a bowl with a spout.

When measuring brown sugar, pack it firmly into a dry measuring cup. It should hold its shape when turned out.

- **Preheat oven to 350°F (180°C)**
- **13- by 9-inch (3 L) cake pan, greased**

FILLING

1¾ cups	semi-sweet chocolate chips	425 mL
1	can (10 oz/300 mL) sweetened condensed milk	1
2 tbsp	butter	25 mL

BASE

2¼ cups	packed brown sugar	550 mL
2	eggs	2
1 cup	butter, melted	250 mL
1 tsp	vanilla	5 mL
2 cups	all-purpose flour	500 mL
1 cup	chopped unblanched almonds	250 mL

1. *Filling:* In a saucepan over low heat, combine chocolate chips, sweetened condensed milk and butter. Heat, stirring constantly, until chocolate is melted and mixture is smooth. Remove from heat and set aside.

2. *Base:* In a bowl, whisk brown sugar, eggs, melted butter and vanilla until smooth. Stir in flour, mixing just until blended. Stir in almonds. Mix well. Spread half in prepared pan. Spread filling evenly over base. Dot spoonfuls of remaining batter on top. Spread lightly with knife to cover filling.

3. Bake in preheated oven until set, 30 to 35 minutes. Let cool completely in pan on rack. Cut into squares.

Variation

For a blond bar, replace the chocolate chips with butterscotch or peanut butter chips, and the almonds with peanuts.

Chocolate Peanut Chews

The combination of peanut butter and chocolate has been a favorite for a long time and will likely always be.

MAKES 24 TO 60 BARS OR SQUARES
(see **Cutting Guide**, page 10)

- **Preparation: 15 minutes**
- **Baking: 15 minutes**
- **Freezing: excellent**

TIPS

When measuring sticky ingredients such as syrup or honey, which are combined with melted butter, measure the melted butter first. (You can also spray the measuring cup with cooking spray.) Then the syrup will slip out of the measuring cup easily.

In this recipe and most others, except for shortbread, hard margarine may be used in place of butter. However, hard margarine likely contains hydrogenated or partially hydrogenated oils, which are unhealthy trans fats. Although soft margarine has a more positive nutritional profile, its consistency differs from butter's so it cannot be used in its place.

- **Preheat oven to 375°F (190°C)**
- **15- by 10- by 1-inch (2 L) jelly roll pan, greased**

BASE

2 cups	quick-cooking rolled oats	500 mL
1 cup	graham wafer crumbs	250 mL
¾ cup	packed brown sugar	175 mL
¼ tsp	baking soda	1 mL
1 cup	chopped peanuts	250 mL
½ cup	butter, melted	125 mL
½ cup	corn syrup	125 mL

TOPPING

1 cup	semi-sweet chocolate chips	250 mL
⅓ cup	creamy peanut butter	75 mL
½ cup	finely chopped peanuts	125 mL

1. *Base:* In a bowl, combine oats, graham wafer crumbs, brown sugar, baking soda and chopped peanuts. In a large measure or small bowl, combine melted butter and corn syrup. Stir into oat mixture, mixing well. Press evenly into prepared pan. Bake in preheated oven until edges are lightly browned, 12 to 15 minutes.

2. *Topping:* In a small saucepan over low heat, melt chocolate chips and peanut butter, stirring constantly, until smooth. Spread evenly over warm base. Sprinkle with finely chopped peanuts. Let cool completely in pan on rack. Cut into bars or squares.

Variation

If you're watching calories, omit the topping. On the plus side, the plain bars pack well for storage.

Chocolate Caramel Cashew Slices

◆

These look great and taste even better. They have lots of caramel, with a nice hit of chocolate and an appealing crunch of cashews.

MAKES 48 SLICES (see Cutting Guide, page 10)

- **Preparation: 20 minutes**
- **Baking: 14 minutes**
- **Freezing: excellent**

TIPS

To retain freshness, store nuts in the freezer. Bring them to room temperature before using in baking.

If you prefer, melt the caramels in the microwave. Combine with the cream and microwave on High until caramels are softened, about 2 minutes. Stir well to blend.

- **Preheat oven to 350°F (180°C)**
- **15- by 10- by 1-inch (2 L) jelly roll pan, greased**

1 cup	butter, softened	250 mL
½ cup	packed brown sugar	125 mL
2 cups	all-purpose flour	500 mL
2 cups	semi-sweet chocolate chips	500 mL
1 lb	soft caramels, unwrapped (about 60)	500 g
⅓ cup	whipping (35%) cream	75 mL
1 cup	coarsely chopped cashews, divided	250 mL

1. In a large bowl, using an electric mixer on medium speed, beat butter and brown sugar until light and creamy, about 3 minutes. Add flour and mix on low speed until crumbly. Press evenly into prepared pan.

2. Bake in preheated oven until golden around edges, 10 to 12 minutes. Sprinkle with chocolate chips. Return to oven to melt chocolate, about 2 minutes. Spread chocolate over base. Let cool in pan on rack or until chocolate is set, about 30 minutes.

3. In a saucepan, combine caramels and whipping cream. Heat over low heat, stirring constantly, until caramels are melted and mixture is smooth. Stir in ¾ cup (175 mL) of the cashews. Spread carefully over chocolate layer. Sprinkle with remaining cashews. Let cool completely in pan on rack. Cut into thin bars.

Variation
Use walnuts, almonds or pecans in place of cashews.

Chocolate Hazelnut Bars

These yummy bars taste like a big chocolate chip oatmeal cookie. They're easy to make and a good choice if you're in a hurry.

MAKES 36 TO 66 BARS (see Cutting Guide, page 10)

- **Preparation: 15 minutes**
- **Baking: 15 minutes**
- **Freezing: excellent**

TIPS

For a softer cookie, prepare these bars the day before you intend to serve them.

When a recipe calls for all-purpose flour, you can substitute whole wheat flour; the texture will be a little drier, and the product will have a nice nutty flavor. I often use half of each kind of flour, for the best qualities of both.

Hazelnuts are also called filberts. If you prefer, remove the outer brown skin before using them in baking. Toast the nuts on a rimmed baking sheet at 350°F (180°C) for about 5 minutes. Transfer the warm nuts to a towel and rub together. The skins should come off in the towel.

- **Preheat oven to 375°F (190°C)**
- **17- by 11- by 1-inch (3 L) jelly roll pan, greased**

1 cup	butter, softened	250 mL
1 cup	packed brown sugar	250 mL
½ cup	granulated sugar	125 mL
2	eggs	2
1 tsp	vanilla	5 mL
1¾ cups	all-purpose flour	425 mL
1 cup	quick-cooking rolled oats	250 mL
1 tsp	baking soda	5 mL
¼ tsp	salt	1 mL
2 cups	semi-sweet chocolate chips	500 mL
1½ cups	coarsely chopped hazelnuts	375 mL

1. In a bowl, using an electric mixer on medium speed, beat butter and brown and granulated sugars until light and creamy, about 3 minutes. Add eggs, one at a time, beating well after each addition. Beat in vanilla. Stir in flour, oats, baking soda and salt, mixing well. Stir in chocolate chips and hazelnuts. Spread dough evenly in prepared pan.

2. Bake in preheated oven until golden, about 15 minutes. Let cool completely in pan on rack. Cut into bars.

Variation

Macadamia nuts make a wonderful substitution for the hazelnuts in this bar.

Chewy Cranberry, Coconut and Chocolate Chip Bars

This bar is particularly nice for holiday entertaining. One pan goes a long way, and the bars keep well.

MAKES 36 TO 66 BARS (see Cutting Guide, page 10)

- **Preparation: 15 minutes**
- **Baking: 15 minutes**
- **Freezing: excellent**

TIPS

I have specified sweetened coconut because it seems to be more readily available than the unsweetened variety. But sweetened and unsweetened coconut can be used interchangeably in any recipe to suit your preference.

It's best to purchase coconut in packages rather than in bulk as it will retain its freshness longer. Coconut purchased in bulk tends to dry out quickly.

Be sure to use the larger jelly roll pan, as recommended, when making this recipe. If you use the smaller 15- by 10-inch (2 L) one, it will overflow.

- **Preheat oven to 375°F (190°C)**
- **17- by 11- by 1-inch (3 L) jelly roll pan, greased**

1 cup	butter, softened	250 mL
¾ cup	granulated sugar	175 mL
¾ cup	packed brown sugar	175 mL
2	eggs	2
2 cups	all-purpose flour	500 mL
1 tsp	baking soda	5 mL
2 cups	milk chocolate chips, divided	500 mL
1 cup	sweetened flaked coconut (see Tips, left)	250 mL
1 cup	dried cranberries	250 mL

1. In a large bowl, using an electric mixer on medium speed, beat butter and granulated and brown sugars until light and creamy, about 3 minutes. Add eggs, one at a time, beating well after each addition. Add flour and baking soda and beat on low speed, mixing well. Stir in 1⅓ cups (325 mL) of the chocolate chips, coconut and cranberries, blending thoroughly. Spread evenly in prepared pan. Sprinkle remaining chocolate chips over top.

2. Bake in preheated oven until set and golden, about 15 minutes. Let cool completely in pan on rack. Cut into bars.

Variations

Substitute dried cherries for the cranberries. Because they're larger than cranberries, use 1 tbsp (15 mL) or so more, and chop them a little.

White chocolate chips in place of the milk chocolate also look nice in this bar, and they create a different but equally great taste.

Chocolate Coconut Squares

◆

Even though these squares are rich, they're so good it's hard to stop at just one. Cut them small to control your consumption.

MAKES 24 SQUARES (see Cutting Guide, page 10)

- **Preparation: 25 minutes**
- **Baking: 40 minutes**
- **Freezing: excellent**

TIPS

The filling is quite thick. If you drop it by small spoonfuls over the entire surface of the bars, you can easily spread it to cover.

To toast almonds, place them on a baking sheet in a 350°F (180°C) oven and stir often until golden, 5 to 10 minutes.

There are a number of ways to melt chocolate chips. You can place them in a double boiler over hot, not boiling, water or in a small saucepan over low heat. In both cases, stir frequently until smooth. Melt them in a microwave oven on Medium power until softened (about 1 minute for ¼ cup/50 mL), then stir until smooth.

- **Preheat oven to 350°F (180°C)**
- **13- by 9-inch (3 L) cake pan, greased**

BASE

4	squares (1 oz/28 g each) unsweetened chocolate, chopped	4
1 cup	butter	250 mL
2 cups	granulated sugar	500 mL
3	eggs	3
1¼ cups	all-purpose flour	300 mL

FILLING

3 cups	unsweetened flaked coconut	750 mL
1	can (10 oz/300 mL) sweetened condensed milk	1
¾ tsp	almond extract	3 mL

TOPPING

1½ cups	semi-sweet chocolate chips, melted (see Tips, left)	375 mL
⅔ cup	sliced almonds, toasted (see Tips, left)	150 mL

1. *Base:* In a saucepan over low heat, melt chocolate and butter, stirring constantly, until smooth. Remove from heat. Stir in sugar until blended. Whisk in eggs, one at a time, mixing lightly after each addition. Stir in flour, mixing well. Spread half of the batter in prepared pan. Set remainder aside.

2. *Filling:* In a bowl, combine coconut, sweetened condensed milk and almond extract, mixing well. Drop by small spoonfuls over base and spread evenly. Cover with reserved batter and spread evenly.

3. Bake in preheated oven until set, 35 to 40 minutes. Let cool completely in pan on rack.

4. *Topping:* Spread melted chocolate chips evenly over baked bar. Sprinkle almonds on top. Chill until chocolate is set, about 30 minutes. Cut into squares.

Variations

For the holiday season, substitute mint extract for the almond and sprinkle crushed candy canes on top.

If nut allergies are a concern, replace the almond extract with vanilla and omit the nuts on top.

Praline Bars

These bars are a real favorite. The crisp toffee crust and chocolate toffee nut top remind me of a chocolate toffee bar.

MAKES 20 TO 54 BARS (see Cutting Guide, page 10)

- **Preparation: 20 minutes**
- **Baking: 20 minutes**
- **Freezing: excellent**

TIPS

My favorite brand of toffee bits is Skor, and I like to buy them in bulk. Others, such as Heath bits, are also available in bulk, but I don't recommend being over-inventoried on this product. If toffee bits become stale, they take longer to soften.

If the chocolate chips aren't melted enough to swirl after standing for 3 minutes, return the pan to the oven for 1 minute.

Be sure to use fresh, pure chocolate chips. When chocolate chips get older or are made from imitation chocolate, they don't melt as easily, making spreading difficult. Store chocolate in a cool, dry place, not in the freezer or refrigerator.

- **Preheat oven to 350°F (180°C)**
- **13- by 9-inch (3 L) cake pan, greased**

CRUST

½ cup	butter	125 mL
½ cup	packed brown sugar	125 mL
1	egg	1
1 cup	all-purpose flour	250 mL
¼ tsp	baking powder	1 mL
¼ cup	toffee bits (see Tips, left)	50 mL
¼ cup	chopped pecans	50 mL

TOPPING

1 cup	semi-sweet chocolate chips	250 mL
1 cup	white chocolate chips	250 mL
¼ cup	toffee bits	50 mL
¼ cup	chopped pecans	50 mL

1. *Crust:* In a large saucepan over low heat, melt butter. Remove from heat. Stir in brown sugar. Whisk in egg, mixing well. Stir in flour and baking powder, mixing well. Stir in toffee bits and pecans. Spread evenly in prepared pan. Bake in preheated oven until edges are lightly browned, 15 to 20 minutes.

2. *Topping:* Sprinkle semi-sweet and white chocolate chips evenly over hot bars. Let stand for 3 minutes to melt chocolate. Swirl lightly with the tip of a knife to create a marbled effect. Sprinkle toffee bits and pecans evenly over top. Let cool completely in pan on rack. Cut into bars.

Variation
Replace pecans with almonds or hazelnuts.

Chocolate Caramel Pecan Bars

I love how these bars combine crisp and chewy textures in one bar. They resemble the popular Turtles or Slow Pokes chocolates.

MAKES 20 TO 54 BARS (see Cutting Guide, page 10)

- **Preparation: 20 minutes**
- **Baking: 20 minutes**
- **Freezing: excellent**

TIPS

If you prefer, use a large wooden spoon to mix the crust.

If the chocolate chips aren't melted enough to swirl after standing for 3 minutes, return the pan to the oven for 1 minute.

Store nuts in the freezer to retain freshness. Let them come to room temperature before using them in baking.

Store brown sugar in a sealed heavy plastic bag. It stays moist and can easily be measured by placing a measuring cup in the bag and packing it into the cup through the bag — no messy hands.

If you're using dark pans, reduce the time slightly to avoid overbaking.

- Preheat oven to 350°F (180°C)
- 13- by 9-inch (3 L) cake pan, greased

CRUST

2 cups	all-purpose flour	500 mL
¾ cup	packed brown sugar	175 mL
½ cup	butter, softened	125 mL
1½ cups	pecan halves	375 mL

CARAMEL FILLING

1 cup	butter	250 mL
¾ cup	packed brown sugar	175 mL

CHOCOLATE GLAZE

1⅓ cups	semi-sweet chocolate chips	325 mL

1. *Crust:* In a large bowl, combine flour, brown sugar and butter. Using an electric mixer on medium speed, beat until crumbly. Press firmly into prepared pan. Sprinkle pecans evenly in a single layer over crust.

2. *Caramel Filling:* In a saucepan over medium heat, combine butter and brown sugar. Cook, stirring constantly, until mixture begins to boil, forming bubbles over the entire surface, about 1½ minutes. Pour evenly over pecans on crust.

3. Bake in preheated oven until caramel is bubbly, about 20 minutes. Remove from oven.

4. *Chocolate Glaze:* Immediately sprinkle chocolate chips evenly over bar. Let stand for 3 minutes to melt chocolate. Swirl lightly with the tip of a knife to create a marbled effect, leaving a few chips whole. Let cool completely in pan on rack. Cut into bars.

Variation

Replace pecans with walnut halves. Cut them in half if large.

Coconut Chocolate Caramel Squares

Packed into a colorful box or tin, these make a wonderful hostess gift.

MAKES 16 TO 36 SQUARES
(see Cutting Guide, page 10)

- **Preparation: 25 minutes**
- **Cooking: 14 minutes**
- **Baking: 24 minutes**
- **Chilling: 4 hours**
- **Freezing: excellent**

TIPS

Be aware that sweetened condensed milk burns very quickly. So don't leave it unattended on the stove.

These bars can be made up to 3 days ahead of serving. Store them in an airtight container in the refrigerator but let stand for about 30 minutes at room temperature before serving.

- **Preheat oven to 350°F (180°C)**
- **8-inch (2 L) square cake pan, lined with parchment paper**

BASE

¾ cup	all-purpose flour	175 mL
⅔ cup	medium flaked coconut	150 mL
½ cup	packed brown sugar	125 mL
1 tsp	baking powder	5 mL
⅓ cup	butter, melted	75 mL

CARAMEL FILLING

1	can (10 oz/300 mL) sweetened condensed milk	1
2 tbsp	butter	25 mL
1 tbsp	corn syrup	15 mL

CHOCOLATE TOPPING

4	squares (1 oz/28 g each) bittersweet chocolate, chopped	4
3 tbsp	butter	45 mL

1. *Base:* In a bowl, combine flour, coconut, brown sugar and baking powder. Stir in melted butter, mixing well. Press evenly into prepared pan. Bake in preheated oven until golden around the edges, 10 to 12 minutes.

2. *Caramel Filling:* In a small heavy saucepan, combine sweetened condensed milk, butter and corn syrup. Cook over medium heat, stirring constantly, until mixture thickens slightly, about 10 minutes. Spread evenly over base. Return to oven and bake until lightly browned around the edges, 10 to 12 minutes. Let cool completely in pan on rack.

3. *Chocolate Topping:* In a small saucepan over low heat, melt chocolate and butter, stirring constantly, until smooth. Spread quickly over filling. Let cool at room temperature for 1 hour. Transfer to refrigerator and chill thoroughly, about 3 hours. Cut into squares.

Variation

Replace coconut with ground almonds and add ½ tsp (2 mL) almond extract to the filling.

Chocolate Almond Toffee Bars

A great treat to enjoy with a cold glass of milk or a steaming cup of coffee.

**MAKES 20 TO 54 BARS
(see Cutting Guide,
page 10)**

- **Preparation: 15 minutes**
- **Baking: 25 minutes**
- **Freezing: excellent**

TIPS

When making bars, line the pan with parchment paper or greased aluminum foil, leaving an overlap on the sides. After they've cooled, chill them briefly to firm them up. Remove them from the pan, pull off the paper and place on a cutting board for easy slicing.

Ovens are often inaccurate so a good oven thermometer is a wise investment. You can check your temperature and adjust the control accordingly. Whenever a range is given, check your bars at the earliest baking time.

- **Preheat oven to 325°F (160°C)**
- **13- by 9-inch (3 L) cake pan, ungreased**

½ cup	butter	125 mL
1 cup	quick-cooking rolled oats	250 mL
1 cup	graham wafer crumbs	250 mL
1¼ cups	semi-sweet chocolate chips	300 mL
1 cup	toffee bits (see Tip, page 54)	250 mL
1 cup	chopped unblanched almonds	250 mL
1	can (10 oz/300 mL) sweetened condensed milk	1

1. Place butter in pan and place in preheated oven until butter melts. Remove from oven. Tilt the pan to cover the bottom evenly with melted butter. Sprinkle oats and graham wafer crumbs evenly over top, pressing with a spatula, if necessary, to ensure sure oats and crumbs are thoroughly moistened.

2. Sprinkle chocolate chips, toffee bits and almonds evenly over base. Drizzle sweetened condensed milk evenly over top. Bake until golden around the edges, 20 to 25 minutes. Let cool completely in pan on rack. Cut into bars.

Variation

For a fruity version, replace half of the chocolate chips with dried cranberries or chopped dried apricots.

White Chocolate Pecan Cranberry Squares

Fresh cranberries add a festive touch to these deliciously decadent squares.

MAKES 24 SQUARES (see Cutting Guide, page 10)

- **Preparation: 25 minutes**
- **Baking: 55 minutes**
- **Freezing: excellent**

TIPS

If you prefer, mix the crust in a food processor. Use cubed cold butter rather than softened. You can also mix the crust in a bowl, cutting cold butter in using a pastry blender, 2 knives or your fingers. Whichever method you use, the mixture should resemble coarse crumbs.

Try a new look for bar cookies: cut them into triangles or diamonds instead of the traditional squares and rectangles. See the Cutting Guide, page 10.

For a fancier presentation, drizzle the cooled bars with melted white chocolate.

- **Preheat oven to 350°F (180°C)**
- **13- by 9-inch (3 L) cake pan, greased**

CRUST

2 cups	all-purpose flour	500 mL
½ cup	granulated sugar	125 mL
¾ cup	butter, softened	175 mL
¼ cup	ground pecans	50 mL

TOPPING

4	eggs	4
1 cup	granulated sugar	250 mL
1 cup	corn syrup	250 mL
3 tbsp	butter, melted	45 mL
1 cup	coarsely chopped pecans	250 mL
¾ cup	coarsely chopped cranberries	175 mL
¾ cup	white chocolate chips	175 mL

1. *Crust:* In a large bowl, combine flour, sugar and butter. Using an electric mixer on low speed, beat until mixture resembles coarse crumbs. Stir in ground pecans. Press evenly into prepared pan. Bake in preheated oven until golden around the edges, 12 to 15 minutes.

2. *Topping:* In a bowl, whisk eggs, sugar, corn syrup and melted butter until blended. Stir in pecans, cranberries and white chocolate chips. Pour evenly over warm crust.

3. Return to oven and bake until set and golden, 35 to 40 minutes. Let cool completely in pan on rack. Cut into squares.

Variation
Replace pecans with walnuts, slivered almonds or cashews.

White Chocolate Cream Bars

These look a bit like Nanaimo bars but taste quite different — they aren't nearly as sweet.

MAKES 18 TO 48 BARS
(see Cutting Guide, page 10)

- **Preparation: 20 minutes**
- **Baking: 35 minutes**
- **Chilling: 2 hours**
- **Freezing: excellent**

TIPS

If serving these at a special occasion, garnish with some shaved white or milk chocolate.

If you prefer, use the microwave to make the topping. Combine the ingredients in a microwave-safe dish and microwave on Medium for about 1 minute, until chocolate is softened. Stir until smooth.

- **Preheat oven to 350°F (180°C)**
- **8-inch (2 L) square cake pan, greased**

BASE

1½ cups	chocolate wafer crumbs	375 mL
⅓ cup	butter, melted	75 mL

FILLING

1 cup	white chocolate chips	250 mL
¾ cup	whipping (35%) cream	175 mL
3	eggs	3
⅓ cup	granulated sugar	75 mL

TOPPING

4	squares (1 oz/28 g each) semi-sweet chocolate, chopped	4
2 tbsp	butter	25 mL

1. *Base:* In a bowl, combine chocolate wafer crumbs and melted butter. Mix well. Press evenly into prepared pan. Bake in preheated oven until set, about 10 minutes.

2. *Filling:* In a saucepan over low heat, combine white chocolate chips and whipping cream. Heat, stirring constantly, until chocolate is melted and mixture is smooth. Remove from heat and let cool for 10 minutes.

3. In a bowl, whisk eggs and sugar until frothy. Add melted chocolate mixture, stirring until smoothly blended. Pour over base. Bake in preheated oven until set and golden, 20 to 25 minutes. Let cool for 20 minutes in pan on rack.

4. *Topping:* In a saucepan over low heat, melt chocolate and butter, stirring constantly, until smooth. Spread evenly over base. Refrigerate until cold, about 2 hours. Cut into bars.

Variations

Replace white chocolate chips with milk chocolate chips.

For a different three-layer treat, use white chocolate in the topping.

Heavenly White Chocolate Macadamia Bars

One bite of these sensational bars and you'll think you're in heaven.

MAKES 20 TO 54 BARS (see Cutting Guide, page 10)

- **Preparation: 20 minutes**
- **Baking: 37 minutes**
- **Freezing: excellent**

TIPS

In this bar, I like the look of coarsely chopped chocolate instead of chips. The irregularity of shreds and chunks gives a more interesting appearance. But you can use 1¼ cups (300 mL) chips if you prefer.

Buy good-quality white chocolate that's flavorful and creamy. Look for cocoa butter, not vegetable shortening, as the main ingredient. Ghirardelli is a reliable brand of white chocolate.

- **Preheat oven to 350°F (180°C)**
- **13- by 9-inch (3 L) cake pan, greased**

CRUST

½ cup	butter, softened	125 mL
½ cup	granulated sugar	125 mL
1½ cups	all-purpose flour	375 mL

TOPPING

1 cup	packed brown sugar	250 mL
¼ cup	granulated sugar	50 mL
½ tsp	baking powder	2 mL
3	eggs	3
1 tsp	vanilla	5 mL
2 tbsp	butter, melted	25 mL
¼ cup	all-purpose flour	50 mL
2 cups	coarsely chopped macadamia nuts	500 mL
8	squares (1 oz/28 g each) white chocolate, coarsely chopped	8

1. *Crust:* In a bowl, using a wooden spoon, beat butter and sugar until light and creamy, about 2 minutes. Add flour and beat until mixture resembles coarse crumbs. Press evenly into prepared pan. Bake in preheated oven until golden around the edges, 10 to 12 minutes.

2. *Topping:* In a bowl, whisk brown and granulated sugars, baking powder, eggs, vanilla and melted butter. Whisk until smooth. Whisk in flour, mixing well. Stir in nuts and chocolate. Spread evenly over crust.

3. Return to oven and bake until top is set and golden, 20 to 25 minutes. Let cool completely in pan on rack. Cut into bars.

Variations

Macadamia nuts are expensive. If the cost seems outrageous, substitute blanched almonds for half of them. You can also use a mixture of macadamia nuts, almonds and Brazil nuts, keeping the total amount at 2 cups (500 mL).

Chocolate Raspberry Crumble Bars

◆

The combo of chocolate and raspberry is a perennial hit.

MAKES 18 TO 48 BARS (see Cutting Guide, page 10)

- Preparation: 20 minutes
- Baking: 35 minutes
- Freezing: excellent

TIPS

If you prefer, use a large wooden spoon to mix the crust.

Use a good-quality, thick jam with great flavor. The taste of the bar is only as good as the ingredients that go in it.

To soften jam for easy spreading, stir it well.

- **Preheat oven to 375°F (190°C)**
- **8-inch (2 L) or 9-inch (2.5 L) square cake pan, greased**

TOPPING

⅔ cup	all-purpose flour	150 mL
½ cup	chopped pecans	125 mL
⅓ cup	packed brown sugar	75 mL
¼ cup	cold butter, cubed	50 mL

CRUST

1¼ cups	all-purpose flour	300 mL
½ cup	packed brown sugar	125 mL
½ cup	butter, softened	125 mL
⅓ cup	raspberry jam	75 mL
1 cup	milk chocolate chips	250 mL

1. *Topping:* In a food processor fitted with a metal blade, combine flour, pecans, brown sugar and butter. Pulse until crumbly. Set aside.

2. *Crust:* In a bowl, combine flour, brown sugar and butter. Using an electric mixer on low speed, beat until crumbly. Press firmly into prepared pan. Bake in preheated oven until edges are lightly browned, 12 to 15 minutes. Spread with jam and sprinkle chocolate chips evenly over top. Sprinkle with topping.

3. Return to oven and bake until lightly browned, 15 to 20 minutes. Let cool completely in pan on rack. Cut into bars.

Variation

Vary the jam to suit your taste. Apricot and strawberry also work well in this recipe.

Creamy Caramel Chocolate Bars

These yummy bars are like caramel-filled chocolate on a cookie crust, with the addition of nuts.

MAKES 18 TO 48 BARS (see Cutting Guide, page 10)

- **Preparation: 20 minutes**
- **Cooking: 10 minutes**
- **Baking: 25 minutes**
- **Freezing: excellent**

TIPS

Cooling the baked crust before you add the filling prevents it from becoming soggy.

Keep a close eye on sweetened condensed milk when cooking. The minute you leave it unattended it will burn.

These squares are very rich. For a pretty presentation, cut them small and serve in small paper cups like the ones boxed chocolates come in.

- **Preheat oven to 350°F (180°C)**
- **9-inch (2.5 L) square cake pan, greased**

CRUST

1 1/4 cups	all-purpose flour	300 mL
1/4 cup	granulated sugar	50 mL
1/2 cup	cold butter, cubed	125 mL

FILLING

1	can (10 oz/300 mL) sweetened condensed milk	1
1/2 cup	granulated sugar	125 mL
1/2 cup	butter	125 mL
2 tbsp	corn syrup	25 mL
1 tsp	vanilla	5 mL
1 cup	coarsely chopped pecans	250 mL

TOPPING

4	squares (1 oz/28 g each) semi-sweet chocolate, chopped	4
2 tbsp	butter	25 mL

1. *Crust:* In a bowl, combine flour and sugar. Using a pastry blender, 2 knives or your fingers, cut in butter until mixture resembles coarse crumbs. Press evenly into prepared pan. Bake in preheated oven until golden, 20 to 25 minutes. Let cool in pan on rack for 15 minutes.

2. *Filling:* In a heavy saucepan over medium heat, combine sweetened condensed milk, sugar, butter and corn syrup. Cook, stirring constantly, until sugar is dissolved and mixture comes to a boil, about 5 minutes. Reduce heat to medium-low and simmer, stirring constantly, until mixture thickens and turns a light caramel color, 6 to 9 minutes. Remove from heat. Stir in vanilla and pecans. Spread evenly over cooled crust. Chill until set, about 1 hour.

3. *Topping:* In a saucepan over low heat, melt chocolate and butter, stirring constantly, until smooth. Spread over filling. Chill for about 30 minutes to set chocolate. Cut into bars.

Variations

Decorate each bar with a pecan half.

Replace pecans with walnuts.

Chocolate Cherry Nut Bars

I love the combination of flavors in these chunky colorful bars. Enjoy with caution — they can quickly become addictive.

MAKES 20 TO 54 BARS (see Cutting Guide, page 10)

- **Preparation: 20 minutes**
- **Baking: 37 minutes**
- **Freezing: excellent**

TIPS

Candied (glacé) cherries darken with age. Look for ones that are a bright color.

Get a head start on your holiday baking. Make an extra pan of these and freeze them.

- **Preheat oven to 350°F (180°C)**
- **13- by 9-inch (3 L) cake pan, greased**

CRUST

1¼ cups	all-purpose flour	300 mL
½ cup	packed brown sugar	125 mL
¾ cup	cold butter, cubed	175 mL

TOPPING

2	eggs	2
⅔ cup	packed brown sugar	150 mL
1½ cups	deluxe salted mixed nuts (no peanuts)	375 mL
1½ cups	halved red and green candied (glacé) cherries	375 mL
1 cup	semi-sweet chocolate chips	250 mL

1. *Crust:* In a bowl, combine flour and brown sugar. Using a pastry blender, 2 knives or your fingers, cut in butter until mixture resembles coarse crumbs. Press evenly into prepared pan. Bake in preheated oven until golden around the edges, 10 to 12 minutes.

2. *Topping:* In a bowl, whisk eggs and brown sugar until blended. Stir in nuts, cherries and chocolate chips, mixing well. Spread evenly over crust.

3. Return to oven and bake until topping is set, 20 to 25 minutes. Let cool completely in pan on rack. Cut into bars.

Variations

Replace semi-sweet chocolate chips with white chocolate chips.

Use all red cherries instead of the red and green mixture.

Replace ½ cup (125 mL) of the cherries with candied (glacé) pineapple.

Add a drizzle of melted white chocolate on cooled bars. It shows off the color nicely.

Chocolate Marshmallow Meringue Bars

A layer of chocolate, nuts and marshmallows hides under a beautiful golden meringue and sits on a soft, buttery crust — delicious, but they won't make a dieter's list.

MAKES 20 TO 54 BARS (see Cutting Guide, page 10)

- **Preparation: 25 minutes**
- **Baking: 30 minutes**
- **Freezing: excellent**

TIPS

Although it's always important to have all your ingredients at room temperature for baking, this is particularly true when making meringue. Otherwise, you won't get the desired volume.

Don't be surprised if your meringue thins out a bit when folding in the brown sugar. Because of the high amount of sugar, it doesn't stay stiff.

To spread the meringue easily over the filling, dip the spatula in hot water.

For the best walnut flavor, buy fresh California walnut halves and chop them, rather than buying prechopped.

- **Preheat oven to 350°F (180°C)**
- **13- by 9-inch (3 L) cake pan, greased**

BASE

½ cup	butter, softened	125 mL
1 cup	granulated sugar	250 mL
1	egg	1
2	egg yolks	2
1½ cups	all-purpose flour	375 mL
1 tsp	baking powder	5 mL
¼ tsp	salt	1 mL

FILLING

1 cup	chopped walnuts	250 mL
1 cup	milk chocolate chips	250 mL
1 cup	miniature marshmallows	250 mL

TOPPING

2	egg whites	2
1 cup	packed brown sugar	250 mL

1. *Base:* In a bowl, using an electric mixer on high speed, beat butter, sugar, egg and egg yolks until light and creamy. Combine flour, baking powder and salt. Stir into creamed mixture until well blended. Spread evenly in prepared pan.

2. *Filling:* Sprinkle walnuts, chocolate chips and marshmallows evenly over batter.

3. *Topping:* In a small bowl, using an electric mixer with clean beaters on high speed, beat egg whites until stiff. Gently fold in brown sugar. Spread evenly over filling.

4. Bake in preheated oven until golden brown, 25 to 30 minutes. Let cool completely in pan on rack. Cut into bars.

Variations

For a stronger hit of chocolate, use semi-sweet instead of milk chocolate chips.

Replace walnuts with pecans.

Fruit Bars and Squares

Fruit bars and squares are extremely varied. They can be plain or fancy or something in between. They may include fresh fruits such as apples and oranges, dried fruits such as apricots and figs, candied fruits and even canned fruits. Some are so much like cake they make great desserts — top with a dollop of whipped cream or a scoop of ice cream to finish them off. Others are perfect finger food, the final embellishment to a cookie tray, passed at festivities during the holiday season. There is so much variety in this chapter, I'm sure you'll find recipes that will become favorites for every occasion.

◄ *Caramel Apple Bars*

Caramel Apple Bars

◆

These bars bring back fond memories of the caramel apples I enjoyed as a kid at fall fairs, exhibitions, and Halloween.

MAKES 20 TO 54 BARS (see Cutting Guide, page 10)

- **Preparation: 25 minutes**
- **Baking: 30 minutes**
- **Freezing: not recommended**

TIPS

Use a firm, crisp apple like Granny Smith or Spartan to avoid a soggy crust.

For a special treat, serve these bars with hot or cold mulled cider.

If you're using a glass baking dish, remember to decrease the oven temperature by 25°F (10°C).

- **Preheat oven to 350°F (180°C)**
- **13- by 9-inch (3 L) cake pan, greased**

2/3 cup	butter, softened	150 mL
3/4 cup	packed brown sugar	175 mL
1 tsp	vanilla	5 mL
1 3/4 cups	quick-cooking rolled oats	425 mL
1 1/2 cups	all-purpose flour	375 mL
1 1/4 tsp	cinnamon	6 mL
2 cups	grated, peeled apple (4 large)	500 mL
1/2 cup	caramel sundae sauce	125 mL
3/4 cup	chopped peanuts	175 mL

1. In a bowl, combine butter, brown sugar and vanilla. Using an electric mixer on medium speed, beat until blended. Add oats, flour and cinnamon. Beat on low speed until crumbly. Set aside 1 1/2 cups (375 mL) for topping. Press remainder into prepared pan. Scatter apples evenly over crust. Sprinkle reserved topping over apples. Drizzle caramel sauce over crumbs. Sprinkle peanuts on top.

2. Bake in preheated oven until top is set and golden, 25 to 30 minutes. Let cool completely in pan on rack. Cut into bars.

Variations

Use half pears and half apples.

Replace peanuts with cashews.

Cherry Lime Squares

Here's a square for all seasons. I love these flavors during the holiday season, but the refreshing combination of fruit is great in the summer as well.

MAKES 24 SQUARES (see Cutting Guide, page 10)

- **Preparation: 25 minutes**
- **Baking: 40 minutes**
- **Freezing: excellent**

TIPS

Always use freshly squeezed lime juice for the best flavor.

To get the most juice out of limes, warm them for about 10 seconds on High in the microwave. Grate the zest off first.

This crust is a little crumbly to cut, but I think it contributes to the appeal of these bars.

- **Preheat oven to 350°F (180°C)**
- **13- by 9-inch (3 L) cake pan, greased**

CRUST

2 cups	all-purpose flour	500 mL
1/2 cup	confectioner's (icing) sugar	125 mL
1 tbsp	grated lime zest	15 mL
1/4 tsp	salt	1 mL
1 cup	cold butter, cubed	250 mL

TOPPING

4	eggs	4
2 cups	granulated sugar	500 mL
1 tbsp	grated lime zest	15 mL
1/3 cup	freshly squeezed lime juice	75 mL
1/4 cup	all-purpose flour	50 mL
1 tsp	baking powder	5 mL
1 cup	chopped dried cherries	250 mL
	Confectioner's (icing) sugar	

1. *Crust:* In a bowl, combine flour, confectioner's sugar, lime zest and salt. Using a pastry blender, 2 knives or your fingers, cut in butter until mixture resembles coarse crumbs. Press evenly into prepared pan. Bake in preheated oven until edges are lightly browned, 12 to 15 minutes.

2. *Topping:* In a bowl, whisk eggs and sugar until blended. Whisk in lime zest and juice, mixing well. Combine flour and baking powder. Whisk into egg mixture until smooth. Stir in cherries. Pour over crust.

3. Return to oven and bake just until set, 20 to 25 minutes. Let cool completely in pan on rack. Chill for 2 hours for easy cutting. Sprinkle with confectioner's sugar. Cut into squares.

Variations

Substitute an equal quantity of lemon juice and zest for the lime.

Add 1/3 cup (75 mL) ground almonds to the crust, along with the flour.

Fruit 'n' Nut Squares

◆

Sweet and yummy, these squares are a bit like fruitcake on a crust. Since they are quite rich, cut them into small bites.

MAKES 24 SQUARES (see Cutting Guide, page 10)

- **Preparation: 25 minutes**
- **Baking: 42 minutes**
- **Freezing: excellent**

TIPS

Theses squares freeze well, so they're a great make-ahead treat for the festive season.

It pays to buy fresh glacé fruit when you're ready to bake rather than using leftovers. When stored, the fruit dries out and forms sugar crystals, which will affect your baked goods.

In my opinion, the tastiest walnuts are from California. Always taste nuts before using to make sure they're not rancid. This is especially true of walnuts as their healthful oils spoil very quickly.

- **Preheat oven to 350°F (180°C)**
- **13- by 9-inch (3 L) cake pan, greased**

CRUST

1¼ cups	all-purpose flour	300 mL
½ cup	granulated sugar	125 mL
½ cup	cold butter, cubed	125 mL
1	egg yolk, beaten	1

TOPPING

1	can (10 oz/300 mL) sweetened condensed milk	1
2 tbsp	all-purpose flour	25 mL
¼ tsp	ground nutmeg	1 mL
2 tbsp	brandy	25 mL
¾ cup	sweetened flaked coconut	175 mL
½ cup	chopped walnuts	125 mL
½ cup	slivered almonds	125 mL
⅔ cup	chopped candied (glacé) cherries	150 mL
⅓ cup	chopped candied (glacé) pineapple	75 mL

1. *Crust:* In a food processor fitted with a metal blade, combine flour, sugar and butter. Process until mixture resembles coarse crumbs. With machine running, add egg yolk, mixing just until moist crumbs form. Press evenly into prepared pan. Bake in preheated oven until golden around edges, 10 to 12 minutes.

2. *Topping:* In a bowl, stir together sweetened condensed milk, flour, nutmeg and brandy until well blended. Stir in coconut, walnuts, almonds, cherries and pineapple, mixing well. Spread evenly over warm crust.

3. Return to oven and bake until set and golden, 25 to 30 minutes. Let cool completely in pan on rack. Cut into squares.

Variations

Replace candied pineapple with candied mixed peel.

Replace brandy with an equal quantity of orange or almond liqueur, or apple juice.

Cranberry Apricot Oat Bars

◆

Apricots and cranberries are a dynamite combination. This flavor combination always seems to be a hit, no matter what you make.

MAKES 20 TO 54 BARS (see Cutting Guide, page 10)

- **Preparation: 20 minutes**
- **Baking: 37 minutes**
- **Freezing: excellent**

TIPS

The filling will spread more easily if, after dropping it over the crust, you let it sit for a minute to warm, then spread gently with a small spatula.

Use regular jam rather than a light variety, which will be quite a bit thinner in consistency.

- **Preheat oven to 350°F (180°C)**
- **13- by 9-inch (3 L) cake pan, greased**

CRUST

2 cups	quick-cooking rolled oats	500 mL
1 1/2 cups	all-purpose flour	375 mL
1 1/2 cups	packed brown sugar	375 mL
1 tsp	baking powder	5 mL
1/2 tsp	baking soda	2 mL
1 tsp	cinnamon	5 mL
1 cup	cold butter, cubed	250 mL

FILLING

2 cups	apricot jam	500 mL
1 1/2 cups	dried cranberries	375 mL
1 tbsp	grated orange zest	15 mL

TOPPING

2/3 cup	slivered almonds	150 mL

1. *Crust:* In a bowl, combine oats, flour, brown sugar, baking powder, baking soda and cinnamon. Using a pastry blender, 2 knives or your fingers, cut in butter until mixture resembles coarse crumbs. Set aside 1 cup (250 mL) for topping. Press remainder evenly into prepared pan. Bake in preheated oven until golden around edges, 10 to 12 minutes.

2. *Filling:* In a bowl, combine apricot jam, dried cranberries and orange zest, mixing well. Drop small spoonfuls over hot crust. Spread gently, leaving a 3/4-inch (2 cm) border of crust.

3. *Topping:* Stir almonds into reserved crumble mixture. Sprinkle evenly over filling.

4. Return to oven and bake until golden, 20 to 25 minutes. Let cool completely in pan on rack. Cut into bars.

Variations

Replace apricot jam with an equal quantity of strawberry jam.

Substitute an equal quantity of cherry jam for the apricot and chopped dried cherries for the cranberries.

Replace almonds with chopped pecans.

Festive Fruit Triangles

This is an attractive candied fruit and almond Florentine cookie on a shortbread crust with a drizzle of chocolate to top it off. Tasty and elegant.

MAKES 48 TO 120 TRIANGLES (see Cutting Guide, page 10)

- **Preparation: 25 minutes**
- **Cooking: 3 minutes**
- **Baking: 20 minutes**
- **Freezing: excellent**

TIPS

If you prefer, buy deluxe mixed candied (glacé) fruit for use in this recipe (the mixture includes cherries and pineapple). Use 1²/₃ cups (400 mL) in place of the cherries and pineapple.

If you don't care for triangles, make these cookies any shape you like. Strips, bars and squares also work well.

- **Preheat oven to 375°F (190°C)**
- **15- by 10- by 1-inch (2 L) jelly roll pan, greased**

CRUST

1½ cups	all-purpose flour	375 mL
½ cup	confectioner's (icing) sugar, sifted	125 mL
½ cup	cold butter, cubed	125 mL
2 tbsp	whipping (35%) cream	25 mL
1 tsp	vanilla	5 mL

TOPPING

¾ cup	butter	175 mL
½ cup	granulated sugar	125 mL
¼ cup	whipping (35%) cream	50 mL
²/₃ cup	chopped red candied (glacé) cherries	150 mL
⅓ cup	chopped green candied (glacé) cherries	75 mL
²/₃ cup	chopped candied (glacé) pineapple	150 mL
1 cup	sliced blanched almonds	250 mL
2	squares (1 oz/28 g each) semi-sweet chocolate, melted	2

1. *Crust:* In a bowl, combine flour and confectioner's sugar. Using a pastry blender, 2 knives or your fingers, cut in butter until mixture resembles coarse crumbs. Stir in whipping cream and vanilla, mixing until dough clings together. Press dough evenly into prepared pan. Chill while preparing topping.

2. *Topping:* In a saucepan over medium heat, combine butter, sugar and whipping cream. Bring to a boil, stirring often. Boil, stirring constantly, until thickened, 1 to 2 minutes. Remove from heat. Stir in red and green cherries, pineapple and almonds. Spread evenly over chilled crust.

3. Bake in preheated oven until top is golden, 15 to 20 minutes. Let cool completely in pan on rack.

4. Drizzle melted chocolate over top. Let cool until chocolate sets, about 1 hour. Cut into squares, then cut into triangles.

> ## Variations
>
> If you prefer, you can use all red or all green cherries.
>
> Omit the chocolate drizzle and dip the triangles in melted chocolate. Use about 8 (1 oz/28 g each) squares.

Apricot Coconut Chews

◆

You don't have to like coconut to love these squares.

MAKES 18 TO 48 BARS OR 16 TO 36 SQUARES
(see Cutting Guide, page 10)

- Preparation: 25 minutes
- Baking: 50 minutes
- Freezing: excellent

TIPS

I have specified sweetened coconut because it seems to be more readily available than the unsweetened variety. But sweetened and unsweetened coconut can be used interchangeably in any recipe to suit your preference.

If your apricots seem very dry, plump them in boiling water for 5 minutes. Pat dry with paper towel before using.

- **Preheat oven to 350°F (180°C)**
- **9-inch (2.5 L) square cake pan, greased**

CRUST

1 cup	all-purpose flour	250 mL
1 cup	graham wafer crumbs	250 mL
1 cup	packed brown sugar	250 mL
½ cup	sweetened flaked coconut	125 mL
½ cup	butter, melted	125 mL

TOPPING

2	eggs	2
1 cup	packed brown sugar	250 mL
1 tbsp	freshly squeezed lemon juice	15 mL
⅓ cup	all-purpose flour	75 mL
½ tsp	baking powder	2 mL
1 cup	chopped dried apricots	250 mL

1. *Crust:* In a bowl, combine flour, graham wafer crumbs, brown sugar and coconut. Stir in melted butter, mixing well. Set aside 1 cup (250 mL) of the mixture for topping. Press remainder evenly into prepared pan. Bake in preheated oven until golden around edges, about 15 minutes.

2. *Topping:* In a bowl, whisk eggs until frothy. Add brown sugar and lemon juice, whisking until smooth. Whisk in flour and baking powder until smooth. Stir in apricots. Spread evenly over base. Sprinkle reserved crust mixture over top.

3. Return to oven and bake until top is set, 30 to 35 minutes. Let cool completely in pan on rack. Cut into bars or squares.

> ## Variations
> Replace coconut in crust with an equal quantity of ground almonds.
>
> Replace graham wafer crumbs with vanilla wafer crumbs.

Cranberry Apricot Pecan Meringue Bars

This crumbly cinnamon meringue tastes particularly delicious with the chewy fruit filling and buttery cookie crust.

MAKES 20 TO 54 BARS (see Cutting Guide, page 10)

- **Preparation: 20 minutes**
- **Baking: 50 minutes**
- **Freezing: not recommended**

TIPS

To cut through meringue neatly, use a hot wet knife.

This is one of the few bars that doesn't freeze well because meringue gets soggy when frozen. But if well wrapped it keeps for about 5 days at room temperature.

- **Preheat oven to 350°F (180°C)**
- **13- by 9-inch (3 L) cake pan, greased**

CRUST

1½ cups	all-purpose flour	375 mL
2 tbsp	granulated sugar	25 mL
⅓ cup	cold butter, cubed	75 mL
2	egg yolks, beaten	2
¼ cup	sour cream	50 mL

FILLING

1 cup	dried cranberries	250 mL
¼ cup	chopped dried apricots	50 mL
⅔ cup	sour cream	150 mL
½ cup	apricot jam	125 mL
2	egg whites	2
Pinch	cream of tartar	Pinch
½ cup	granulated sugar	125 mL
½ tsp	cinnamon	2 mL
⅓ cup	finely chopped pecans	75 mL

1. *Crust:* In a bowl, combine flour and sugar. Using a pastry blender, 2 knives or your fingers, cut in butter until mixture resembles coarse crumbs. Stir in egg yolks and sour cream, mixing well. Press evenly into prepared pan. Bake in preheated oven until light golden, 15 to 20 minutes.

2. *Filling:* In a bowl, combine cranberries, apricots, sour cream and jam, mixing well. Spread evenly over warm crust. In a clean bowl, beat egg whites and cream of tartar until soft peaks form. Gradually add sugar and cinnamon, beating until stiff peaks form. Carefully spread meringue over cranberry-apricot mixture. Sprinkle with pecans.

3. Return to oven and bake until light brown, 25 to 30 minutes. Let cool completely in pan on rack. Cut into bars.

Variation

Replace pecans with unblanched almonds.

Marmalade Bars

These tasty bars couldn't be easier. Keep a jar of marmalade on hand to prepare them at a moment's notice.

MAKES 18 TO 48 BARS (see Cutting Guide, page 10)

- **Preparation: 20 minutes**
- **Baking: 35 minutes**
- **Freezing: excellent**

TIPS

When making bars, use jams that are fairly stiff in consistency. Lighter, lower-sugar versions are too moist and too loose to set firmly.

A drizzle of confectioner's (icing) sugar mixed with a little orange juice to make a pouring consistency looks nice on these bars. Add after they've cooled.

If you're a ginger lover, add 3 tbsp (45 mL) finely chopped crystallized ginger to the marmalade.

- **Preheat oven to 350°F (180°C)**
- **9-inch (2.5 L) square cake pan, greased**

BASE

2 cups	all-purpose flour	500 mL
¾ cup	packed brown sugar	175 mL
¾ cup	butter, softened	175 mL
2 tsp	grated orange zest	10 mL
¼ tsp	ground ginger	1 mL
Pinch	salt	Pinch
1	egg, beaten	1

TOPPING

1 cup	orange marmalade	250 mL
3 tbsp	all-purpose flour	45 mL

1. *Base:* In a bowl, combine flour, brown sugar, butter, orange zest, ginger and salt. Using an electric mixer on medium speed, beat until crumbly, about 2 minutes. Add egg and mix to form a soft dough. Set aside one-third of the dough for topping. Press remainder evenly into prepared pan.

2. *Topping:* Spread marmalade evenly over crust. Stir flour into reserved dough and work with fingers until crumbly. Sprinkle over marmalade.

3. Bake in preheated oven until golden, 30 to 35 minutes. Let cool completely in pan on rack. Cut into bars.

Variations

Try making these bars with other kinds of jam. Red ones like sour cherry, strawberry and plum, look and taste great.

Replace ginger with nutmeg.

Cranberry Coconut Oat Bars

I like these bars because they aren't too sweet. They're also easy to make and freeze well.

MAKES 18 TO 48 BARS (see Cutting Guide, page 10)

- **Preparation: 25 minutes**
- **Baking: 40 minutes**
- **Freezing: excellent**

TIPS

Be sure to use regular quick-cooking oats, not the instant variety that just requires the addition of boiling water. Large flake rolled oats also work well in this recipe.

For added flavor, toast oats before using. To toast oats, spread in a thin layer on a large rimmed baking sheet. Bake in a 350°F (180°C) oven for about 10 minutes, stirring often until lightly browned. Let cool completely before using.

- **Preheat oven to 350°F (180°C)**
- **9-inch (2.5 L) square cake pan, greased**

CRUST

½ cup	butter, melted	125 mL
⅓ cup	granulated sugar	75 mL
1 cup	all-purpose flour	250 mL
½ cup	quick-cooking rolled oats (see Tips, left)	125 mL

TOPPING

2	eggs	2
1 cup	packed brown sugar	250 mL
⅓ cup	all-purpose flour	75 mL
½ tsp	baking powder	2 mL
¾ tsp	cinnamon	3 mL
1⅓ cups	dried cranberries	325 mL
1 cup	unsweetened flaked coconut	250 mL

1. *Crust:* In a bowl, combine melted butter, sugar, flour and oats, mixing well. Press evenly into prepared pan. Bake in preheated oven until lightly browned, about 15 minutes. Let cool in pan on rack.

2. *Topping:* In a large bowl, whisk eggs and brown sugar until blended. Whisk in flour, baking powder and cinnamon until blended. Stir in dried cranberries and coconut. Spread evenly over cooled base.

3. Return to oven and bake until set and golden, 20 to 25 minutes. Let cool completely in pan on rack. Cut into bars.

Variations

Replace ⅓ cup (75 mL) of the dried cranberries with chopped dried apricots.

Replace cinnamon with 1 tsp (5 mL) grated orange zest.

Blueberry Cheesecake Bars

These bars are just like cheesecake — but smaller in size.

MAKES 20 TO 54 BARS (see Cutting Guide, page 10)

- **Preparation: 30 minutes**
- **Baking: 45 minutes**
- **Freezing: not recommended**

TIPS

Be sure to have eggs and cream cheese at room temperature for smooth blending.

If you've forgotten to remove eggs from the refrigerator to allow them to come to room temperature, place them in a bowl of warm water for a few minutes.

To soften cream cheese in a microwave, place an unwrapped 8 oz (250 g) block in a microwaveable bowl. Microwave on High for 15 seconds. Add 15 seconds for each additional block of cream cheese.

- **Preheat oven to 350°F (180°C)**
- **13- by 9-inch (3 L) cake pan, greased**

CRUST

2 cups	all-purpose flour	500 mL
½ cup	granulated sugar	125 mL
⅔ cup	cold butter, cubed	150 mL

FILLING

2	pkg (8 oz/250 g each) cream cheese, softened	2
¾ cup	granulated sugar	175 mL
2	eggs	2
1 tbsp	grated lemon zest	15 mL
1 tbsp	freshly squeezed lemon juice	15 mL
1 cup	blueberry jam	250 mL
1 cup	fresh blueberries	250 mL

1. *Crust:* In a bowl, combine flour and sugar. Using a pastry blender, 2 knives or your fingers, cut in butter until mixture resembles coarse crumbs. Press evenly into prepared pan. Bake in preheated oven until edges are lightly browned, 12 to 15 minutes. Let cool in pan on rack.

2. *Filling:* In a bowl, using an electric mixer on medium speed, beat cream cheese and sugar until smooth. Add eggs and lemon zest and juice, beating until smooth.

3. Spread jam evenly over crust. Sprinkle blueberries on top. Drop cream cheese mixture by spoonfuls over berries, then spread evenly. Return to oven and bake just until set, 25 to 30 minutes. Let cool completely in pan on rack. Cut into bars.

Variation

Try replacing blueberry jam and fresh blueberries with strawberry or raspberry jam and sliced fresh strawberries or fresh raspberries.

Frosted Banana Bars

These yummy bars taste like a mini version of banana cake. How can you go wrong?

MAKES 36 TO 48 BARS (see Cutting Guide, page 10)

- **Preparation: 25 minutes**
- **Baking: 25 minutes**
- **Freezing: excellent**

TIP

The riper the banana the better the flavor in baked goods. I like to buy extra bananas so I always have some that are at the baking stage. I prefer to use them fresh rather than mashing and freezing them. Frozen bananas always seem too wet, which means you need to adjust the recipe.

- **Preheat oven to 375°F (190°C)**
- **15- by 10- by 1-inch (2 L) jelly roll pan, greased**

BATTER

½ cup	butter, softened	125 mL
1½ cups	granulated sugar	375 mL
1 cup	sour cream	250 mL
2	eggs	2
1½ cups	mashed ripe banana (3 large bananas)	375 mL
1½ tsp	vanilla	7 mL
2 cups	all-purpose flour	500 mL
1 tsp	baking soda	5 mL
½ tsp	salt	2 mL
½ cup	chopped walnuts	125 mL

FROSTING

¼ cup	butter, softened	50 mL
2 cups	confectioner's (icing) sugar, sifted	500 mL
¼ cup	milk	50 mL
1 tsp	vanilla	5 mL

1. *Batter:* In a large bowl, using an electric mixer on low speed, beat butter, sugar, sour cream and eggs for 1 minute. Beat in mashed bananas and vanilla. Combine flour, baking soda and salt. On low speed, beat into creamed mixture, mixing until smooth. Stir in walnuts. Spread evenly in prepared pan.

2. Bake in preheated oven until a toothpick inserted in center comes out clean, 20 to 25 minutes. Let cool completely in pan on rack.

3. *Frosting:* In a saucepan, over medium heat, heat butter until it melts and turns a delicate brown color, about 10 minutes. Remove from heat. Stir in confectioner's sugar, milk and vanilla. Beat until smooth and spreadable. Spread quickly over cooled bars. Let cool until set. Cut into bars.

Variation

Replace walnuts with pecans or omit the nuts if allergies are a concern.

Apple Streusel Squares

With a tender melt-in-your-mouth crust, a tart apple filling and walnut streusel topping, these delicious squares taste like old fashioned apple pie in a new shape.

MAKES 24 TO 60 SQUARES (see Cutting Guide, page 10)

- **Preparation: 40 minutes**
- **Cooking: 16 minutes**
- **Baking: 55 minutes**
- **Freezing: not recommended**

TIPS

There seems to be a lot of steps in this recipe, but each is easy and the large yield is well worth the extra time.

If you prefer, mix the crust in a food processor.

You'll need about 3 lb (1.5 kg) or 8 large apples to make these squares.

Use Golden Delicious apples or Matsu apples for a great flavor and texture.

Because ovens are often not accurate in their temperature, a good oven thermometer is a worthwhile investment. Set your timer for the minimum recommended time. You can always bake a little longer but you can't fix an overbaked product.

- **Preheat oven to 375°F (190°C)**
- **15- by 10- by 1-inch (2 L) jelly roll pan, greased**

STREUSEL TOPPING

1 cup	all-purpose flour	250 mL
1 cup	chopped walnuts	250 mL
½ cup	packed brown sugar	125 mL
½ cup	butter, softened	125 mL
1 tsp	cinnamon	5 mL

CRUST

3 cups	all-purpose flour	750 mL
⅓ cup	granulated sugar	75 mL
1 cup	cold butter, cubed	250 mL

FILLING

3 tbsp	butter	45 mL
7 cups	sliced (½ inch/1 cm), cored, peeled apples	1.75 L
1 cup	dried cranberries	250 mL
½ cup	packed brown sugar	125 mL
1 tsp	cinnamon	5 mL
2 tbsp	cornstarch	25 mL
3 tbsp	freshly squeezed lemon juice	45 mL

1. *Streusel Topping:* In a bowl, combine flour, walnuts, brown sugar, butter and cinnamon. Mix with a wooden spoon, then knead until the dough comes together. Shape into a ball. Cover and chill until ready to use.

2. *Crust:* In a bowl, combine flour and sugar. Using a pastry blender, 2 knives or your fingers, cut in butter until mixture resembles coarse crumbs. Press evenly into prepared pan. Bake in preheated oven until lightly browned all over, about 20 minutes. (Don't worry if crust cracks a little).

3. *Filling:* In a large skillet, melt butter over medium heat. Add apples, cranberries, brown sugar and cinnamon. Cook, stirring occasionally, until apples are tender-crisp, about 15 minutes. In a small bowl, combine cornstarch and lemon juice, mixing until smooth. Stir into apples and cook, stirring, until slightly thickened, about 1 minute. Spoon evenly over warm crust. Crumble chilled streusel mixture evenly over fruit.

4. Return to oven and bake until golden, 30 to 35 minutes. Let cool completely in pan on rack. Cut into squares.

Crunchy Raisin Pecan Bars with Broiled Topping

These bars are easy as well as delicious. A crunchy coconut nut topping is baked right on, so you don't need to add a frosting later.

MAKES 20 TO 54 BARS (see Cutting Guide, page 10)

- Preparation: 25 minutes
- Baking: 37 minutes
- Freezing: excellent

TIPS

To ease cleanup, rather than combining the dry ingredients in a bowl (Step 1), place a large piece of waxed paper on the counter. Spread the flour on the paper and sprinkle with the baking powder, baking soda, salt and cinnamon. Using the paper as a funnel, transfer the dry ingredients to the butter mixture.

The topping can burn quickly. Watch it carefully so it just gets to the bubbly, golden brown stage.

I recommend the use of unsweetened coconut in this recipe because it won't burn as quickly under the broiler. Leave the door slightly ajar and watch closely when broiling.

- Preheat oven to 350°F (180°C)
- 13- by 9-inch (3 L) cake pan, greased

BAR

1½ cups	all-purpose flour	375 mL
1 tsp	baking powder	5 mL
1 tsp	baking soda	5 mL
½ tsp	salt	2 mL
1 tsp	cinnamon	5 mL
1 cup	quick-cooking rolled oats	250 mL
1¼ cups	boiling water	300 mL
½ cup	butter, softened	125 mL
1½ cups	packed brown sugar	375 mL
2	eggs	2
1¼ cups	raisins	300 mL

TOPPING

¼ cup	butter	50 mL
¾ cup	packed brown sugar	175 mL
¼ cup	half-and-half (10%) cream	50 mL
1¼ cups	chopped pecans	300 mL
1 cup	unsweetened flaked coconut	250 mL

1. *Bar:* Combine flour, baking powder, baking soda, salt and cinnamon. Place oats in a bowl. Add boiling water and mix to moisten oats. Let stand for 5 to 10 minutes.

2. In a bowl, using an electric mixer on medium speed, beat butter, brown sugar and eggs until light. Stir in flour mixture and oats, mixing well. Stir in raisins. Spread evenly in prepared pan.

3. Bake in preheated oven until a toothpick inserted in center comes out clean, 30 to 35 minutes. Do not remove from pan.

4. *Topping:* Preheat broiler. In a saucepan over low heat, melt butter. Stir in brown sugar, cream, pecans and coconut, mixing well. Remove from heat. Spread evenly over hot bar. Broil 6 inches (15 cm) below element, until topping is bubbly and golden brown, 1 to 2 minutes. Let cool completely in pan on rack. Cut into bars.

Almond Cranberry Lemon Bars

Lemon juice enhances the tart flavor of cranberries in these wonderful almond bars.

MAKES 20 TO 54 BARS (see Cutting Guide, page 10)

- **Preparation: 25 minutes**
- **Baking: 65 minutes**
- **Freezing: excellent**

TIPS

If you prefer, you can mix the crust in a food processor. Use cubed cold butter, not softened. You can also mix the crust in a bowl, cutting in the cold butter using a pastry blender, 2 knives or your fingers. Whichever method you use, the mixture should resemble coarse crumbs.

When freezing bars and squares, chill the whole bar well before cutting. Cut as desired then wrap tightly in plastic wrap, individually or 6 per package. Freeze for up to 3 months.

To get the maximum amount of juice from lemons, warm them in the microwave on High for 30 seconds or place in a bowl of boiling water for a minute.

- **Preheat oven to 350°F (180°C)**
- **13- by 9-inch (3 L) cake pan, greased**

CRUST

2 cups	all-purpose flour	500 mL
1/3 cup	confectioner's (icing) sugar, sifted	75 mL
1 cup	butter, softened	250 mL

TOPPING

1 1/4 cups	dried cranberries	300 mL
7	eggs	7
2 1/4 cups	granulated sugar	550 mL
4 tsp	grated lemon zest	20 mL
3/4 cup	freshly squeezed lemon juice	175 mL
1/4 cup	butter, melted	50 mL
1/2 cup	all-purpose flour	125 mL
2 tsp	baking powder	10 mL
1 1/4 cups	ground or finely chopped almonds	300 mL
	Confectioner's (icing) sugar for dusting	

1. *Crust:* In a bowl, combine flour, confectioner's sugar and butter. Using an electric mixer on low speed, beat until crumbly. Press evenly into prepared pan. Bake in preheated oven until edges are lightly browned, 12 to 15 minutes.

2. *Topping:* Reduce oven temperature to 325° (160°C). Sprinkle dried cranberries evenly over crust. In a bowl, using an electric mixer on high speed, beat eggs and sugar until light and slightly thickened, about 5 minutes. Stir in lemon zest and juice, melted butter, flour, baking powder and ground almonds, mixing well. Pour over cranberries.

3. Return to oven and bake until set and golden, about 50 minutes. Let cool completely in pan on rack. Cut into bars. Dust with confectioner's sugar before serving.

Variations
Replace almonds with hazelnuts.
Replace dried cranberries with dried blueberries or cherries.

Lemony Lemon Squares

If, like me, you enjoy lots of lemon flavor, you'll love these squares. They really make you pucker up.

MAKES 16 TO 36 SQUARES
(see Cutting Guide, page 10)

- **Preparation: 20 minutes**
- **Baking: 45 minutes**
- **Freezing: excellent**

TIPS

For less pucker-up lemon flavor, decrease the lemon juice to ⅓ cup (75 mL) and the flour to 2 tbsp (25 mL).

Just before serving, dust these squares lightly with confectioner's (icing) sugar, if desired. Don't do it too far ahead as it will soak into the topping on standing.

Don't worry if these squares crack on top during cooling. The fabulous flavor outweighs the cracked appearance.

- **Preheat oven to 350°F (180°C)**
- **8-inch (2 L) square cake pan, greased**

CRUST

1 cup	all-purpose flour	250 mL
¼ cup	granulated sugar	50 mL
½ cup	cold butter, cubed	125 mL

TOPPING

3	eggs	3
1 cup	granulated sugar	250 mL
3 tbsp	all-purpose flour	45 mL
2 tsp	grated lemon zest	10 mL
½ cup	freshly squeezed lemon juice	125 mL

1. *Crust:* In a bowl, combine flour and sugar. Using a pastry blender, 2 knives or your fingers, cut in butter until mixture resembles coarse crumbs. Press evenly into prepared pan. Bake in preheated oven until lightly browned around the edges, 12 to 15 minutes.

2. *Topping:* In a bowl, whisk eggs, sugar, flour, lemon zest and juice just until smooth. Don't overbeat. Pour over crust.

3. Return to oven and bake just until set, 25 to 30 minutes. Let cool completely in pan on rack. Cut into squares.

Variation

You can transform these into a citrus square by substituting an equal quantity of lime juice and zest for half of the lemon juice and zest.

Apricot Orange Almond Bars

The combination of a crisp crust with a tangy apricot almond topping is delightful. Nothing fancy, just plain good.

MAKES 20 TO 54 BARS (see Cutting Guide, page 10)

- **Preparation: 25 minutes**
- **Cooking: 10 minutes**
- **Baking: 45 minutes**
- **Freezing: excellent**

TIPS

For convenience, chop the apricots in a food processor fitted with a steel blade. Process just until finely chopped but not mushy.

Bars with an acid such as lemon juice in the filling should not be stored in the baking pan because the acid cuts into the pan. Line the pan with parchment paper for easy removal.

- **Preheat oven to 350°F (180°C)**
- **13- by 9-inch (3 L) cake pan, greased**

CRUST

2 cups	all-purpose flour	500 mL
¾ cup	butter, softened	175 mL
½ cup	granulated sugar	125 mL

FILLING

2 cups	dried apricots, finely chopped	500 mL
½ cup	water	125 mL
¼ cup	orange liqueur	50 mL
2 tsp	freshly squeezed lemon juice	10 mL
2	eggs	2
⅓ cup	granulated sugar	75 mL
1 cup	chopped toasted almonds	250 mL

GLAZE

½ cup	confectioner's (icing) sugar, sifted	125 mL
2 tbsp	orange liqueur	25 mL

1. *Crust:* In a bowl, combine flour, sugar and butter. Using an electric mixer on low speed, beat until crumbly. Press evenly into prepared pan. Bake in preheated oven until golden around the edges, 12 to 15 minutes. Let cool in pan on rack.

2. *Filling:* In a saucepan over medium heat, bring apricots, water, orange liqueur and lemon juice to a boil. Reduce heat and simmer, stirring occasionally, until apricots are tender and liquid is evaporated, about 10 minutes. Remove from heat. Let cool. Stir in eggs and sugar until blended. Spread evenly over crust. Sprinkle with almonds.

3. Return to oven and bake until top is set and golden, 25 to 30 minutes. Let cool completely in pan on rack.

4. *Glaze:* In a bowl, combine confectioner's sugar and orange liqueur, stirring until smooth. Drizzle over filling. Let stand until set. Cut into bars.

Variations

Hazelnuts work well in place of almonds.

Replace orange liqueur with almond liqueur.

Pear and Mincemeat Oatmeal Bars

Prepared mincemeat gives you a head start on these fabulous bars. Take them along with some eggnog or sparkling cider as a hostess gift for a holiday party.

MAKES 20 TO 54 BARS (see Cutting Guide, page 10)

- **Preparation: 20 minutes**
- **Baking: 30 minutes**
- **Freezing: excellent**

TIPS

For baking, pears should be ripe but firm.

Try cutting these bars in large squares and serve them slightly warm with a scoop of French vanilla or eggnog ice cream.

Prepared mincemeats vary considerably among brands. Experiment and pick your favorite before using it in baking.

- **Preheat oven to 375°F (190°C)**
- **13- by 9-inch (3 L) cake pan, greased**

BASE

¾ cup	butter, softened	175 mL
¾ cup	packed brown sugar	175 mL
1½ cups	all-purpose flour	375 mL
1¼ cups	quick-cooking rolled oats	300 mL
¾ cup	chopped walnuts	175 mL
1 tsp	cinnamon	5 mL
½ tsp	baking soda	2 mL
½ tsp	salt	2 mL

FILLING

2	large Anjou or Bartlett pears, peeled, cored and chopped	2
1 cup	prepared mincemeat	250 mL
1 tsp	grated lemon zest	5 mL
1 tbsp	freshly squeezed lemon juice	15 mL

1. *Base:* In a bowl, using an electric mixer on medium speed, beat butter and brown sugar until blended. Stir in flour, oats, walnuts, cinnamon, baking soda and salt, mixing until crumbly. Set aside 1½ cups (375 mL) for topping. Press remainder evenly into prepared pan. Set aside.

2. *Filling:* In a bowl, combine pears, mincemeat and lemon zest and juice, mixing well. Spread evenly over crust. Sprinkle reserved topping evenly over mincemeat mixture.

3. Bake in preheated oven until top is golden brown, 25 to 30 minutes. Let cool completely in pan on rack. Cut into bars.

Variation

Replace lemon juice with an equal quantity of rum or brandy.

Replace pears with apple.

Pineapple Squares

◆

These squares have been in my family for as long as I can remember. They were one of my grandmother's specialties, probably because they're easy to make and use only a few ingredients, all shelf stable.

MAKES 16 TO 36 SQUARES (see Cutting Guide, page 10)

- Preparation: 25 minutes
- Baking: 37 minutes
- Freezing: excellent

TIPS

Use a good-quality crushed pineapple that has coarse chunks and a high fruit to juice ratio.

I have specified sweetened coconut because it seems to be more readily available than the unsweetened variety. But sweetened and unsweetened coconut can be used interchangeably in any recipe to suit your preference.

Bars and squares always taste better when enjoyed with a hot cup of tea or coffee. To personalize a cookie gift, pack them with a mug or teacup containing a package of gourmet coffee or herbal tea bags.

- Preheat oven to 350°F (180°C)
- 8-inch (2 L) square cake pan, greased

CRUST

½ cup	butter, softened	125 mL
¼ cup	granulated sugar	50 mL
1⅓ cups	all-purpose flour	325 mL
¼ tsp	baking powder	1 mL

FILLING

1	can (19 oz/540 mL) crushed pineapple, well drained	1

TOPPING

¼ cup	butter, melted	50 mL
½ cup	granulated sugar	125 mL
1	egg	1
1 tsp	vanilla	5 mL
1¼ cups	sweetened flaked coconut	300 mL

1. *Crust:* In a bowl, using an electric mixer on medium speed, beat butter and sugar until blended. Stir in flour and baking powder, mixing until crumbly. Press evenly into prepared pan. Bake in preheated oven until golden around edges, 10 to 12 minutes. Let cool for 30 minutes.

2. *Filling:* Spread pineapple evenly over cooled crust.

3. *Topping:* In a bowl, whisk melted butter, sugar, egg and vanilla until well blended. Stir in coconut. Spread evenly over pineapple.

4. Return to oven and bake until set, 20 to 25 minutes. Let cool completely in pan on rack. Cut into squares.

Variations

Add ¼ cup (50 mL) ground almonds to the crust and replace the vanilla with ½ tsp (2 mL) almond extract.

Use shredded coconut for a slightly different texture in the topping.

Coconut Lemon Squares

If you're a fan of lemon bars but long for a change every now and again, you'll love the addition of coconut and apple to these tart, intensely lemon-flavored squares. It makes a very nice change.

MAKES 16 TO 36 SQUARES
(see Cutting Guide, page 10)

- **Preparation: 25 minutes**
- **Cooking: 15 minutes**
- **Baking: 42 minutes**
- **Freezing: excellent**

TIPS

The little time it takes to grate fresh citrus peel is worth the effort when you taste the burst of fresh flavor it adds to baked goods.

Use only the colored surface of the peel, not the bitter white part. Hand graters and zesters are convenient, but if you don't have one, you can use a vegetable peeler to remove a thin layer of peel. Finely mince the peel with a sharp knife.

Prepare extra zest. You can keep it on hand in the freezer in small resealable plastic bags.

- **Preheat oven to 325°F (160°C)**
- **8-inch (2 L) square cake pan, greased**

CRUST

¾ cup	all-purpose flour	175 mL
2 tbsp	granulated sugar	25 mL
⅓ cup	cold butter, cubed	75 mL

FILLING

¾ cup	grated, cored, peeled apple (1 large)	175 mL
	Grated zest and juice of 1 lemon	
1	egg, beaten	1
1 tsp	butter	5 mL

TOPPING

1½ cups	sweetened shredded coconut (see Tips, page 104)	375 mL
¼ cup	granulated sugar	50 mL
1	egg	1
1 tbsp	butter, melted	15 mL

1. *Crust:* In a bowl, combine flour and sugar. Using a pastry blender, 2 knives or your fingers, cut in butter until mixture resembles coarse crumbs. Press evenly into prepared pan. Bake in preheated oven until golden around edges, 10 to 12 minutes.

2. *Filling:* In a saucepan, combine grated apple, lemon zest and juice, egg and butter. Cook over medium heat, stirring constantly, until slightly thickened, 12 to 15 minutes. Spread evenly over warm crust.

3. *Topping:* In a bowl, combine coconut, sugar, egg and melted butter, mixing well. Drop by spoonfuls over filling and spread carefully.

4. Return to oven and bake until set and golden, 25 to 30 minutes. Let cool completely in pan on rack. Cut into squares.

Variation
Replace ⅓ cup (75 mL) of the coconut with finely chopped almonds.

Cranberry Orange Apricot Bars

Here's a tasty bar that isn't too sweet. It's particularly enjoyable during the holiday season when there are plenty of other sweet treats available.

MAKES 18 TO 48 BARS
(see Cutting Guide, page 10)

- **Preparation: 25 minutes**
- **Baking: 42 minutes**
- **Freezing: excellent**

TIP

Spices don't last forever. Their flavor comes from volatile oils that lose their punch over time. Buy in small amounts, which will be used fairly quickly. To ensure optimum flavor, keep spices in airtight containers in a cool, dry place. Put the date of purchase on the container.

- **Preheat oven to 350°F (180°C)**
- **9-inch (2.5 L) square cake pan, greased**

CRUST

1 cup	all-purpose flour	250 mL
1/3 cup	packed brown sugar	75 mL
1/3 cup	cold butter, cubed	75 mL

FILLING

1/2 cup	golden raisins	125 mL
1/2 cup	dried cranberries	125 mL
1/2 cup	chopped dried apricots	125 mL
1/3 cup	freshly squeezed orange juice	75 mL
2	eggs	2
1 cup	packed brown sugar	250 mL
1/3 cup	all-purpose flour	75 mL
1/2 tsp	cinnamon	2 mL
1/3 cup	chopped pecans	75 mL

1. *Crust:* In a bowl, combine flour and brown sugar. Using a pastry blender, 2 knives or your fingers, cut in butter until mixture resembles coarse crumbs. Press evenly into prepared pan. Bake in preheated oven until golden around the edges, 10 to 12 minutes.

2. *Filling:* In a saucepan, combine raisins, cranberries, apricots and orange juice. Bring to a boil over medium heat. Remove from heat and let stand for 20 minutes. Liquid should be absorbed. If necessary, drain off any excess.

3. In a bowl, whisk eggs and brown sugar until blended. Add flour and cinnamon, whisking until smooth. Stir in pecans and reserved fruit mixture. Spread evenly over crust.

4. Return to oven and bake until top is set and golden, 25 to 30 minutes. Let cool completely in pan on rack. Cut into bars.

Variations

Replace raisins with chopped dates or dried figs.
Replace orange juice with apple juice, brandy or water.

Raspberry Almond Holiday Bars

Here's a delicious and colorful bar to jazz up your holiday cookie tray. Swirls of pink and green batter on a shortbread crust, topped with snowy white almond-flavored frosting, fit right into the festive season.

MAKES 18 TO 48 BARS (see Cutting Guide, page 10)

- **Preparation: 25 minutes**
- **Baking: 47 minutes**
- **Freezing: excellent**

TIPS

Although the filling has a tender but dense, cake-like texture, it doesn't contain any leavening agents such as baking soda or baking powder. Beating the eggs into the batter provides the lift.

Add a sprinkling of toasted, sliced almonds after the bar has been frosted.

If you want to make a big batch of these bars, double the recipe. Bake in a 13- by 9-inch (3 L) pan for 35 to 40 minutes.

- **Preheat oven to 350°F (180°C)**
- **8-inch (2 L) square cake pan, greased**

CRUST

1 cup	all-purpose flour	250 mL
3 tbsp	granulated sugar	45 mL
1/3 cup	cold butter, cubed	75 mL

FILLING

1/2 cup	raspberry jam	125 mL
1/2 cup	butter, softened	125 mL
2/3 cup	granulated sugar	150 mL
2	eggs	2
2/3 cup	all-purpose flour	150 mL
1/4 tsp	salt	1 mL
	Red and green food coloring	

FROSTING

2 tbsp	butter, softened	25 mL
2 cups	confectioner's (icing) sugar, sifted	500 mL
2 tbsp	half-and-half (10%) cream	25 mL
1 tsp	almond extract	5 mL

1. *Crust:* In a bowl, combine flour and sugar. Using a pastry blender, 2 knives or your fingers, cut in butter until mixture resembles coarse crumbs. Press evenly into prepared pan. Bake in preheated oven until light golden around edges, 10 to 12 minutes.

2. *Filling:* Spread jam evenly over crust. In a bowl, using an electric mixer on medium speed, beat butter and sugar until blended, about 3 minutes. Add eggs, one at a time, beating lightly after each addition. Stir in flour and salt, mixing well. Divide batter evenly between 2 bowls. Add red food coloring to one of the bowls a few drops at a time, stirring, to make pastel pink. Using green food coloring, repeat with the other bowl to make pastel green. Drop small spoonfuls of each batter alternately over jam. Tap pan gently on counter to even out batter.

3. Return to oven and bake until top is set and golden, 30 to 35 minutes. Let cool completely in pan on rack.

4. *Frosting:* In a bowl, using an electric mixer on medium speed, beat butter, confectioner's sugar, cream and almond extract until smooth and creamy. Spread over filling. Cut into bars.

Raspberry Coconut Squares

These squares are similar to Raspberry Coconut Walnut Slices (see recipe, page 152) but different enough that I wanted to include them. I love them both and can't decide which I like better.

MAKES 16 TO 36 SQUARES
(see Cutting Guide, page 10)

- **Preparation: 25 minutes**
- **Baking: 42 minutes**
- **Freezing: excellent**

TIPS

Chill the bars for easy cutting but serve at room temperature for the nicest flavor.

Try these bars slightly warm with a scoop of French vanilla ice cream or raspberry sherbet.

When cutting bars containing flaked or shredded coconut, use a straight blade like a chef's knife and cut straight down. A serrated knife drags the coconut down rather than cutting it.

- **Preheat oven to 425°F (220°C)**
- **9-inch (2.5 L) square cake pan, greased**

CRUST

1 1/4 cups	all-purpose flour	300 mL
1/4 cup	granulated sugar	50 mL
1/2 cup	cold butter, cubed	125 mL
3 tbsp	cold water	45 mL

TOPPING

1/3 cup	raspberry jam	75 mL
2	eggs	2
1/2 cup	packed brown sugar	125 mL
2 cups	sweetened flaked coconut	500 mL

1. *Crust:* In a bowl, combine flour and sugar. Using a pastry blender, 2 knives or your fingers, cut in butter until mixture resembles coarse crumbs. Add water and, using a fork, mix until moistened. Press firmly into prepared pan. Bake in preheated oven until golden around edges, 10 to 12 minutes. Reduce oven temperature to 350°F (180°C).

2. *Topping:* Spread jam evenly over crust, leaving a 1/2-inch (1 cm) border of crust. In a small bowl, using an electric mixer on high speed, beat eggs until frothy. Gradually add sugar, beating until mixture is thick, about 5 minutes. Stir in coconut, mixing well until moistened. Drop by spoonfuls over jam and, using a spatula or the back of a spoon, carefully spread evenly.

3. Return to oven and bake until topping is light golden, 25 to 30 minutes. Let cool completely in pan on rack. Chill (see Tips, left). Cut into squares.

Variations

Replace 1/2 cup (125 mL) of the coconut with finely chopped almonds.

Use strawberry, peach or pineapple jam.

Coconut Lemon Bars

The tart lemon flavor mingles beautifully with the crunchy almonds in this easy-to-make bar.

MAKES 20 TO 54 BARS (see Cutting Guide, page 10)

- **Preparation: 20 minutes**
- **Baking: 50 minutes**
- **Freezing: excellent**

TIPS

If you prefer, mix the crust using an electric mixer on medium speed. It will take about 3 minutes.

Using a toothbrush makes cleaning a zester or grater easier.

When a microwave isn't handy and you have hard butter, here's how to soften it quickly: set it in a dish and leave a heated saucepan upside down over the dish for a few minutes.

- **Preheat oven to 325°F (160°C)**
- **13- by 9-inch (3 L) cake pan, greased**

CRUST

¾ cup	butter, softened	175 mL
½ cup	granulated sugar	125 mL
1½ cups	all-purpose flour	375 mL
⅓ cup	fine coconut	75 mL

TOPPING

4	eggs	4
1½ cups	granulated sugar	375 mL
¼ cup	all-purpose flour	50 mL
1½ tbsp	grated lemon zest	22 mL
⅓ cup	freshly squeezed lemon juice	75 mL
1⅓ cups	sliced almonds	325 mL
	Confectioner's (icing) sugar, optional	

1. *Crust:* In a bowl, using a wooden spoon, beat butter and sugar until smooth and creamy. Stir in flour and coconut, mixing until thoroughly blended. Press evenly into prepared pan. Bake in preheated oven until golden, 20 to 25 minutes.

2. *Topping:* In a bowl, whisk eggs and sugar until blended. Whisk in flour and lemon zest, mixing until smooth. Whisk in lemon juice. Pour evenly over crust. Sprinkle almonds evenly over top.

3. Return to oven and bake until topping is set and almonds are golden, 20 to 25 minutes. Let cool completely in pan on rack. Before serving, dust lightly with confectioner's sugar, if desired. Cut into bars.

Variation

Replace half of the lemon zest and juice with lime for a citrus bar.

Raspberry Criss-Cross Squares

This variation on the classic Austrian Linzer Torte is delicious, but very easy to make, unlike the original.

MAKES 16 TO 36 SQUARES (see Cutting Guide, page 10)

- **Preparation: 25 minutes**
- **Baking: 30 minutes**
- **Freezing: excellent**

TIPS

Look for a jam that has a bright red color. It will darken a little during baking, so the brighter it is to start, the nicer it will be after baking.

Omit the glaze if time is a factor or if you would rather not have a leftover egg white. The glaze makes the lattice a nice golden color.

When adding liquid such as water, milk or egg to pastry crumbs, toss the mixture lightly with a fork to keep it crumbly. When you use a spoon, it tends to mash the crumbs, making the dough tough.

- **Preheat oven to 375°F (190°C)**
- **9-inch (2.5 L) square cake pan, greased**

DOUGH

1¼ cups	all-purpose flour	300 mL
½ cup	packed brown sugar	125 mL
⅓ cup	ground almonds	75 mL
¼ cup	granulated sugar	50 mL
2 tsp	grated lemon zest	10 mL
½ tsp	baking powder	2 mL
¼ tsp	salt	1 mL
¾ tsp	cinnamon	3 mL
½ cup	cold butter, cubed	125 mL
1	egg, beaten	1
1 tsp	almond extract	5 mL

TOPPING

1 cup	raspberry jam	250 mL
2 tbsp	all-purpose flour	25 mL
1 tbsp	water (approx.)	15 mL

GLAZE, OPTIONAL

1	egg yolk	1
1 tsp	milk	5 mL

1. *Dough:* In a bowl, combine flour, brown sugar, ground almonds, granulated sugar, lemon zest, baking powder, salt and cinnamon. Using a pastry blender, 2 knives or your fingers, cut in butter until mixture resembles coarse crumbs. Add egg and almond extract. Mix with a fork until moistened. Set ½ cup (125 mL) of the mixture aside for topping. Press remainder evenly into prepared pan.

2. *Topping:* Spread jam evenly over base. Add 2 tbsp (25 mL) flour to reserved dough and stir with a fork to blend. Stir in water until dough holds together, adding a little more if necessary. Divide into 10 portions and roll each into pencil-like strips. Crisscross strips diagonally over jam to form a lattice.

3. *Glaze (if using):* Mix together egg yolk and milk. Brush over lattice.

4. Bake in preheated oven until golden, 25 to 30 minutes. Let cool completely in pan on rack. Cut into squares.

Lemon-Frosted Cherry Bars

The tart flavors of lemon and sour cherry combine in a bar that's not too sweet. It makes a refreshing treat at the end of a busy day.

MAKES 18 TO 48 BARS
(see Cutting Guide, page 10)

- **Preparation: 30 minutes**
- **Baking: 47 minutes**
- **Chilling: 1 hour**
- **Freezing: excellent**

TIPS

If there are large pieces of fruit in the jam, chop them to get an even distribution of pieces over the crust.

When you only need a little lemon juice, poke holes in a whole lemon with a fork or the tip of a knife and squeeze out the juice required. The lemon can then be refrigerated and will keep longer than a cut lemon.

- **Preheat oven to 350°F (180°C)**
- **9-inch (2.5 L) square cake pan, greased**

CRUST

1 cup	all-purpose flour	250 mL
¼ cup	granulated sugar	50 mL
⅓ cup	cold butter, cubed	75 mL

FILLING

½ cup	sour cherry jam	125 mL
½ cup	butter, softened	125 mL
⅔ cup	granulated sugar	150 mL
2	eggs	2
⅔ cup	all-purpose flour	150 mL
2 tsp	grated lemon zest	10 mL

LEMON FROSTING

2 tbsp	butter, softened	25 mL
1½ cups	confectioner's (icing) sugar, sifted	375 mL
2 tsp	grated lemon zest	10 mL
1 to 2 tbsp	freshly squeezed lemon juice	15 to 25 mL

1. *Crust:* In a bowl, combine flour and sugar. Using a pastry blender, 2 knives or your fingers, cut in butter until mixture resembles coarse crumbs. Press evenly into prepared pan. Bake in preheated oven until golden around edges, 10 to 12 minutes. Let cool in pan on rack for 15 minutes.

2. *Filling:* Spread jam evenly over crust. In a bowl, using an electric mixer on medium speed, beat butter, sugar and eggs for 3 minutes. On low speed, beat in flour and lemon zest, mixing well. Drop filling by spoonfuls over jam and, using a spatula or the back of a spoon, spread evenly.

3. Return to oven and bake until top is set and golden, 30 to 35 minutes. Let cool completely in pan on rack.

4. *Lemon Frosting:* In a bowl, using an electric mixer on medium speed, beat butter, confectioner's sugar and lemon zest and juice until light and creamy. Spread evenly over cooled bars. Chill until frosting is firm, about 1 hour. Cut into bars.

Variation

Replace cherry jam with blackcurrant or strawberry.

Party Pink Coconut Squares

This creamy, soft frosting is a perfect match for a moist coconut filling and graham wafer crust.

MAKES 16 TO 36 SQUARES
(see Cutting Guide, page 10)

- **Preparation: 30 minutes**
- **Baking: 37 minutes**
- **Chilling: 1 hour**
- **Freezing: excellent**

TIPS

I have specified sweetened coconut because it seems to be more readily available than the unsweetened variety. But sweetened and unsweetened coconut can be used interchangeably in any recipe to suit your preference.

The smooth, rich, creamy texture of the frosting is thanks to the long beating. It may seem to have a lot of liquid for a frosting, but believe me, it's wonderful.

I like the pastel pink frosting, but if you prefer, leave it plain or color it other pastel colors.

This bar cuts very nicely. It looks pretty cut into small squares and put into tiny pastel paper cups.

- **Preheat oven to 350°F (180°C)**
- **9-inch (2.5 L) square cake pan, greased**

CRUST

1½ cups	graham wafer crumbs	375 mL
¼ cup	packed brown sugar	50 mL
1 tbsp	all-purpose flour	15 mL
½ cup	butter, melted	125 mL

FILLING

1	can (10 oz/300 mL) sweetened condensed milk	1
2 cups	sweetened fine or medium coconut	500 mL

FROSTING

½ cup	butter, softened	125 mL
2 cups	confectioner's (icing) sugar, sifted	500 mL
1 tbsp	half-and-half (10%) cream	15 mL
1 tbsp	boiling water	15 mL
2	drops red food coloring	2

1. *Crust:* In a bowl, combine graham wafer crumbs, brown sugar, flour and melted butter, mixing well until all ingredients are moistened. Press evenly into prepared pan. Bake in preheated oven until firm, 10 to 12 minutes.

2. *Filling:* In a bowl, combine sweetened condensed milk and coconut, mixing until coconut is thoroughly moistened. Spread evenly over crust, being careful not to break the delicate crust.

3. Return to oven and bake until filling is set and top is light golden, 20 to 25 minutes. Let cool completely in pan on rack.

4. *Frosting:* In a small bowl, using an electric mixer on low speed, beat butter and confectioner's (icing) sugar for 2 minutes. Add cream. Beat on medium speed until smooth, about 2 minutes. Add boiling water and beat for 2 minutes. Add food coloring and beat until very smooth and creamy, about 2 minutes. Spread evenly over filling. Chill until frosting is firm, about 1 hour. Cut into squares.

Variation

Add ½ tsp (2 mL) almond extract to the filling.

Nut Bars
and Squares

If you enjoy eating nuts — and now that nutritionists tell us including moderate amounts of nuts in our diets is a healthy strategy, you can do this guilt-free — there are lots of recipes to choose from in this chapter. Almost every kind of nut is featured, but since nuts are usually interchangeable, you can adapt most recipes to include your favorites or the kind you have on hand.

I've included recipes to meet the needs of every occasion. Many of the bars contain two layers, which include a cookie-like crust pressed into the pan and a topping that includes an abundance of nuts, often mixed with other ingredients such as fruit and chocolate. There are also single-layer bars, where nuts are combined with mixtures of other yummy ingredients scattered through a cookie dough. These bars have only one step in the method and are particularly quick and easy.

Overloaded Nut Squares

The topping soaks into the crust of these squares, making the base more cake-like, which is a refreshing change from the crisp shortbread base usually found in bars. The softer texture goes well with the overload of crunchy, chunky mixed nuts on top.

MAKES 24 SQUARES
(see Cutting Guide, page 10)

- **Preparation: 20 minutes**
- **Baking: 50 minutes**
- **Freezing: excellent**

TIPS

If you don't have buttermilk, here's a handy substitute: Place 1 tbsp (15 mL) lemon juice or vinegar in a measuring cup and add milk to make 1 cup (250 mL). Let stand for 5 minutes, then stir. Add to recipe.

If the filling is sticky, make cutting easier by running a knife around the edge of the pan as soon as you remove it from the oven. Let bars cool completely before cutting. Bars with a soft filling or frosting are usually easier to cut neatly if they're first chilled until firm.

- **Preheat oven to 350°F (180°C)**
- **13- by 9-inch (3 L) cake pan, greased**

CRUST

1¾ cups	all-purpose flour	425 mL
⅓ cup	packed brown sugar	75 mL
¾ cup	butter, softened	175 mL

TOPPING

1⅔ cups	granulated sugar	400 mL
¼ cup	all-purpose flour	50 mL
3	eggs	3
1 cup	buttermilk (see Tips, left)	250 mL
¼ cup	butter, melted and cooled	50 mL
1 tsp	vanilla	5 mL
2 cups	coarsely chopped deluxe salted mixed nuts (no peanuts)	500 mL

1. *Crust:* In a bowl, combine flour, brown sugar and butter. Using an electric mixer on low speed, beat until crumbly. Press evenly into prepared pan. Bake in preheated oven until golden around edges, 12 to 15 minutes.

2. *Topping:* In a bowl, combine sugar and flour. Whisk in eggs, buttermilk, melted butter and vanilla, whisking just until smooth. Stir in nuts. Pour over crust.

3. Return to oven and bake until topping is set and golden, 30 to 35 minutes. Let cool completely in pan on rack. Cut into squares.

Variation

I like the flavor of salted nuts in these bars, but if you're trying to cut down on salt, make your own mixture of nuts using unsalted pecans, almonds, hazelnuts, cashews and Brazil nuts.

Crunchy Caramel Almond Squares

These squares are one of the simplest recipes in the book. They're also one of my favorites. With a recipe like this, there's no excuse for not making homemade treats.

MAKES 24 TO 60 SQUARES
(see Cutting Guide, page 10)

- **Preparation: 5 minutes**
- **Baking: 10 minutes**
- **Freezing: excellent**

TIPS

Be careful not to boil the sugar mixture or it will become sugary and too thick.

Try making these squares into ice cream sandwiches by placing a scoop of ice cream on one square, then topping with another.

Instead of cutting this bar into neat squares, break it into irregular pieces after it has cooled. Lift the bar off the pan in large pieces, then break into smaller ones.

- **Preheat oven to 375°F (190°C)**
- **15- by 10- by 1-inch (2 L) jelly roll pan, greased**

28	graham crackers	28
1 cup	butter	250 mL
1 cup	packed brown sugar	250 mL
1½ cups	sliced almonds	375 mL

1. In prepared pan, arrange graham crackers in single layer. Set aside.

2. In a saucepan, melt butter over medium heat. Whisk in brown sugar until combined. Bring just to a boil, reduce heat to low and simmer for 2 minutes. (Do not boil.) Remove from heat. Stir in almonds. Quickly pour over crackers and spread evenly to cover.

3. Bake in preheated oven until golden and bubbly, about 10 minutes. Let cool in pan on rack for 10 minutes. Cut into squares. Let cool completely.

Variations

I like the look of unblanched almonds, which are available presliced in some bulk stores, although you'll get the same flavor using the blanched variety.

Substitute an equal quantity of sliced hazelnuts for the almonds.

Spread or drizzle melted chocolate over the squares.

Raspberry Almond Bars

◆

The combination of raspberry and almond is always delicious. Add a shortbread crust and creamy butter frosting and the results are nothing short of sensational.

MAKES 20 TO 54 BARS (see Cutting Guide, page 10)

- Preparation: 30 minutes
- Baking: 37 minutes
- Chilling: 1 hour
- Freezing: excellent

TIPS

Be sure to buy almond paste, not marzipan, which contains a much higher proportion of sugar. Squeeze the almond paste to make sure it's soft and fresh. It tends to harden in storage, which makes it difficult to blend smoothly.

If you prefer, make the crust in a food processor. Just substitute cold butter, cubed, for the softened.

- **Preheat oven to 350°F (180°C)**
- **13- by 9-inch (3 L) cake pan, greased**

CRUST

½ cup	butter, softened	125 mL
½ cup	packed brown sugar	125 mL
1 tsp	vanilla	5 mL
1½ cups	all-purpose flour	375 mL
¼ tsp	salt	1 mL
¾ cup	raspberry jam	175 mL

FILLING

8 oz	almond paste (see Tips, left)	250 g
½ cup	granulated sugar	125 mL
1 tsp	vanilla	5 mL
3	eggs	3

BUTTERY CHOCOLATE FROSTING

2 tbsp	butter, softened	25 mL
1½ cups	confectioner's (icing) sugar, sifted	375 mL
1 tsp	vanilla	5 mL
2 to 3 tbsp	milk	25 to 45 mL
1	square (1 oz/28 g) semi-sweet chocolate, melted	1

1. *Crust:* In a bowl, using a wooden spoon, beat butter, brown sugar and vanilla until smooth and creamy, about 2 minutes. Stir in flour and salt, mixing until crumbly. Press evenly into prepared pan. Bake in preheated oven until golden around edges, 10 to 12 minutes. Let cool slightly. Spread jam evenly over warm crust, leaving a ½-inch (1 cm) border of crust.

2. *Filling:* In a food processor fitted with a metal blade, process almond paste, sugar and vanilla until smoothly blended. Add eggs, one at a time, pulsing a few times after each addition. Process until smooth. Spread evenly over jam.

3. Return to oven and bake until set and golden, 20 to 25 minutes. Let cool completely in pan on rack.

4. *Buttery Chocolate Frosting:* In a bowl, using an electric mixer on medium speed, beat butter, confectioner's sugar and vanilla just until combined. Gradually beat in milk, adding just enough to make a spreadable consistency. Beat in melted chocolate. Spread over filling. Chill for 1 hour to firm up frosting. Cut into bars.

Maraschino Cherry and Almond Bars

Here's a colorful holiday bar to brighten up a cookie tray. I love the almond flavor with the cherries.

MAKES 18 TO 48 BARS (see Cutting Guide, page 10)

- **Preparation: 30 minutes**
- **Baking: 37 minutes**
- **Freezing: excellent**

TIPS

Red maraschino cherries are flavored with almond. If you'd like a stronger almond flavor in the topping, add ½ tsp (2 mL) almond extract.

Green maraschino cherries are often flavored with mint, but they work in this recipe.

- **Preheat oven to 350°F (180°C)**
- **9-inch (2.5 L) square cake pan, greased**

CRUST

1 cup	all-purpose flour	250 mL
¼ cup	confectioner's (icing) sugar	50 mL
½ cup	cold butter, cubed	125 mL

TOPPING

2	eggs	2
½ cup	granulated sugar	125 mL
¼ cup	all-purpose flour	50 mL
½ tsp	baking powder	2 mL
1 cup	sliced almonds	250 mL
1 cup	drained red maraschino cherries, chopped	250 mL

GLAZE, OPTIONAL

½ cup	confectioner's (icing) sugar, sifted	125 mL
¼ tsp	almond extract	1 mL
2 tsp	reserved maraschino cherry juice	10 mL
1 to 2 tsp	milk	5 to 10 mL

1. *Crust:* In a bowl, combine flour and confectioner's sugar. Using a pastry blender, 2 knives or your fingers, cut in butter until mixture resembles coarse crumbs. Press evenly into prepared pan. Bake in preheated oven until golden around the edges, 10 to 12 minutes.

2. *Topping:* In a bowl, whisk eggs and sugar until blended. Whisk in flour and baking powder, mixing well. Stir in almonds and cherries. Spread evenly over crust.

3. Return to oven and bake until topping is set and golden, 20 to 25 minutes. Let cool completely in pan on rack.

4. *Glaze (if using):* In a small bowl, combine confectioner's sugar, almond extract and cherry juice. Gradually whisk in enough milk to make a smooth, pourable consistency. Drizzle over top of cooled bars. Let glaze set. Cut into bars.

Butterscotch Peanut Squares

A crisp crust and chewy caramel top with lots of peanuts in the middle make these bars the perfect partner for a cold glass of milk.

MAKES 24 TO 60 SQUARES (see Cutting Guide, page 10)

- **Preparation: 15 minutes**
- **Baking: 27 minutes**
- **Freezing: excellent**

TIPS

Like all nuts, peanuts become rancid quickly because they're high in fat. Keep them in your freezer in airtight containers to retain freshness. Taste nuts before using to make sure they're fresh.

If you prefer, you can mix the crust in a bowl. Combine the flour and brown sugar, then cut in butter using a pastry blender, 2 knives or your fingers. Whichever method you use, the mixture should resemble coarse crumbs.

- **Preheat oven to 350°F (180°C)**
- **15- by 10- by 1-inch (2 L) jelly roll pan, greased**

CRUST

1½ cups	all-purpose flour	375 mL
¾ cup	packed brown sugar	175 mL
½ cup	cold butter, cubed	125 mL

TOPPING

3½ cups	salted peanuts	875 mL
½ cup	corn syrup	125 mL
2 tbsp	butter	25 mL
1 tbsp	water	15 mL
1 cup	butterscotch chips	250 mL

1. *Crust:* In a food processor fitted with a metal blade, combine flour, brown sugar and butter. Process until mixture resembles coarse crumbs. Press evenly into prepared pan. Bake in preheated oven until golden around edges, 10 to 12 minutes.

2. *Topping:* Sprinkle peanuts over crust. In a saucepan over low heat, combine corn syrup, butter, water and butterscotch chips. Cook, stirring often, until chips are melted and mixture is smooth. Pour evenly over peanuts.

3. Return to oven and bake until set, 12 to 15 minutes. Let cool completely in pan on rack. Cut into squares.

Variations

Replace butterscotch chips with peanut butter chips or semi-sweet chocolate chips.

Use dry-roasted peanuts for an extra-crunchy filling.

Apricot Almond Bars

The almond paste gives these bars a strong but appealing almond flavor. I find it works particularly well with a tart apricot jam.

MAKES 20 TO 54 BARS (see Cutting Guide, page 10)

- **Preparation: 25 minutes**
- **Baking: 40 minutes**
- **Freezing: excellent**

TIPS

Almond paste is a mixture of ground almonds and sugar. Marzipan is too, but it has a much higher sugar content. It's sold in tubes, cans or pieces, by weight, in the baking section of supermarkets.

Use cold butter when cutting it into a dry mixture with a pastry blender or in a food processor. Let it soften if you're using a mixer or beating with a spoon.

- **Preheat oven to 350°F (180°C)**
- **13- by 9-inch (3 L) cake pan, greased**

CRUST

1½ cups	all-purpose flour	375 mL
¼ cup	granulated sugar	50 mL
½ cup	butter, softened	125 mL

TOPPING

7½ oz	almond paste, crumbled	200 g
½ cup	all-purpose flour	125 mL
¼ cup	granulated sugar	50 mL
¼ cup	butter, softened	50 mL
1 cup	apricot jam	250 mL
½ cup	sliced almonds	125 mL

1. *Crust:* In a bowl, combine flour, sugar and butter. Using an electric mixer on low speed, beat until crumbly. Press evenly into prepared pan. Bake in preheated oven until golden all over, 12 to 15 minutes.

2. *Topping:* In a bowl, combine almond paste, flour and sugar. Using a pastry blender, 2 knives or your fingers, cut in butter until mixture resembles coarse crumbs. Set aside.

3. Spread jam over crust, leaving a ½-inch (1 cm) border of crust. Sprinkle almond paste mixture evenly over top. Sprinkle sliced almonds evenly over topping.

4. Return to oven and bake until top is set and golden, 20 to 25 minutes. Let cool completely in pan on rack. Cut into bars.

Variations

Use other soft spreads, such as raspberry or peach jam or marmalade.

Dust with confectioner's (icing) sugar or drizzle with a mixture of ⅔ cup (150 mL) confectioner's (icing) sugar and 1 to 2 tbsp (15 to 25 mL) milk.

Peanut Butter Candy Bars

Kids young and old love these bars. A generous layer of caramel peanuts smothers a tender, melt-in-your-mouth crust.

MAKES 36 TO 48 BARS (see Cutting Guide, page 10)

- **Preparation: 20 minutes**
- **Baking: 27 minutes**
- **Freezing: excellent**

TIPS

It's always best to use the pan size recommended in a recipe because it's the one in which the recipe was tested. However, if you don't have a jelly roll pan, you can use two 9-inch (2.5 L) square pans. In any recipe, check for doneness 5 minutes before the minimum time suggested.

When serving bars like these, which may stick to the plate, first dust the plate lightly with fine sugar.

- **Preheat oven to 350°F (180°C)**
- **15- by 10- by 1-inch (2 L) jelly roll pan, greased**

CRUST

2 cups	all-purpose flour	500 mL
½ cup	packed brown sugar	125 mL
¾ cup	butter, softened	175 mL

TOPPING

2 cups	peanuts	500 mL
1¼ cups	milk chocolate chips	300 mL
3 tbsp	all-purpose flour	45 mL
1½ cups	caramel sundae sauce	375 mL

1. *Crust:* In a bowl, combine flour, brown sugar and butter. Using an electric mixer on low speed, beat until crumbly. Press evenly into prepared pan. Bake in preheated oven until golden around the edges, 10 to 12 minutes.

2. *Topping:* Sprinkle peanuts and chocolate chips evenly over crust. In a small bowl, stir flour into sundae sauce, mixing until smooth. Pour evenly over peanuts and chocolate chips.

3. Return to oven and bake until caramel is bubbly, 12 to 15 minutes. Let cool completely in pan on rack. Cut into bars.

Variations

Substitute semi-sweet chocolate chips for the milk chocolate chips.

Use butterscotch sundae sauce if you prefer a milder caramel flavor.

Raspberry Hazelnut Bars

◆

These bars, which feature a light and tender nut top on a layer of jam and a shortbread crust, are a favorite in Austria. They're pretty delicious on this side of the ocean, too.

MAKES 20 TO 54 BARS (see Cutting Guide, page 10)

- **Preparation: 20 minutes**
- **Baking: 47 minutes**
- **Freezing: excellent**

TIPS

Hazelnuts are also called filberts.

It's not a mistake — there's no flour in the topping. The ground hazelnuts take its place.

When folding stiff egg whites into a stiff batter, add one-quarter of the egg whites first and stir them into the batter to soften it. Then gently fold in the remaining egg whites. This helps keep the mixture light, tender and airy.

- **Preheat oven to 325°F (160°C)**
- **13- by 9-inch (3 L) cake pan, greased**

CRUST

1¼ cups	all-purpose flour	300 mL
3 tbsp	granulated sugar	45 mL
1 cup	cold butter, cubed	250 mL

TOPPING

½ cup	raspberry jam	125 mL
3 tbsp	butter, softened	45 mL
1¼ cups	granulated sugar	300 mL
6	eggs, separated	6
1⅔ cups	coarsely ground hazelnuts	400 mL

1. *Crust:* In a bowl, combine flour and sugar. Using a pastry blender, 2 knives or your fingers, cut in butter until mixture resembles coarse crumbs. Press evenly into prepared pan. Bake in preheated oven until golden around edges, 10 to 12 minutes. Let cool on rack for 30 minutes.

2. *Topping:* Spread jam evenly over cooled crust, leaving a ½-inch (1 cm) border. In a bowl, using an electric mixer on medium speed, beat butter and sugar until blended. In a small bowl, using an electric mixer on high speed, beat egg yolks until light and creamy, about 5 minutes. Stir into butter mixture along with ground hazelnuts, mixing well. In a clean bowl, using an electric mixer with clean beaters on high speed, beat egg whites until stiff, shiny peaks form. Gently fold into nut mixture. Spread carefully over jam.

3. Return to oven and bake until topping is set and golden, 30 to 35 minutes. Let cool completely in pan on rack. Cut into bars.

Variations

Use raspberry, strawberry or pineapple jam.
Substitute unblanched ground almonds for the hazelnuts.

Mom's Dream Cake

For as long as I can remember, my mother, who was fond of nuts of any kind, loved making — and eating — these delicious bars.

MAKES 16 TO 48 BARS OR SQUARES (see Cutting Guide, page 10)

- **Preparation: 20 minutes**
- **Baking: 42 minutes**
- **Freezing: excellent**

TIPS

Shortbread crusts like this can be prepared quickly in a food processor. They can also be mixed with an electric mixer on low speed or with a wooden spoon when using softened butter. Whichever method you choose, the butter should be evenly distributed throughout the mixture, so it resembles coarse crumbs.

I have specified sweetened coconut because it seems to be more readily available than the unsweetened variety. But sweetened and unsweetened coconut can be used interchangeably in any recipe to suit your preference.

- **Preheat oven to 350°F (180°C)**
- **9-inch (2.5 L) square cake pan, greased**

CRUST

1 cup + 2 tbsp	all-purpose flour	275 mL
3 tbsp	granulated sugar	45 mL
1/4 tsp	salt	1 mL
1/2 cup	cold butter, cubed	125 mL

TOPPING

2	eggs	2
1 1/4 cups	packed brown sugar	300 mL
1 tsp	vanilla	5 mL
2 tbsp	all-purpose flour	25 mL
1 tsp	baking powder	5 mL
1 cup	chopped walnuts	250 mL
1/2 cup	sweetened flaked coconut	125 mL

1. *Crust:* In a bowl, combine flour, sugar and salt. Using a pastry blender, 2 knives or your fingers, cut in butter until mixture resembles coarse crumbs. Press evenly into prepared pan. Bake in preheated oven until golden around edges, 10 to 12 minutes.

2. *Topping:* In a bowl, whisk eggs, brown sugar and vanilla until smooth. Whisk in flour and baking powder, mixing well. Stir in walnuts and coconut. Spread evenly over crust.

3. Return to oven and bake until topping is set and golden, 25 to 30 minutes. Let cool completely in pan on rack. Cut into bars or squares.

> ## Variations
> Replace walnuts with pecans or almonds.
>
> Add 1/3 cup (75 mL) chopped red candied (glacé) cherries to topping.

Maple Nut Bars

These delicious bars start with a shortbread crust and add a slightly gooey maple topping loaded with your favorite nuts. What could be better?

MAKES 20 TO 54 BARS (see Cutting Guide, page 10)

- **Preparation: 25 minutes**
- **Baking: 40 minutes**
- **Freezing: excellent**

TIPS

If you prefer, mix the crust in a food processor. Use cold butter rather than softened. You can also mix the crust in a bowl, cutting in cold cubed butter using a pastry blender, 2 knives or your fingers.

Use pure maple syrup for baking. Pancake syrup doesn't have enough maple flavor and can react differently in baking.

Buy California walnuts for baking. If you have the time, buy walnut halves and chop them rather than using pieces. They're fresher and of a higher quality.

In all your baking, you can replace all-purpose flour with unbleached all-purpose flour if you prefer. They are interchangeable.

- **Preheat oven to 350°F (180°C)**
- **13- by 9-inch (3 L) cake pan, greased**

CRUST

1 cup	butter, softened	250 mL
½ cup	packed brown sugar	125 mL
2 cups	all-purpose flour	500 mL

TOPPING

3	eggs	3
1 cup	packed brown sugar	250 mL
¼ cup	pure maple syrup	50 mL
2 tbsp	butter, melted	25 mL
¼ cup	all-purpose flour	50 mL
½ tsp	baking powder	2 mL
1 cup	coarsely chopped pecans	250 mL
¾ cup	sliced hazelnuts	175 mL
⅔ cup	coarsely chopped walnuts	150 mL

1. *Crust:* In a bowl, using an electric mixer on medium speed, beat butter and brown sugar until smooth and creamy. On low speed, beat in flour until thoroughly blended and crumbly. Press evenly into prepared pan. Bake in preheated oven until golden around edges, 12 to 15 minutes.

2. *Topping:* In a bowl, whisk eggs, brown sugar, maple syrup and melted butter until smoothly blended. Whisk in flour and baking powder. Mix well. Stir in hazelnuts and walnuts. Spread evenly over warm crust.

3. Return to oven and bake until topping is set, 20 to 25 minutes. Let cool completely in pan on rack. Cut into bars.

Variation

Use the same quantities of your favorite combination of nuts. To make the texture more interesting, use a combination of sliced and chopped nuts.

Lots of Pecan Cranberry Bars

◆

Featuring a caramel topping with lots of pecans and dried cranberries throughout, these bars are simple to make and delicious to eat.

MAKES 18 TO 48 BARS (see Cutting Guide, page 10)

- **Preparation: 20 minutes**
- **Cooking: 2 to 5 minutes**
- **Baking: 37 minutes**
- **Freezing: excellent**

TIP

Always use the size of pan recommended in your recipe. The difference between an 8-inch (2 L) and 9-inch (2.5 L) square pan can mean the difference between a dry, overbaked, crumbly bar if your pan is too large or an underbaked heavy flop if it's too small.

- **Preheat oven to 350°F (180°C)**
- **8-inch (2 L) square cake pan, greased**

CRUST

1 cup	all-purpose flour	250 mL
1 tbsp	granulated sugar	15 mL
¼ cup	cold butter, cubed	50 mL
2 tbsp	water	25 mL

TOPPING

⅓ cup	whipping (35%) cream	75 mL
½ cup	packed brown sugar	125 mL
2 tbsp	liquid honey	25 mL
¾ cup	dried cranberries	175 mL
¾ cup	coarsely chopped pecans	175 mL
½ cup	pecan halves	125 mL

1. *Crust:* In a food processor fitted with a metal blade, combine flour, sugar and butter. Process until mixture resembles coarse crumbs. Add water and pulse a few times until well blended. Press evenly into prepared pan. Bake in preheated oven until golden around edges, 10 to 12 minutes.

2. *Topping:* In a saucepan, combine whipping cream, brown sugar and honey. Bring to a boil over medium heat, stirring frequently. Boil for 1 minute. Remove from heat. Stir in cranberries, chopped pecans and pecan halves. Spread evenly over crust.

3. Return to oven and bake until topping is set and golden, 20 to 25 minutes. Let cool completely in pan on rack. Cut into bars.

> ## Variations
> Replace pecans with walnuts.
> Replace dried cranberries with chopped dried cherries.

Caramel Almond Squares

A chewy caramel and almond topping covers a shortbread crust. These luscious squares are quick and easy to make.

MAKES 16 TO 36 SQUARES
(see Cutting Guide, page 10)

- **Preparation: 20 minutes**
- **Baking: 50 minutes**
- **Freezing: excellent**

TIPS

Many bars do not contain eggs, which means people with egg allergies have lots of choice.

Be careful not to cook the caramel topping too long or it will be too thick. Bring it just to a boil, then remove from heat.

- **Preheat oven to 350°F (180°C)**
- **9-inch (2.5 L) square cake pan, greased**

CRUST

1 cup	butter, softened	250 mL
1 cup	confectioner's (icing) sugar	250 mL
2 cups	all-purpose flour	500 mL

TOPPING

1 cup	packed brown sugar	250 mL
1 cup	sliced almonds	250 mL
1/3 cup	butter	75 mL
2 tbsp	water	25 mL
1 tsp	vanilla	5 mL
3/4 tsp	freshly squeezed lemon juice	3 mL

1. *Crust:* In a bowl, using an electric mixer on medium speed, beat butter with confectioner's sugar until creamy. Stir in flour, mixing until fine crumbs form. Press evenly into prepared pan. Bake in preheated oven until golden, 25 to 30 minutes.

2. *Topping:* In a saucepan, combine brown sugar, almonds, butter, water, vanilla and lemon juice. Bring to a boil over medium-high heat, stirring occasionally. Pour over crust.

3. Return to oven and bake until topping is bubbly and golden, 15 to 20 minutes. Let cool in pan on rack for 5 minutes. Run a knife along the edges to loosen. Let cool completely. Cut into squares.

Variations

Replace almonds with sliced hazelnuts.
Replace vanilla with 1/4 tsp (1 mL) almond extract.

Lemon Walnut Bars

These bars are a favorite. I love the way the tart lemon glaze sets off the crisp crust and nutty filling.

MAKES 20 TO 54 BARS (see Cutting Guide, page 10)

- **Preparation: 20 minutes**
- **Baking: 32 minutes**
- **Freezing: excellent**

TIP

I like to use freshly squeezed lemon juice when baking because it has the best flavor. If your recipe calls for grated lemon zest, remember to remove the zest before juicing.

- **Preheat oven to 350°F (180°C)**
- **13- by 9-inch (3 L) cake pan, greased**

CRUST

½ cup	butter, softened	125 mL
½ cup	granulated sugar	125 mL
2 tsp	grated lemon zest	10 mL
1¼ cups	all-purpose flour	300 mL

FILLING

2	eggs	2
1 cup	packed brown sugar	250 mL
¼ cup	all-purpose flour	50 mL
¼ tsp	baking powder	1 mL
1 tsp	grated lemon zest	5 mL
1 cup	finely chopped walnuts	250 mL

LEMON GLAZE

1 tbsp	butter, softened	15 mL
1 cup	confectioner's (icing) sugar, sifted	250 mL
2 tbsp	freshly squeezed lemon juice	25 mL

1. *Crust:* In a bowl, using an electric mixer on medium speed, beat butter, sugar and lemon zest until creamy. Gradually stir in flour to form a soft, crumbly dough. Press evenly into prepared pan. Bake in preheated oven until golden around edges, 10 to 12 minutes.

2. *Filling:* In a bowl, whisk eggs, brown sugar, flour, baking powder and lemon zest, mixing well. Stir in walnuts. Spread evenly over crust.

3. Return to oven and bake until set and golden, 15 to 20 minutes.

4. *Lemon Glaze:* In a bowl, using an electric mixer on medium speed, beat butter until smooth. Gradually add confectioner's sugar and lemon juice, mixing until smooth. Spread evenly over hot filling. Let cool completely in pan on rack. Cut into bars.

Variation
Replace almonds with hazelnuts.

Sour Cherry Almond Bars

A not-too-sweet, easy-to-make bar that combines the mouthwatering flavors of sour cherries and almonds.

MAKES 18 TO 48 BARS (see Cutting Guide, page 10)

- **Preparation: 20 minutes**
- **Cooling: 30 minutes**
- **Baking: 42 minutes**
- **Freezing: excellent**

TIPS

If you want to make a bigger batch of these bars — you can stash some in the freezer — double the recipe and bake in a 13- by 9-inch (3 L) cake pan for 30 to 35 minutes.

To prevent the jam from sticking to the pan, line it with parchment or greased foil.

- **Preheat oven to 350°F (180°C)**
- **8-inch (2 L) square cake pan, greased**

CRUST

1 cup	all-purpose flour	250 mL
½ cup	ground almonds	125 mL
⅓ cup	packed brown sugar	75 mL
⅓ cup	cold butter, cubed	75 mL
¼ tsp	almond extract	1 mL

TOPPING

¾ cup	sour cherry jam	175 mL
1 tbsp	freshly squeezed lemon juice	15 mL
¼ tsp	almond extract	1 mL
1 cup	sliced almonds	250 mL

1. *Crust:* In a food processor fitted with a metal blade, combine flour, ground almonds and brown sugar. Pulse to combine. Add butter and almond extract. Process until mixture resembles coarse crumbs. Press evenly into prepared pan. Bake in preheated oven until golden around the edges, 10 to 12 minutes. Let cool for 30 minutes.

2. *Topping:* In a bowl, combine jam, lemon juice and almond extract, mixing well. Spread evenly over crust, leaving a ½-inch (1 cm) border of crust. Sprinkle with sliced almonds.

3. Return to oven and bake until topping is bubbly and almonds are light golden, 25 to 30 minutes. Let cool completely in pan on rack. Cut into bars.

Variation

You can also use other kinds of jam in this recipe. Raspberry and peach work well with the flavorings.

Chocolate-Glazed Almond Squares

These squares combine two favorites — cookies and candy. It's no wonder they don't last long.

MAKES 16 TO 36 SQUARES
(see **Cutting Guide**, page 10)

- **Preparation: 25 minutes**
- **Baking: 27 minutes**
- **Freezing: excellent**

TIPS

Corn syrup comes in white and golden colors. The white is used mainly for candy making while the golden is used for baking.

To cut bars neatly, use a sharp knife in a gentle sawing motion to avoid squashing the filling.

- **Preheat oven to 350°F (180°C)**
- **8-inch (2 L) square cake pan, greased**

CRUST

¼ cup	butter, softened	50 mL
⅔ cup	confectioner's (icing) sugar, sifted	150 mL
½ cup	ground almonds	125 mL
¼ cup	all-purpose flour	50 mL

TOPPING

⅓ cup	butter	75 mL
½ cup	packed brown sugar	125 mL
½ cup	corn syrup (see Tips, left)	125 mL
1 tbsp	water	15 mL
1 tbsp	freshly squeezed lemon juice	15 mL
¾ cup	sliced almonds	175 mL
¼ tsp	almond extract	1 mL

GLAZE, OPTIONAL

1	square (1 oz/28 g) semi-sweet chocolate, chopped	1
1 tbsp	butter	15 mL

1. *Crust:* In a bowl, using an electric mixer on medium speed, beat butter and confectioner's sugar until creamy. On low speed, beat in ground almonds and flour, mixing until crumbly. Press evenly into prepared pan. Bake in preheated oven until golden around the edges, 10 to 12 minutes.

2. *Topping:* In a saucepan, melt butter over medium heat. Add brown sugar, corn syrup, water and lemon juice, whisking until smooth. Bring to a boil over medium-high heat and boil for 3 minutes, stirring constantly, until thickened. Remove from heat. Stir in almonds and almond extract. Spread evenly over crust.

3. Return to oven and bake until topping is set and golden, about 15 minutes. Let cool completely in pan on rack.

4. *Glaze (if using):* In a saucepan over low heat, melt chocolate and butter, stirring until smooth. Drizzle over topping. Let cool until chocolate is set, about 30 minutes. Cut into squares.

Caramel Peanut Squares

Dieters, beware. These are definitely not on your list.

MAKES 24 SQUARES (see Cutting Guide, page 10)

- **Preparation: 15 minutes**
- **Baking: 35 minutes**
- **Freezing: excellent**

TIPS

Look for good-quality caramel sauce that's thick and has a rich caramel flavor. If it's thin, add an additional 1 tbsp (15 mL) flour.

I like to use salted peanuts in this recipe because the salt complements the caramel flavor. But if you're trying to decrease your salt intake, unsalted peanuts work well, too.

- **Preheat oven to 350°F (180°C)**
- **13- by 9-inch (3 L) cake pan, greased**

1²/₃ cups	all-purpose flour, divided	400 mL
²/₃ cup	quick-cooking rolled oats	150 mL
½ cup	packed brown sugar	125 mL
¾ tsp	baking soda	3 mL
½ cup	butter, melted	125 mL
1½ cups	caramel sundae sauce	375 mL
1²/₃ cups	peanut butter chips	400 mL
1 cup	coarsely chopped peanuts	250 mL

1. In a bowl, combine 1⅓ cups (325 mL) of the flour, oats, brown sugar and baking soda. Stir well. Stir in melted butter, mixing well. Press evenly into prepared pan. Bake in preheated oven until edges are lightly browned, about 10 minutes.

2. In another bowl, combine caramel sauce and remaining ⅓ cup (75 mL) of the flour, mixing until smooth. Sprinkle peanut butter chips and chopped peanuts over warm crust. Drizzle caramel mixture evenly over top.

3. Return to oven and bake until bubbly and browned, 20 to 25 minutes. Let cool completely in pan on rack. Cut into squares.

Chocolate Raspberry Hazelnut Squares

Four delightful layers — shortbread, raspberry jam, ground hazelnuts and a chocolate drizzle — stacked to make up an attractive square.

MAKES 16 TO 36 SQUARES
(see Cutting Guide, page 10)

- Preparation: 30 minutes
- Baking: 40 minutes
- Cooling: 30 minutes
- Freezing: excellent

TIPS

For optimum flavor, toast the hazelnuts before you grind them. Place whole hazelnuts on a baking sheet and toast in a 350°F (180°C) oven for 5 to 10 minutes, stirring occasionally, until golden. Immediately transfer to a clean tea towel and rub together to remove skins. One cup (250 mL) hazelnuts weighs about 3.8 oz (100 g).

When spreading jam over a tender cookie crust, stir it well first. This will soften the jam and make it easier to spread evenly.

- Preheat oven to 350°F (180°C)
- 9-inch (2.5 L) square cake pan, greased

CRUST

½ cup	butter, softened	125 mL
⅓ cup	confectioner's (icing) sugar, sifted	75 mL
2	egg yolks, beaten	2
1⅓ cups	all-purpose flour	325 mL

TOPPING

⅔ cup	raspberry jam	150 mL
2	egg whites	2
¼ tsp	cream of tartar	1 mL
½ cup	granulated sugar	125 mL
1 cup	toasted hazelnuts, ground	250 mL

CHOCOLATE DRIZZLE

1	square (1 oz/28 g) semi-sweet chocolate, chopped	1
1 tbsp	butter	15 mL

1. *Crust:* In a bowl, using an electric mixer on medium speed, beat butter and confectioner's sugar until smooth and creamy. On low speed, beat in egg yolks and flour, mixing until blended. Press evenly into prepared pan. Bake in preheated oven until golden around the edges, 12 to 15 minutes.

2. *Topping:* Spread jam over crust, leaving a ½-inch (1 cm) border of crust. In a bowl, using an electric mixer on high speed, beat egg whites and cream of tartar until soft peaks form. Gradually add sugar, beating until stiff peaks form. Fold in ground hazelnuts. Drop by spoonfuls on top of jam and carefully spread to edges.

3. Return to oven and bake until topping is lightly browned, 20 to 25 minutes. Let cool completely in pan on rack.

4. *Chocolate Drizzle:* In a small saucepan over low heat, melt chocolate and butter, stirring until smooth. Drizzle over squares. Let cool until chocolate is set, about 30 minutes. Cut into squares.

Toffee Almond Triangles

The crisp, candy-like oatmeal crust is a perfect match for the thin caramel almond top.

MAKES 48 TRIANGLES (see Cutting Guide, page 10)

- **Preparation: 20 minutes**
- **Cooking: 2 minutes**
- **Baking: 32 minutes**
- **Freezing: excellent**

TIPS

When deciding on bars and squares to include on an assorted cookie tray or in a gift box, look for a variety of textures, colors and shapes. That way, you're sure to have something that will please everyone.

- **Preheat oven to 350°F (180°C)**
- **13- by 9-inch (3 L) cake pan, greased**

CRUST

1 cup	all-purpose flour	250 mL
1 cup	quick-cooking rolled oats	250 mL
1 cup	packed brown sugar	250 mL
1 tsp	baking soda	5 mL
½ cup	cold butter, cubed	125 mL

TOPPING

½ cup	corn syrup	125 mL
⅓ cup	packed brown sugar	75 mL
¼ cup	butter	50 mL
¼ cup	whipping (35%) cream	50 mL
1⅔ cups	sliced almonds	400 mL
1 tsp	vanilla	5 mL

1. *Crust:* In a food processor fitted with a metal blade, combine flour, oats, brown sugar, baking soda and butter. Process until crumbly. Press evenly into prepared pan. Bake in preheated oven until golden around the edges, 10 to 12 minutes.

2. *Topping:* In a heavy saucepan over medium-high heat, combine corn syrup, brown sugar, butter and whipping cream. Cook, stirring, until mixture boils. Remove from heat. Stir in almonds and vanilla. Pour over crust, using a spatula or the back of a spoon to spread evenly.

3. Return to oven and bake until topping is bubbly, 15 to 20 minutes. Let cool completely in pan on rack. Cut into squares, then triangles.

Variations

You can also make the crust using half all-purpose and half whole wheat flour.

For a less rich, more intense caramel flavor, replace the whipping cream with evaporated milk.

Bite-Size Pecan Pie

I love pecan pie, but because it's so rich, I always feel guilty eating an entire piece. Enjoying it in smaller bites in these squares makes me feel less self-indulgent.

**MAKES 16 TO 36 SQUARES
(see Cutting Guide, page 10)**

- **Preparation: 20 minutes**
- **Baking: 47 minutes**
- **Freezing: excellent**

TIPS

Bars like these, with a slightly soft topping, will be easier to cut if they're cold.

Use a sharp serrated knife in a sawing motion to cut neat pieces.

If you like the filling a little gooey, underbake slightly. Bake a little longer for a firmer texture.

- **Preheat oven to 350°F (180°C)**
- **9-inch (2.5 L) square cake pan, greased**

CRUST

1⅓ cups	all-purpose flour	325 mL
3 tbsp	granulated sugar	45 mL
½ cup	cold butter, cubed	125 mL

TOPPING

2	eggs	2
½ cup	granulated sugar	125 mL
½ cup	corn syrup	125 mL
2 tbsp	butter, melted	25 mL
1¾ cups	coarsely chopped pecans	425 mL

1. *Crust:* In a bowl, combine flour and sugar. Using a pastry blender, 2 knives or your fingers, cut in butter until mixture resembles coarse crumbs. Press evenly into prepared pan. Bake in preheated oven until golden around the edges, 10 to 12 minutes.

2. *Topping:* In a bowl, whisk eggs, sugar, corn syrup and melted butter until smoothly blended. Stir in pecans. Pour evenly over crust.

3. Return to oven and bake until set and golden, 25 to 35 minutes. Let cool completely in pan on rack. Cut into squares.

Variations

Replace pecans with walnuts and half of the corn syrup with pure maple syrup.

Decrease pecans to 1¼ cups (300 mL) and add ½ cup (125 mL) dried cranberries or raisins.

Chewy Toffee Almond Squares

These bars have a delicate candy-like base and a crunchy layer of sliced almonds covered by a thin, chewy caramel coating. It's a mouthwatering combination.

**MAKES 24 SQUARES
(see Cutting Guide, page 10)**

- **Preparation: 20 minutes**
- **Cooking: 12 minutes**
- **Baking: 30 minutes**
- **Freezing: excellent**

TIPS

Toffee bits are available in bags. They're broken pieces of the toffee part of Heath or Skor bars (no chocolate).

I have specified sweetened coconut because it seems to be more readily available than the unsweetened variety. But sweetened and unsweetened coconut can be used interchangeably in any recipe to suit your preference.

If your coconut seems dry, sprinkle it with a little milk and let it stand until softened.

- **Preheat oven to 350°F (180°C)**
- **13- by 9-inch (3 L) cake pan, greased**

CRUST

1 cup	butter, softened	250 mL
½ cup	granulated sugar	125 mL
2 cups	all-purpose flour	500 mL

TOPPING

1 ⅓ cups	toffee bits (see Tips, left)	325 mL
¾ cup	corn syrup	175 mL
1 cup	sliced almonds, divided	250 mL
¾ cup	sweetened flaked coconut, divided (see Tips, left)	175 mL

1. *Crust:* In a bowl, using an electric mixer on medium speed, beat butter and sugar until smooth, about 2 minutes. On low speed, gradually add flour, beating until well blended and crumbly. Press evenly into prepared pan. Bake in preheated oven until edges are lightly browned, 12 to 15 minutes.

2. *Topping:* In a saucepan over medium heat, combine toffee bits and corn syrup. Cook, stirring constantly, until toffee is melted, about 12 minutes. Stir in ½ cup (125 mL) of the almonds and ½ cup (125 mL) of the coconut. Spread evenly over crust, leaving ½-inch (1 cm) border of crust. Sprinkle remaining almonds and coconut over top.

3. Return to oven and bake until bubbly and golden, about 15 minutes. Let cool completely in pan on rack. Cut into squares.

Variations

Cut these squares into triangles for an interesting alternative shape.

Use unblanched sliced almonds for an attractive top. The taste is the same as the blanched variety, but I like the contrasting colors.

Apricot Pecan Bars

A tender shortbread crust, a layer of apricot jam and crunchy but chewy pecan meringue make one great bar.

MAKES 18 TO 48 BARS (see Cutting Guide, page 10)

- **Preparation: 25 minutes**
- **Baking: 37 minutes**
- **Freezing: excellent**

TIPS

When making meringue, be sure your bowl and beaters are clean and free of any trace of grease. Otherwise, your egg whites won't stiffen.

When beating egg whites, have them at room temperature to ensure the best volume.

To fancy these up, drizzle melted chocolate over top.

- **Preheat oven to 350°F (180°C)**
- **9-inch (2.5 L) square cake pan, greased**

CRUST

½ cup	butter, softened	125 mL
½ cup	confectioner's (icing) sugar, sifted	125 mL
2	egg yolks	2
1¼ cups	all-purpose flour	300 mL

TOPPING

¾ cup	apricot jam	175 mL
2	egg whites	2
Pinch	cream of tartar	Pinch
½ cup	granulated sugar	125 mL
1¼ cups	ground toasted pecans	300 mL

1. *Crust:* In a bowl, using an electric mixer on medium speed, beat butter, confectioner's sugar and egg yolks until smooth. Gradually add flour, mixing on low speed until well blended. Press firmly into prepared pan. Bake in preheated oven until golden around edges, 10 to 12 minutes. Let cool for 15 minutes.

2. *Topping:* Spread jam evenly over crust. In a bowl, using an electric mixer on high speed, beat egg whites and cream of tartar until soft peaks form. Gradually add sugar, beating until stiff peaks form. Fold in pecans. Drop by spoonfuls on top of jam and spread carefully to edges.

3. Return to oven and bake until lightly browned, 20 to 25 minutes. Let cool completely in pan on rack. Cut into bars.

Variation

Other kinds of jam, such as marmalade and peach, also work well in this recipe.

Caramel Cappuccino Bars

The combination of coffee flavor and crunchy toffee bits makes these bars an outstanding coffee time treat.

MAKES 20 TO 54 BARS
(see Cutting Guide, page 10)

- **Preparation: 25 minutes**
- **Baking: 45 minutes**
- **Freezing: excellent**

TIPS

My favorite brand of toffee bits is Skor bits and I like to buy them in bulk. Others, such as Heath bits are also available in bulk.

If you don't have instant espresso coffee powder, use double the amount of regular instant coffee granules. Use the back of a spoon to grind them to a fine powder before combining with water.

I prefer to leave the coffee powder dry in the crust, but you can dissolve it in 2 tsp (10 mL) hot water if you prefer.

To make a wonderful Valentine gift, cut these bars into heart shapes using a cookie cutter.

- **Preheat oven to 325°F (160°C)**
- **13- by 9-inch (3 L) cake pan, greased**

CRUST

½ cup	butter, softened	125 mL
¾ cup	packed brown sugar	175 mL
2 tsp	instant espresso coffee powder	10 mL
1¼ cups	all-purpose flour	300 mL
⅓ cup	ground almonds	75 mL
⅔ cup	toffee bits (see Tips, left)	150 mL

TOPPING

1 tbsp	instant espresso coffee powder (see Tips, left)	15 mL
2 tsp	hot water	10 mL
1 cup	granulated sugar	250 mL
⅔ cup	sweetened condensed milk	150 mL
3	eggs	3
2 tbsp	all-purpose flour	25 mL
½ tsp	baking powder	2 mL
⅓ cup	toffee bits	75 mL
¼ cup	finely chopped almonds	50 mL

1. *Crust:* In a bowl, using an electric mixer on medium speed, beat butter, brown sugar and coffee powder until light and creamy. Add flour and ground almonds and mix on low speed until thoroughly blended. Press evenly into prepared pan. Sprinkle toffee bits evenly over crust. Press in lightly. Bake in preheated oven until lightly browned all over, 12 to 15 minutes.

2. *Topping:* In a bowl, dissolve espresso powder in hot water. Whisk in sugar, sweetened condensed milk and eggs until smooth. Whisk in flour and baking powder, mixing well. Pour evenly over crust.

3. Return to oven and bake until topping is golden, 25 to 30 minutes. Remove from oven and immediately sprinkle toffee bits and almonds evenly over top. Let cool completely in pan on rack. Cut into bars.

Variation

If you prefer a milder coffee flavor, use half the suggested amount of espresso coffee powder.

Chewy Cherry Date and Nut Bars

The combination of dates and nuts has been popular for years. They fit into the "comfort food" category, and so do these bars.

MAKES 20 TO 54 BARS (see Cutting Guide, page 10)

- **Preparation: 30 minutes**
- **Baking: 40 minutes**
- **Chilling: 1 hour**
- **Freezing: excellent**

TIPS

For a bar that's less sweet, omit the frosting and dust lightly with confectioner's (icing) sugar.

The easiest way to cut dates is to use kitchen shears sprayed with cooking spray. Be sure your dates are soft. They'll be easier to cut and taste better in your baking.

Confectioner's (icing) sugar is often lumpy. Measure it, then sift it in a sifter or sieve before adding to your other ingredients.

For dusting confectioner's (icing) sugar over a bar, use a small sieve with a very fine mesh.

- **Preheat oven to 350°F (180°C)**
- **13- by 9-inch (3 L) cake pan, greased**

CRUST

¾ cup	butter, softened	175 mL
½ cup	granulated sugar	125 mL
2 cups	all-purpose flour	500 mL

FILLING

2	eggs	2
1½ cups	packed brown sugar	375 mL
1 tsp	vanilla	5 mL
2 tbsp	all-purpose flour	25 mL
½ tsp	baking powder	2 mL
1¼ cups	chopped walnuts, toasted	300 mL
1 cup	candied (glacé) cherries, quartered	250 mL
½ cup	chopped dates	125 mL

FROSTING

½ cup	butter, softened	125 mL
2 cups	confectioner's (icing) sugar, sifted	500 mL
2 tbsp	milk	25 mL
1 tbsp	lemon juice	15 mL

1. *Crust:* In a bowl, using an electric mixer on medium speed, beat butter and sugar until creamy. Beat in flour, mixing until crumbly. Press evenly into prepared pan. Bake in preheated oven until golden all over, 12 to 15 minutes. Let cool in pan on rack.

2. *Filling:* In a bowl, whisk eggs, brown sugar and vanilla until blended. Whisk in flour and baking powder, mixing until smooth. Stir in walnuts, cherries and dates. Spread evenly over cooled crust.

3. Return to oven and bake until top is set and golden, 20 to 25 minutes. Let cool completely in pan on rack.

4. *Frosting:* In a bowl, using an electric mixer on medium speed, beat butter, half of the confectioner's sugar, milk and lemon juice until light and creamy. Gradually add remaining confectioner's sugar, beating until smooth. Spread evenly over cooled filling. Refrigerate until frosting is firm, about 1 hour. Cut into bars.

Double Almond Strawberry Jam Squares

These bars are an example of how the simplest things often taste the best.

MAKES 16 TO 36 SQUARES
(see Cutting Guide, page 10)

- **Preparation: 25 minutes**
- **Baking: 45 minutes**
- **Freezing: excellent**

TIPS

For the best flavor, grind nuts just before using.

If you prefer, use unbleached flour in all your baking. Unbleached and regular all-purpose flours are interchangeable.

- **Preheat oven to 350°F (180°C)**
- **9-inch (2.5 L) square cake pan, greased**

CRUST

1 cup	all-purpose flour	250 mL
¼ cup	confectioner's (icing) sugar, sifted	50 mL
½ cup	cold butter, cubed	125 mL
¼ cup	ground almonds	50 mL

TOPPING

¾ cup	firmly packed ground almonds	175 mL
⅓ cup	granulated sugar	75 mL
2 tbsp	butter, softened	25 mL
1	egg	1
½ tsp	almond extract	2 mL
1 tbsp	all-purpose flour	15 mL
¾ cup	strawberry jam	175 mL
¾ cup	sliced almonds	175 mL

1. *Crust:* In a bowl, combine flour and confectioner's sugar. Using a pastry blender, 2 knives or your fingers, cut in butter until mixture resembles coarse crumbs. Press evenly into bottom of prepared pan. Bake in preheated oven until golden all over, 12 to 15 minutes. Let cool for 15 minutes.

2. *Topping:* In a bowl, combine ground almonds, sugar, butter, egg and almond extract. Using a wooden spoon, mix until smooth. Stir in flour. Spread jam evenly over base. Drop filling by spoonfuls over jam and, using a spatula or the back of a spoon, spread evenly. Sprinkle sliced almonds evenly over top.

3. Return to oven and bake until set and golden, 25 to 30 minutes. Let cool completely in pan on rack. Cut into squares.

Variation
Replace strawberry jam with apricot or blueberry.

Frosted Carrot Nut Bars

Here's a great way to enjoy carrot cake in a bite-size form.

MAKES 18 TO 48 BARS (see Cutting Guide, page 10)

- **Preparation: 25 minutes**
- **Baking: 30 minutes**
- **Freezing: excellent**

TIPS

To ease cleanup, rather than combining the dry ingredients in a bowl, place a large piece of waxed paper on the counter. Spread the flour on the paper. Sprinkle with the baking soda, cinnamon, nutmeg and cloves. Using the paper as a funnel, transfer the dry ingredients to the chocolate mixture.

Minimizing the number of times you open the oven door and the amount of time you keep it open helps maintain the oven temperature, which is important to successful baking.

- **Preheat oven to 350°F (180°C)**
- **9-inch (2.5 L) square cake pan, greased**

BAR

1/4 cup	butter, softened	50 mL
2/3 cup	packed brown sugar	150 mL
1	egg	1
1 tsp	vanilla	5 mL
1 cup	all-purpose flour	250 mL
1 tsp	baking soda	5 mL
3/4 tsp	cinnamon	3 mL
1/4 tsp	ground nutmeg	1 mL
1/4 tsp	ground cloves	1 mL
1 cup	shredded carrots	250 mL
1/2 cup	chopped walnuts	125 mL

FROSTING

1 1/2 cups	confectioner's (icing) sugar, sifted	375 mL
1/4 cup	butter, softened	50 mL
1 tsp	grated lemon zest	5 mL
1 to 2 tbsp	milk	15 to 25 mL
1/4 cup	finely chopped walnuts	50 mL

1. *Bar:* In a bowl, using an electric mixer on medium speed, beat butter, brown sugar, egg and vanilla until light and creamy, about 3 minutes. Combine flour, baking soda, cinnamon, nutmeg and cloves. Stir into butter mixture, mixing well. Stir in carrots and walnuts. Spread evenly in prepared pan.

2. Bake in preheated oven until a toothpick inserted in center comes out clean, 25 to 30 minutes. Let cool completely in pan on rack.

3. *Frosting:* In a bowl, using an electric mixer on medium speed, beat confectioner's sugar, butter and lemon zest, adding just enough milk to make a smooth, spreadable consistency. Spread evenly over cooled bar. Sprinkle walnuts evenly over top. Cut into bars.

Variation

Replace walnuts with dried cranberries.

Raspberry Coconut Walnut Bars

◆

A bit chewy and a little gooey, but a big success. These look messy when cut, but that's why they're so delicious.

MAKES 18 TO 48 BARS (see Cutting Guide, page 10)

- **Preparation: 25 minutes**
- **Baking: 37 minutes**
- **Freezing: excellent**

TIPS

The jam will ooze during baking. Line the pan completely with parchment paper (overhanging the sides), so the bars will be easy to remove.

Combine crust ingredients in a food processor for convenience.

Store nuts in the freezer to retain their freshness. Label the package with the date so you'll be sure to rotate the containers and use in order.

- **Preheat oven to 425°F (220°C)**
- **9-inch (2.5 L) square cake pan, lined with parchment paper**

CRUST

1⅓ cups	all-purpose flour	325 mL
⅓ cup	packed brown sugar	75 mL
½ tsp	baking powder	2 mL
½ cup	cold butter, cubed	125 mL
1	egg, beaten	1

TOPPING

⅓ cup	raspberry jam	75 mL
2	eggs	2
1 cup	packed brown sugar	250 mL
¾ cup	chopped walnuts	175 mL
¾ cup	sweetened flaked coconut	175 mL
2 tbsp	all-purpose flour	25 mL
2 tsp	freshly squeezed lemon juice	10 mL
1 tsp	baking powder	5 mL

1. *Crust:* In a bowl, combine flour, brown sugar and baking powder. Using a pastry blender, 2 knives or your fingers, cut in butter until mixture resembles coarse crumbs. Add egg and, using a fork, mix thoroughly until moistened. Press mixture evenly into prepared pan. Bake in preheated oven until golden around the edges, 10 to 12 minutes. Reduce oven temperature to 350°F (180°C).

2. *Topping:* Spread jam evenly over crust, leaving a ½-inch (1 cm) border of crust. In a bowl, whisk eggs and brown sugar until blended. Stir in walnuts, coconut, flour, lemon juice and baking powder, mixing well. Spread evenly over jam.

3. Return to oven and bake until topping is set and golden, 20 to 25 minutes. Let cool completely in pan on rack. Cut into bars.

Variations

Strawberry and apricot jam work well in these bars.

Replace flaked coconut with shredded coconut for a different texture.

Cranberry Raspberry Almond Bars

With their bright red filling, these bars are a great choice for holiday baking. The large pan makes a lot of bars, but they keep and freeze well, allowing you to get a head start on the festive season.

MAKES 36 TO 48 BARS (see Cutting Guide, page 10)

- Preparation: 25 minutes
- Baking: 37 minutes
- Freezing: excellent

TIPS

If you're using frozen cranberries, pat them dry with paper towel to eliminate excess moisture.

Buy good-quality jam. The flavor of this bar is highly dependent on the jam.

You can use regular jam in place of seedless, but the flavor will not be as robust.

When jam is baked, the sugar caramelizes, causing it to stick to the pan. This makes cleanup difficult. Leaving a small border of crust around the jam helps alleviate this problem.

- **Preheat oven to 350°F (180°C)**
- **15- by 10- by 1-inch (2 L) jelly roll pan, greased**

CRUST

2 cups	quick-cooking rolled oats	500 mL
1¼ cups	all-purpose flour	300 mL
⅓ cup	ground almonds	75 mL
1⅓ cups	packed brown sugar	325 mL
1 tsp	baking powder	5 mL
½ tsp	baking soda	2 mL
1 cup	cold butter, cubed	250 mL

FILLING

1½ cups	seedless raspberry jam (see Tips, left)	375 mL
1 cup	fresh or frozen (thawed) cranberries	250 mL
1 tbsp	grated lemon zest	15 mL

TOPPING

1¼ cups	sliced almonds	300 mL

1. *Crust:* In a bowl, combine oats, flour, ground almonds, brown sugar, baking powder and baking soda. Using a pastry blender, 2 knives or your fingers, cut in butter until mixture resembles coarse crumbs. Set 1¼ cups (300 mL) aside for topping. Press remainder evenly into prepared pan. Bake in preheated oven until golden around edges, 10 to 12 minutes.

2. *Filling:* In a bowl, combine jam, cranberries and lemon zest. Drop spoonfuls over crust. Spread evenly, leaving a ½-inch (1 cm) border of crust.

3. *Topping:* Stir almonds into reserved crumb mixture. Sprinkle over filling. Return to oven and bake until golden, 20 to 25 minutes. Let cool completely in pan on rack. Cut into bars.

Variation
Other flavors of jam, such as strawberry, cherry or blueberry, also work well in this recipe.

Lemon Almond Bars

Here's a traditional favorite, but with a touch of almonds. It's an exquisite combination.

MAKES 20 TO 54 BARS (see Cutting Guide, page 10)

- **Preparation: 15 minutes**
- **Baking: 45 minutes**
- **Freezing: excellent**

TIPS

Lemons often contain a lot of seeds, so be sure to strain the juice before using.

A medium lemon yields 2 to 3 tbsp (25 to 45 mL) juice and 1 tbsp (15 mL) zest.

- **Preheat oven to 350°F (180°C)**
- **13- by 9-inch (3 L) cake pan, greased**

ALMOND CRUST

1¾ cups	all-purpose flour	425 mL
⅔ cup	ground almonds	150 mL
⅓ cup	granulated sugar	75 mL
1 cup	cold butter, cubed	250 mL

TOPPING

4	eggs	4
2 cups	granulated sugar	500 mL
2 tsp	grated lemon zest	10 mL
⅓ cup	freshly squeezed lemon juice	75 mL
¼ cup	all-purpose flour	50 mL
1 tsp	baking powder	5 mL
	Confectioner's (icing) sugar, optional	

1. *Almond Crust:* In a bowl, combine flour, almonds and sugar. Using a pastry blender, 2 knives or your fingers, cut in butter until mixture resembles coarse crumbs. Press evenly into prepared pan. Bake in preheated oven until golden around edges, 12 to 15 minutes. Let cool in pan on rack for 10 minutes.

2. *Topping:* In a bowl, whisk eggs, sugar, lemon zest and juice until blended. Combine flour and baking powder. Whisk into egg mixture, whisking until smooth. Pour over crust.

3. Return to oven and bake just until set and light golden, 25 to 30 minutes. Let cool completely in pan on rack. Cut into bars. Sprinkle with confectioner's sugar before serving, if desired.

Variation

Replace ground almonds with ground hazelnuts.

Apricot Walnut Squares

I love the way the tangy apricots set off the sweet brown sugar topping. The addition of walnuts is, for me, the pièce de résistance, but if you're not a fan, replace them with almonds (see Variations).

MAKES 16 TO 36 SQUARES (see Cutting Guide, page 10)

- **Preparation: 25 minutes**
- **Baking: 47 minutes**
- **Freezing: excellent**

TIP

To chop apricots easily, use kitchen shears. Lightly spray the blades with vegetable oil spray.

- **Preheat oven to 350°F (180°C)**
- **9-inch (2.5 L) cake pan, greased**

1 cup	dried apricots	250 mL
	Boiling water	
CRUST		
1 cup	all-purpose flour	250 mL
1/4 cup	granulated sugar	50 mL
1/2 cup	cold butter, cubed	125 mL
TOPPING		
2	eggs	2
1 cup	packed brown sugar	250 mL
1 tsp	baking powder	5 mL
1/4 tsp	salt	1 mL
1 1/4 tsp	vanilla	6 mL
1 cup	chopped walnuts	250 mL

1. In a small bowl, combine apricots with boiling water to cover. Let stand until apricots are softened, about 15 minutes. Drain well and chop. Set aside.

2. *Crust:* In a food processor fitted with a metal blade, combine flour, sugar and butter. Process until mixture resembles coarse crumbs. Press evenly into prepared pan. Bake in preheated oven until golden around edges, 10 to 12 minutes.

3. *Topping:* In a bowl, whisk eggs, brown sugar, baking powder, salt and vanilla until blended. Stir in walnuts and reserved apricots. Spread evenly over warm crust.

4. Return to oven and bake until set and golden, 30 to 35 minutes. Let cool completely in pan on rack. Cut into squares.

Variations

Replace one-third of the apricots with 1/3 cup (75 mL) dried cranberries.

Replace walnuts with almonds and vanilla with 1/2 tsp (2 mL) almond extract.

Caramel Honey Pecan Bars

◆

There's nothing I'd want to change in these bars, which are a favorite in my family. The honey gives them a special flavor. Making a large pan is a good idea because they go quickly.

MAKES 40 TO 48 BARS (see Cutting Guide, page 10)

- **Preparation: 15 minutes**
- **Cooking: 7 minutes**
- **Baking: 30 minutes**
- **Freezing: excellent**

TIPS

It takes a little extra time, but if you place the pecans right side up before adding the syrup, your squares will be more visually appealing.

Look for large, light-colored pecans, and taste them before using to ensure they have a fresh, nutty taste. It doesn't make sense to spoil the bar by using nuts that aren't up to par.

- **Preheat oven to 350°F (180°C)**
- **15- by 10- by 1-inch (2 L) jelly roll pan, greased**

CRUST

½ cup	pecan halves	125 mL
2½ cups	all-purpose flour	625 mL
1 cup	cold butter, cubed	250 mL
⅓ cup	granulated sugar	75 mL
1	egg, beaten	1

FILLING

3½ cups	pecan halves	875 mL
¾ cup	butter	175 mL
½ cup	liquid honey	125 mL
¾ cup	packed brown sugar	175 mL
½ tsp	cinnamon	2 mL
¼ cup	whipping (35%) cream	50 mL

1. *Crust*: In a food processor, process pecans until fine. Add flour, butter, brown sugar and egg. Process until mixture resembles coarse crumbs. Press evenly into prepared pan. Bake in preheated oven until edges are lightly browned, 12 to 15 minutes.

2. *Filling*: Sprinkle pecans evenly over hot crust. Set aside. In large heavy saucepan over medium-high heat, melt butter and honey. Add brown sugar and cinnamon and boil, stirring constantly, until mixture is a rich caramel color, 5 to 7 minutes. Remove from heat. Stir in whipping cream, mixing well. Pour evenly over pecans.

3. Return to oven and bake until top is bubbly, about 15 minutes. Let cool completely in pan on rack. Cut into bars.

Apple Pecan Bars

These bars remind me of an apple nut cake in bite-size form. It's nice to be able to pop them in your mouth without having to use a plate and fork.

MAKES 18 TO 48 BARS (see Cutting Guide, page 10)

- **Preparation: 20 minutes**
- **Baking: 35 minutes**
- **Freezing: excellent**

TIPS

Choose apples that are best for baking. Apples that are too wet, like McIntosh, will make your bars too gooey. Firmer apples, such as Granny Smith, Northern Spy and Spartan, work well for baking.

Using the largest holes on a box grater, grate the apple fairly coarsely for use in this recipe. Since the apple will turn brown quickly when exposed to air, grate it just before using.

- **Preheat oven to 350°F (180°C)**
- **9-inch (2.5 L) square cake pan, greased**

6 tbsp	butter	90 mL
1 cup	packed brown sugar	250 mL
2	eggs	2
1 cup	all-purpose flour	250 mL
1 tsp	baking powder	5 mL
¾ tsp	cinnamon	3 mL
¼ tsp	salt	1 mL
¼ tsp	ground nutmeg	1 mL
¾ cup	chopped pecans	175 mL
1	medium apple, peeled and coarsely grated (see Tips, left)	1

1. In a large saucepan, melt butter over medium heat. Stir in brown sugar. Bring mixture to a boil, stirring often. Remove from heat and let cool to room temperature. Add eggs, one at a time, whisking until smooth.

2. Combine flour, baking powder, cinnamon, salt and nutmeg. Add to saucepan, mixing until smooth. Stir in pecans and grated apple, mixing well. Spread evenly in prepared pan.

3. Bake in preheated oven until a toothpick inserted in center comes out clean, 25 to 35 minutes. Let cool completely in pan on rack. Cut into bars.

Variations

Replace the apple with a pear.

Dried cranberries are a nice touch in autumn. Add ½ cup (125 mL) to the batter.

Applesauce Praline Bars

Not only does applesauce give these bars a great flavor, but it also helps to keep them moist. In fact, they actually taste better the second day. The crunchy praline topping is the crowning touch.

MAKES 20 TO 54 BARS (see Cutting Guide, page 10)

- **Preparation: 25 minutes**
- **Baking: 35 minutes**
- **Freezing: excellent**

TIPS

Peel and chop apples just before using to prevent them from turning brown.

Golden Delicious apples work particularly well in these bars.

This recipe works well with chunky applesauce, so homemade is ideal. Use unsweetened applesauce since there's already sugar in the batter. If your applesauce is sweetened, decrease the amount of sugar in the batter to 1/3 cup (75 mL).

- **Preheat oven to 350°F (180°C)**
- **13- by 9-inch (3 L) cake pan, greased**

BATTER

1/4 cup	butter, softened	50 mL
1/2 cup	packed brown sugar	125 mL
1	egg	1
1 tsp	vanilla	5 mL
1 cup	unsweetened applesauce (see Tips, left)	250 mL
1 1/2 cups	all-purpose flour	375 mL
1 tsp	cinnamon	5 mL
1/2 tsp	baking powder	2 mL
1/2 tsp	baking soda	2 mL
1/4 tsp	ground cloves	1 mL
1/4 tsp	salt	1 mL
1 1/2 cups	chopped, peeled apples (2 large apples)	375 mL
2/3 cup	chopped pecans	150 mL

TOPPING

2/3 cup	packed brown sugar	150 mL
3 tbsp	butter, softened	45 mL
1 tbsp	all-purpose flour	15 mL
1 tsp	cinnamon	5 mL
1 cup	chopped pecans	250 mL

1. *Batter:* In a bowl, using an electric mixer on medium speed, beat butter and brown sugar until light and fluffy. Add egg and vanilla, beating well. Stir in applesauce just until blended. (The mixture will look curdled).

2. Combine flour, cinnamon, baking powder, baking soda, cloves and salt. Add to batter, mixing on low speed just until blended. Stir in apples and pecans. Spread batter evenly in prepared pan.

3. *Topping:* In a bowl, combine brown sugar, butter, cinnamon and flour. Blend with a fork until crumbly. Stir in pecans. Crumble the mixture evenly over batter.

4. Bake in preheated oven until set and golden, 30 to 35 minutes. Let cool completely in pan on rack. Cut into bars.

Good for You, Too

I've tried to make these recipes healthy and delicious, using ingredients that are readily available. You won't need to shop in specialty stores to make these bars. Although they aren't designed for special diets, some are nut-free, lactose-free or egg-free. They use ingredients that nutritionists say are good for us: nuts and seeds; dried fruits; and whole grain cereals, such as oats, bran and wheat germ. I've tried to cut down on sugar and fat and increase dietary fiber, keeping the calories as low as possible without sacrificing flavor. I've used unbleached flour because some people avoid flour that has been chemically bleached. If you enjoy the nutty taste and slightly drier texture, you can substitute whole wheat flour, which contains more fiber, for all or half of the all-purpose flour called for.

Enjoy the recipes in this chapter as guilt-free snacks and treats. The key to healthy eating is moderation, so when eating these bars and squares, as well as others in the book, bear in mind that the richer it is, the smaller you cut it. Often a small taste of something delicious is far more satisfying than a big piece of mediocrity.

Crispy Cereal Bars

These no-bake bars are a great way for kids to enjoy their breakfast cereal. Add a glass of milk and they'll be happy campers.

MAKES 20 TO 54 BARS
(see **Cutting Guide,**
page 10)

- **Preparation: 15 minutes**
- **Baking: 10 minutes**
- **Freezing: excellent**

TIP

Lightly butter an offset spatula or the back of a spoon to press the cereal mixture into the pan. It keeps it from sticking to the gooey mixture. You can also use your fingers — butter them, too, to ease sticking.

- **Preheat oven to 350°F (180°C)**
- **13- by 9-inch (3 L) cake pan, ungreased**

1 cup	quick-cooking rolled oats	250 mL
1/4 cup	butter	50 mL
8 oz	marshmallows (about 40 regular size)	250 g
1 tsp	vanilla	5 mL
5 cups	crisp rice cereal	1.25 L
3/4 cup	raisins	175 mL
1/3 cup	sunflower seeds	75 mL
1/3 cup	chopped dried apricots	75 mL
1/4 cup	chopped unblanched almonds	50 mL

1. Sprinkle oats evenly in pan. Bake in preheated oven, stirring occasionally, until lightly toasted, about 10 minutes. Transfer to a bowl and let cool for 15 minutes. Spray pan lightly with cooking spray. Set aside.

2. In a large saucepan, combine butter and marshmallows. Cook over low heat, stirring often, until melted and smooth. Remove from heat. Stir in vanilla. Stir in oats, cereal, raisins, sunflower seeds, apricots and almonds, mixing well. Using an offset spatula or the back of a spoon, press mixture evenly into prepared pan. Let cool completely, about 1 hour. Cut into bars.

Variations

If you prefer a nut-free bar, omit the almonds.

Replace raisins with dried cranberries.

Replace almonds with another type of nut.

Replace sunflower seeds with pumpkin seeds.

Replace apricots with dried apples.

Three-Simple-Steps Squares

Here's a healthy version of an old classic. I think I prefer it to the original layered bar. If you're watching calories, cut these squares in half into triangles.

MAKES 24 SQUARES (see Cutting Guide, page 10)

- **Preparation: 20 minutes**
- **Baking: 25 minutes**
- **Freezing: excellent**

TIPS

Store wheat germ in the freezer to keep it fresh.

Sweetened and unsweetened coconut are interchangeable in recipes. I have specified unsweetened in this recipe with a view to reducing sugar consumption.

- **Preheat oven to 350°F (180°C)**
- **13- by 9-inch (3 L) cake pan, ungreased**

½ cup	butter	125 mL
1 cup	graham wafer crumbs	250 mL
⅓ cup	wheat germ (see Tips, left)	75 mL
1	can (10 oz/300 mL) light sweetened condensed milk	1
1 cup	chopped dried apricots	250 mL
¾ cup	dried cranberries	175 mL
¾ cup	unsweetened flaked coconut	175 mL
½ cup	chopped unblanched almonds	125 mL
⅓ cup	pumpkin seeds	75 mL

1. Place butter in cake pan and melt in preheated oven. Remove from oven and tilt pan to cover bottom evenly with melted butter. Combine graham wafer crumbs and wheat germ. Sprinkle evenly over butter, pressing with an offset spatula or the back of a spoon to moisten.

2. Drizzle sweetened condensed milk evenly over crumbs. Sprinkle apricots, cranberries, coconut, almonds and pumpkin seeds over top. Press in lightly.

3. Bake in preheated oven until lightly browned around edges, 20 to 25 minutes. Let cool completely in pan on rack. Cut into squares.

Variations

Replace dried cranberries with raisins, chopped dried cherries or chopped dried figs.

Replace pumpkin seeds with sunflower seeds.

Replace almonds with pecans or walnuts.

Tropical Fruit and Nut Bars

A lighter version of an old-time favorite.

MAKES 18 TO 48 BARS (see Cutting Guide, page 10)

- Preparation: 20 minutes
- Baking: 45 minutes
- Freezing: excellent

TIP

Older baking recipes tend to be high in fat, sugar and salt, ingredients we are trying to cut back on. Experiment with your favorite recipes by decreasing these ingredients by about 25% and see how they turn out. You may prefer the lighter version.

- **Preheat oven to 350°F (180°C)**
- **8-inch (2 L) square cake pan, greased**

¾ cup	dried apricots, chopped	175 mL
¼ cup	dried cherries	50 mL
¼ cup	dried mango, chopped	50 mL
CRUST		
1 cup	unbleached all-purpose flour	250 mL
¼ cup	packed brown sugar	50 mL
¼ cup	cold butter, cubed	50 mL
TOPPING		
2	eggs	2
½ cup	packed brown sugar	125 mL
1 tsp	freshly squeezed lemon juice	5 mL
½ cup	pine nuts	125 mL

1. In a saucepan, combine apricots and cherries with water to cover. Bring to a boil, then remove from heat. Stir in mango and let stand while preparing crust.

2. *Crust:* In a bowl, combine flour and brown sugar. Using a pastry blender, 2 knives or your fingers, cut in butter until mixture resembles coarse crumbs. Press firmly into prepared pan. Bake in preheated oven until lightly browned around the edges, 12 to 15 minutes.

3. *Topping:* In a bowl, whisk eggs, brown sugar and lemon juice until smooth. Stir in pine nuts and apricot mixture, mixing well. Spread evenly over crust.

4. Return to oven and bake until topping is set and golden, 25 to 30 minutes. Let cool completely in pan on rack. Cut into bars.

Variations

Replace dried cranberries with dried cherries or an equal quantity of dried apricots.

Replace almonds with pecans.

Chewy Honey Apple Fig Bars

In these moist, chewy bars, I've used applesauce to replace the fat. It also adds great flavor.

MAKES 20 TO 54 BARS (see Cutting Guide, page 10)

- **Preparation: 25 minutes**
- **Baking: 25 minutes**
- **Freezing: excellent**

TIP

Because honey replaces sugar in these bars, they have a dense, moist, chewy texture and a delightful honey flavor. Often you see both honey and sugar in a recipe because using honey only would result in too much liquid, which interferes with proper baking.

- **Preheat oven to 350°F (180°C)**
- **13- by 9-inch (3 L) cake pan, greased**

1 cup	unbleached all-purpose flour	250 mL
¾ cup	whole wheat flour	175 mL
1 tsp	baking soda	5 mL
1 tsp	cinnamon	5 mL
½ tsp	ground ginger	2 mL
¼ tsp	ground nutmeg	1 mL
1	egg	1
1 cup	liquid honey	250 mL
½ cup	unsweetened applesauce	125 mL
2 tsp	grated lemon zest	10 mL
¾ cup	finely chopped dried figs	175 mL
¾ cup	finely chopped dried apricots	175 mL
½ cup	chopped pecans	125 mL

1. In a bowl, combine all-purpose and whole wheat flours, baking soda, cinnamon, ginger and nutmeg. In a separate bowl, whisk egg, honey, applesauce and lemon zest until smooth. Stir into dry ingredients, mixing well. Stir in figs, apricots and pecans. Spread evenly in prepared pan.

2. Bake in preheated oven until top is set and lightly browned, 20 to 25 minutes. Let cool completely in pan on rack. Cut into bars.

Variations

Replace apricots with figs for an all-fig bar.

Replace almonds with walnuts.

Apricot Seed Bars

Packed full of dried fruits and seeds, these bars make a great addition to a backpack, if you're hiking or biking.

MAKES 20 TO 54 BARS, see Cutting Guide, page 10

- **Preparation: 20 minutes**
- **Baking: 30 minutes**
- **Freezing: excellent**

TIPS

To prevent sticking, use cooking spray to get a light, even coating of grease on baking pans.

To ease cleanup rather than combining the dry ingredients in a bowl (in Step 1), place a large piece of waxed paper on the counter. Spread the flour on the paper and sprinkle the baking soda, salt and cinnamon over it. Using the paper as a funnel, transfer the dry ingredients to the egg mixture.

- **Preheat oven to 350°F (180°C)**
- **13- by 9-inch (3 L) cake pan, greased**

¾ cup	butter, softened	175 mL
¾ cup	packed brown sugar	175 mL
1	egg	1
1 cup	unbleached all-purpose flour	250 mL
½ tsp	baking soda	2 mL
¼ tsp	salt	1 mL
¾ tsp	cinnamon	3 mL
1 cup	quick-cooking rolled oats	250 mL
¾ cup	finely chopped dried apricots	175 mL
¾ cup	dried cranberries	175 mL
¼ cup	sesame seeds	50 mL
¼ cup	flax seeds	50 mL
¼ cup	sunflower seeds	50 mL

1. In a bowl, using an electric mixer on medium speed, beat butter, brown sugar and egg until smooth and creamy. Combine flour, baking soda, salt and cinnamon. Stir into creamed mixture, mixing well. Stir in rolled oats, apricots, cranberries, sesame seeds, flax seeds and sunflower seeds. Spread evenly in prepared pan.

2. Bake in preheated oven until top is set and golden, 25 to 30 minutes. Let cool completely in pan on rack. Cut into bars.

Variations
Replace cranberries with chopped dried figs or raisins.
Add ⅓ cup (75 mL) chopped almonds along with the seeds.

Orange Cream Cheese Brownies

This is a very moist cake-like brownie, with a nice orange flavor in every bite. It doesn't contain any butter and uses less sugar than most brownies. It looks great, too, making it a nice dessert or coffee-time treat.

MAKES 18 TO 48 BARS OR 16 TO 36 SQUARES
(see Cutting Guide, page 10)

- **Preparation: 25 minutes**
- **Baking: 30 minutes**
- **Freezing: excellent**

TIPS

To ease cleanup, rather than combining the dry ingredients in a bowl, (in Step 2), place a large piece of waxed paper on the counter. Spread the flour on the paper and sift the cocoa powder and baking powder over it. Using the paper as a funnel, transfer the dry ingredients to the egg mixture.

For thinner, less cake-like bars, bake these in a 9-inch (2.5 L) square cake pan for 20 to 25 minutes.

These make a nice dessert topped with a scoop of orange sherbet.

- **Preheat oven to 350°F (180°C)**
- **8-inch (2 L) square cake pan, greased**

FILLING

4 oz	light cream cheese, softened	125 g
2 tbsp	granulated sugar	25 mL
2 tbsp	2% milk	25 mL
1 tbsp	grated orange zest	15 mL

BATTER

1 cup	packed brown sugar	250 mL
⅓ cup	2% plain yogurt	75 mL
¼ cup	vegetable oil	50 mL
1	egg	1
1	egg white	1
¾ cup	unbleached all-purpose flour	175 mL
½ cup	unsweetened cocoa powder, sifted	125 mL
1 tsp	baking powder	5 mL

1. *Filling:* In a small bowl, using an electric mixer on low speed, beat cream cheese and sugar until blended, about 3 minutes. Add milk and orange zest, beating until smooth. Set aside.

2. *Batter:* In a bowl, whisk brown sugar, yogurt, oil, egg and egg white until blended. Combine flour, cocoa and baking powder. Stir into egg mixture, mixing well.

3. Spread half of the brownie batter in prepared pan. Spread filling evenly over top. Drop remaining batter by spoonfuls over filling. Swirl batters together lightly with small spatula or knife to make a marbled effect.

4. Bake in preheated oven until set, 25 to 30 minutes. Let cool completely in pan on rack. Cut into bars or squares.

Variations

For a plain marble brownie, replace orange zest with 1 tsp (5 mL) vanilla.

Replace yogurt with light sour cream.

Lighten-Up Cookie Bars

This is a lighter version of one of my favorite bar cookies, and it's still very delicious.

MAKES 20 TO 54 BARS
(see Cutting Guide, page 10)

- **Preparation: 25 minutes**
- **Baking: 25 minutes**
- **Freezing: excellent**

TIPS

Miniature chocolate chips are great to use when you're trying to cut down on calories. There are a lot more chips per bar than with regular chips, so you can reduce the quantity and still get a good chocolate impact in every bite.

If you like the nutty flavor of whole wheat, you can reverse the proportions of the unbleached all-purpose and whole wheat flour. You'll increase your fiber intake.

- **Preheat oven to 375°F (190°C)**
- **13- by 9-inch (3 L) cake pan, greased**

½ cup	butter, softened	125 mL
¾ cup	granulated sugar	175 mL
¾ cup	packed brown sugar	175 mL
½ cup	unsweetened applesauce	125 mL
1	egg	1
1 tsp	vanilla	5 mL
1½ cups	unbleached all-purpose flour	375 mL
1 cup	whole wheat flour	250 mL
1 tsp	baking soda	5 mL
½ tsp	salt	2 mL
¾ cup	miniature chocolate chips	175 mL
¾ cup	chopped dried apricots	175 mL
¾ cup	dried cranberries	175 mL
½ cup	sunflower seeds	125 mL

1. In a bowl, using an electric mixer on medium speed, beat butter, granulated and brown sugars, applesauce, egg and vanilla until creamy, about 3 minutes. Combine all-purpose and whole wheat flours, baking soda and salt. Stir into creamed mixture, mixing well. Stir in chocolate chips, apricots, cranberries and sunflower seeds. Spread evenly in prepared pan.

2. Bake in preheated oven until light golden, about 25 minutes. Let cool completely in pan on rack. Cut into bars.

Variations

Replace apricots with chopped dates or raisins.

Replace dried cranberries with chopped dried pineapple or mango.

Replace sunflower seeds with chopped almonds.

Oatmeal Crisps

Enjoy your morning oats baked in a bar rather than warm in a cereal bowl. Accompany with a glass of cold milk for more nutrients.

**MAKES ABOUT
24 PIECES**

- **Preparation: 15 minutes**
- **Cooking: 1 minute**
- **Baking: 15 minutes**
- **Freezing: excellent**

TIPS

Store these crisps in a tightly covered container with waxed paper between the layers to prevent them from becoming soft. They also freeze well for up to 3 months.

Use cooking spray to grease pans. It doesn't burn like butter.

- **Preheat oven to 350°F (180°C)**
- **13- by 9-inch (3 L) cake pan, lined with aluminum foil and greased**

⅔ cup	butter	150 mL
⅔ cup	packed brown sugar	150 mL
2⅔ cups	old-fashioned (large-flake) rolled oats	650 mL
1 tsp	cinnamon	5 mL
Pinch	salt	Pinch

1. In a large saucepan, melt butter over medium heat. Add brown sugar. Cook, stirring constantly, until sugar is melted and mixture is smooth, about 1 minute. Stir in oats, cinnamon and salt, mixing until oats are thoroughly moistened. Press evenly into prepared pan.

2. Bake in preheated oven until top is golden, about 15 minutes. Let cool completely in pan on rack. Break into irregular pieces.

Variations

Decrease oats to 2⅓ cups (575 mL) and add ⅓ cup (75 mL) toasted wheat germ.

Add ¼ cup (50 mL) sesame or flax seeds.

Pick-Me-Up Bars

This dense, slightly chewy bar is a great boost if you're experiencing an afternoon lull and is an ideal after-school snack.

**MAKES 18 TO 48 BARS
(see Cutting Guide,
page 10)**

- **Preparation: 20 minutes**
- **Baking: 20 minutes**
- **Freezing: excellent**

TIPS

When baking, you can usually use 1 whole egg in place of 2 egg whites or vice versa. However, in desserts like custards, where the yolk is needed for thickening, this rule doesn't apply.

Small seeds, like sesame, flax and sunflower, can easily be added to your favorite cookie and bar recipes in small amounts.

- **Preheat oven to 350°F (180°C)**
- **8-inch (2 L) square cake pan, greased**

1 cup	graham wafer crumbs	250 mL
⅔ cup	packed brown sugar	150 mL
½ cup	whole wheat flour	125 mL
½ cup	butterscotch chips	125 mL
⅓ cup	quick-cooking rolled oats	75 mL
⅓ cup	sunflower seeds	75 mL
1 tsp	baking powder	5 mL
2	egg whites (see Tips, left)	2
1 tbsp	vegetable oil	15 mL
1½ tsp	vanilla	7 mL

1. In a bowl, combine graham wafer crumbs, brown sugar, flour, butterscotch chips, oats, sunflower seeds and baking powder.

2. In a separate bowl, whisk egg whites, oil and vanilla until blended. Stir into dry ingredients, mixing well. Press evenly into prepared pan.

3. Bake in preheated oven until top is golden, about 20 minutes. Let cool completely in pan on rack. Cut into bars.

Variations

Replace whole wheat flour with all-purpose, but be aware that you'll lose some of the health benefits, such as added fiber.

Replace sunflower seeds with a mixture of sesame and flax seeds.

Date and Applesauce Squares

This moist square has a soft, cake-like texture. It gets its wonderful flavor from applesauce and dates.

MAKES 16 TO 36 SQUARES (see Cutting Guide, page 10)

- **Preparation: 20 minutes**
- **Baking: 30 minutes**
- **Freezing: excellent**

TIP

To ease cleanup, rather than combining the dry ingredients in a bowl, (Step 2) place a large piece of waxed paper on the counter. Spread the flours on the paper. Sprinkle with the baking powder, baking soda, cinnamon and cloves. Using the paper as a funnel, transfer the dry ingredients to the butter mixture.

- **Preheat oven to 350°F (180°C)**
- **8-inch (2 L) square cake pan, greased**

¼ cup	butter, softened	50 mL
½ cup	packed brown sugar	125 mL
1	egg	1
1 tbsp	grated orange zest	15 mL
1 tsp	vanilla	5 mL
1 cup	unbleached all-purpose flour	250 mL
½ cup	whole wheat flour	125 mL
½ tsp	baking powder	2 mL
½ tsp	baking soda	2 mL
1 tsp	cinnamon	5 mL
¼ tsp	ground cloves	1 mL
1 cup	unsweetened applesauce	250 mL
¾ cup	raisins	175 mL

1. In a large bowl, using an electric mixer on low speed, beat butter, brown sugar, egg, orange zest and vanilla until blended, about 3 minutes.
2. Combine all-purpose and whole wheat flours, baking powder, baking soda, cinnamon and cloves. Stir into creamed mixture alternately with applesauce, making 3 additions and mixing lightly after each addition. Stir in raisins. Spread evenly in prepared pan.
3. Bake in preheated oven until a toothpick inserted in center comes out clean, 25 to 30 minutes. Let cool completely in pan on rack. Cut into squares.

Variations

Replace orange zest with lemon zest.

Replace raisins with dried cranberries or cherries.

Apple Cinnamon Bars

These bars are nice to pack in your kids' lunch boxes or to have waiting after school with juice or a mug of hot chocolate.

MAKES 18 TO 48 BARS (see Cutting Guide, page 10)

- **Preparation: 25 minutes**
- **Baking: 50 minutes**
- **Freezing: not recommended**

TIPS

Cut these bars into small squares for bite-size finger food or cut larger pieces to serve for dessert with ice cream or Cheddar cheese.

If you're serving these for dessert, you can double the recipe and bake in a 13- by 9-inch (3 L) pan.

Dust lightly with confectioner's (icing) sugar if desired.

- **Preheat oven to 350°F (180°C)**
- **9-inch (2.5 L) square cake pan, greased**

CRUST

1 cup	unbleached all-purpose flour	250 mL
1 cup	whole wheat flour	250 mL
½ cup	granulated sugar	125 mL
½ tsp	baking powder	2 mL
¼ tsp	salt	1 mL
⅔ cup	cold butter, cubed	150 mL
1	egg, beaten	1

FILLING

⅓ cup	granulated sugar	75 mL
2 tbsp	all-purpose flour	25 mL
1 tsp	cinnamon	5 mL
2 lb	tart cooking apples, peeled, cored and thinly sliced (5½ cups/1.375 L)	1 kg
1 tbsp	freshly squeezed lemon juice	15 mL

1. *Crust:* In a bowl, combine all-purpose and whole wheat flours, sugar, baking powder and salt. Using a pastry blender, 2 knives or your fingers, cut in butter until mixture resembles coarse crumbs. Add egg and, using a fork, mix until thoroughly blended. Press half of the mixture (about 2 cups/500 mL) evenly into prepared pan. Set aside remainder.

2. *Filling:* In a large bowl, combine sugar, flour, cinnamon, apples and lemon juice, mixing well. Layer evenly over crust. Sprinkle remaining crumble mixture over top.

3. Bake in preheated oven until apples are tender and crust is golden, 45 to 50 minutes. Let cool completely in pan on rack. Cut into bars.

Variation

Decrease apples to 5 cups (1.25 L) and add 1 cup (250 mL) fresh cranberries.

Fabulous Fig Bars

These bars are a childhood favorite. I'm not sure whether I love making these for the taste of the moist fig filling in the buttery crust or just for the memories.

MAKES 18 TO 48 BARS, (see Cutting Guide, page 10)

- **Preparation: 35 minutes**
- **Cooking: 25 minutes**
- **Cooling: 30 minutes**
- **Baking: 35 minutes**
- **Freezing: excellent**

TIPS

I like to use a combination of Calimyrna (golden) and Mission (black) figs in this recipe.

If your dough seems soft after mixing, chill for 30 to 60 minutes. It will roll out much more easily.

Don't worry if the dough tears when you transfer it to the pan. You can patch any tears by pressing it together with your fingertips. The bottom crust can extend a bit up the side before filling. The top crust is trimmed to fit over it.

This recipe can be doubled and baked in a 13- by 9-inch (3 L) pan.

- **Preheat oven to 350°F (180°C)**
- **8-inch (2 L) square cake pan, greased**

FILLING

8 oz	dried figs, chopped	250 g
1 cup	water	250 mL
1 tbsp	freshly squeezed lemon juice	15 mL

CRUST

¾ cup	unbleached all-purpose flour	175 mL
½ cup	whole wheat flour	125 mL
¾ tsp	baking powder	3 mL
¾ tsp	cinnamon	3 mL
Pinch	salt	Pinch
¼ cup	butter, softened	50 mL
½ cup	granulated sugar	125 mL
1	egg	1

1. *Filling:* In a saucepan, combine figs, water and lemon juice. Bring to a boil over medium heat, reduce heat to low and simmer, uncovered, until water is absorbed and figs are tender, about 25 minutes. Let cool to lukewarm. Transfer to a food processor and purée. Set aside until cool, about 30 minutes.

2. *Crust:* Combine all-purpose and whole wheat flours, baking powder, cinnamon and salt. In a large bowl, using an electric mixer on medium speed, beat butter, sugar and egg until light and creamy, about 3 minutes. On low speed, gradually add dry ingredients, mixing just until dough comes together. Using floured hands, knead dough to form a smooth ball. Divide in half.

3. Between 2 sheets of waxed paper, roll out one half of the dough to an 8-inch (20 cm) square. Remove top sheet of waxed paper and transfer dough upside down into prepared pan. Remove second sheet of waxed paper. Spread cooled fig filling evenly over dough. Repeat rolling with other half of dough. Trim edges to make an even square. Place over filling.

4. Bake in preheated oven until crust is golden, 30 to 35 minutes. Let cool completely in pan on rack. Cut into bars.

Coconut Almond Raspberry Bars

A little like soft store-bought jam-filled granola bars but with a whole lot more flavor.

MAKES 18 TO 48 BARS (see Cutting Guide, page 10)

- **Preparation: 20 minutes**
- **Baking: 30 minutes**
- **Freezing: excellent**

TIPS

I suggest lining the pan with parchment or greased aluminum foil because the jam will stick and caramelize on the pan making it difficult to cut.

Although sweetened and unsweetened coconut are interchangeable in baking, I recommend the use of unsweetened in this recipe to cut down on sugar.

- **Preheat oven to 350°F (180°C)**
- **9-inch (2.5 L) square cake pan, greased and lined with parchment or greased aluminum foil**

1¾ cups	quick-cooking rolled oats	425 mL
1 cup	unbleached all-purpose flour	250 mL
1 cup	packed brown sugar	250 mL
¼ cup	unsweetened flaked coconut	50 mL
1 tsp	baking powder	5 mL
¼ tsp	salt	1 mL
¾ cup	butter, melted	175 mL
¾ cup	raspberry jam	175 mL
1 tsp	grated lemon zest	5 mL
⅔ cup	sliced almonds	150 mL

1. In a large bowl, combine oats, flour, brown sugar, coconut, baking powder and salt. Stir in melted butter, mixing well. Press two-thirds of the mixture evenly into prepared pan. Set remainder aside.

2. In a bowl, combine jam and lemon zest. Spread evenly over crust, leaving a ½-inch (1 cm) border of crust. Stir almonds into reserved crust mixture and sprinkle over jam. Pat down lightly.

3. Bake in preheated oven until top is golden, 25 to 30 minutes. Let cool completely in pan on rack. Cut into bars.

Variations

Replace raspberry jam with strawberry, apricot, peach or cherry.

Replace almonds with sliced hazelnuts.

Replace some of the all-purpose flour with whole wheat flour for a little more fiber.

Fruit and Seed Granola Bars

You won't be tempted to buy granola bars again after making these tasty nibblers. Keep a supply on hand for lunch-box treats.

MAKES 36 TO 48 BARS (see Cutting Guide, page 10)

- **Preparation: 20 minutes**
- **Baking: 25 minutes**
- **Freezing: excellent**

TIPS

If you prefer a chewy texture, underbake these bars. Bake longer for crisp bars.

Vary the dried fruit and seeds to suit your taste. A mixture looks nice, but you can use just one fruit and one kind of seed.

- **Preheat oven to 350°F (180°C)**
- **15- by 10- by 1-inch (2 L) jelly roll pan, greased**

1 cup	butter, softened	250 mL
1 cup	packed brown sugar	250 mL
½ cup	corn syrup	125 mL
3 cups	quick-cooking rolled oats	750 mL
1 cup	whole wheat flour	250 mL
½ tsp	baking soda	2 mL
1 tsp	cinnamon	5 mL
1 cup	crisp rice cereal	250 mL
¾ cup	raisins	175 mL
¾ cup	chopped dried apricots	175 mL
¼ cup	sunflower seeds	50 mL
¼ cup	pumpkin seeds	50 mL
¼ cup	flax seeds	50 mL

1. In a small saucepan over medium heat, heat butter and brown sugar, stirring until butter is melted and mixture is smooth. Stir in corn syrup.

2. In a large bowl, combine rolled oats, whole wheat flour, baking soda, cinnamon, cereal, raisins, apricots, and sunflower, pumpkin and flax seeds. Pour sugar mixture over top. Mix until ingredients are moistened. Press evenly into prepared pan.

3. Bake in preheated oven until top is light golden, 20 to 25 minutes. Let cool completely in pan. Cut into bars.

Variations

Add ½ cup (125 mL) chopped almonds, pecans or peanuts to the dry ingredients.

Replace whole wheat flour with unbleached all-purpose, or use half of each kind.

Apple Fruit Bars

A moist, cake-like bar that's as good for dessert as it is for snack time.

MAKES 20 TO 54 BARS (see Cutting Guide, page 10)

- **Preparation: 20 minutes**
- **Baking: 30 minutes**
- **Freezing: excellent**

TIPS

If you're concerned about fat and cholesterol, replace 1 egg with 2 egg whites. When your recipe calls for 2 eggs, use 1 whole egg and 2 egg whites.

Add ¼ cup (50 mL) flax seeds to increase the fiber content.

- **Preheat oven to 350°F (180°C)**
- **13- by 9-inch (3 L) cake pan, greased**

2	eggs	2
¾ cup	packed brown sugar	175 mL
½ cup	vegetable oil	125 mL
½ cup	unbleached all-purpose flour	125 mL
½ cup	whole wheat flour	125 mL
1 tsp	baking soda	5 mL
¾ tsp	cinnamon	3 mL
¼ tsp	ground nutmeg	1 mL
2 cups	chopped, peeled apples (2 to 3 apples)	500 mL
⅔ cup	dried cranberries	150 mL
½ cup	chopped dates	125 mL

1. In a bowl, whisk eggs, brown sugar and oil. Combine all-purpose and whole wheat flours, baking soda, cinnamon and nutmeg. Stir into egg mixture, mixing until blended. Stir in apples, cranberries and dates, mixing well. Spread evenly in prepared pan.

2. Bake in preheated oven until set and golden, 25 to 30 minutes. Let cool completely in pan on rack. Cut into bars.

Variations

Replace dried cranberries with raisins.
Replace dates with chopped dried apricots.

High-Energy Granola Bars

This granola bar is nice and chewy but not too sweet, with lots of healthy, tasty ingredients. It's also easy to make. Take a few to work for an afternoon energy boost.

MAKES 20 TO 54 BARS (see Cutting Guide, page 10)

- **Preparation: 20 minutes**
- **Baking: 20 minutes**
- **Freezing: excellent**

TIPS

Underbaking granola bars gives them a chewy texture, whereas baking for a little longer makes a crisp bar. Use whichever technique your family prefers.

After cutting, wrap these into individual bars so they're ready to pack in lunch boxes or knapsacks when needed.

- **Preheat oven to 350°F (180°C)**
- **13- by 9-inch (3 L) cake pan, greased**

½ cup	butter, melted	125 mL
¾ cup	corn syrup	175 mL
2 cups	quick-cooking rolled oats	500 mL
¾ cup	natural bran	175 mL
½ cup	chopped unblanched almonds	125 mL
½ cup	sunflower seeds	125 mL
⅓ cup	chopped apricots	75 mL
⅓ cup	chopped dates	75 mL
⅓ cup	chopped dried cranberries	75 mL
¼ cup	wheat germ	50 mL
¼ cup	pumpkin seeds	50 mL
¼ cup	flax seeds	50 mL
¼ cup	sesame seeds	50 mL

1. In a bowl, combine melted butter and corn syrup. Stir in rolled oats, bran, almonds, sunflower seeds, apricots, dates, cranberries, wheat germ, pumpkin seeds, flax seeds and sesame seeds, mixing well until all ingredients are moistened. Press evenly into prepared pan.

2. Bake in preheated oven until top is golden, 15 to 20 minutes. Let cool completely in pan. Cut into bars.

Variations

There's no end to the variety of dried fruit combinations you can use. Dried cranberries, cherries, raisins, mango and papaya all work well in this recipe. Just keep the total amount to 1 cup (250 mL).

Replace almonds with your favorite nut.

Mixed Fruit Bran Bars

Enjoy your breakfast bran flakes in an easy-to-eat-on-the-run fruit and fiber bar.

MAKES 20 TO 54 BARS (see Cutting Guide, page 10)

- **Preparation: 20 minutes**
- **Baking: 25 minutes**
- **Freezing: excellent**

TIPS

When choosing a healthy snack, look for those containing dried fruits, such as apricots and dates, which are high in iron and fiber. And they taste great!

For added fiber, substitute whole wheat flour for all or half of the all-purpose.

- **Preheat oven to 375°F (190°C)**
- **13- by 9-inch (3 L) cake pan, greased**

2 cups	bran flake cereal	500 mL
1 cup	unbleached all-purpose flour	250 mL
⅔ cup	packed brown sugar	150 mL
2 tsp	baking soda	10 mL
¼ tsp	salt	1 mL
1 cup	buttermilk	250 mL
2 tbsp	vegetable oil	25 mL
2	eggs	2
1 tbsp	grated lemon zest	15 mL
¾ cup	chopped dried apricots	175 mL
½ cup	chopped dried apples	125 mL
½ cup	chopped dates	125 mL
½ cup	dried cranberries	125 mL
⅓ cup	chopped pecans	75 mL

1. In a food processor fitted with a metal blade, combine cereal, flour, brown sugar, baking soda and salt. Pulse until coarsely chopped, about 1 minute. Add buttermilk, vegetable oil, eggs and lemon zest and process until cereal is crushed and mixture is blended. Stir in apricots, apples, dates, cranberries and pecans. Spread evenly in prepared pan.

2. Bake in preheated oven until set and golden, 20 to 25 minutes. Let cool completely in pan on rack. Cut into bars.

Variations

Replace lemon zest with orange or tangerine zest.

Replace dried cranberries with chopped dried cherries or raisins.

Honey Granola Breakfast Bars

Keep some of these on hand for the days when the need for a little extra sleep takes priority over a sit-down breakfast. They also make a great pick-me-up any time of the day.

MAKES 20 TO 54 BARS (see Cutting Guide, page 10)

- **Preparation: 20 minutes**
- **Baking: 30 minutes**
- **Freezing: excellent**

TIPS

Ground flax is available in the health food section of grocery stores or specialty health food stores. Keep it handy in the freezer so you can add a little to baking.

Always use liquid honey unless specified otherwise.

When making these bars, measure the oil in your measuring cup first, then measure the honey. That way, the honey will slip easily out of the cup without sticking.

- Preheat oven to 350°F (180°C)
- 13- by 9-inch (3 L) cake pan, greased

2 cups	old-fashioned (large-flake) rolled oats	500 mL
1 cup	whole wheat flour	250 mL
¾ cup	packed brown sugar	175 mL
¼ cup	wheat germ	50 mL
¼ cup	ground flax seeds	50 mL
1 tsp	cinnamon	5 mL
½ tsp	salt	2 mL
1	egg	1
½ cup	vegetable oil	125 mL
½ cup	liquid honey	125 mL
1 tsp	vanilla	5 mL
¾ cup	raisins	175 mL
½ cup	chopped dried apricots	125 mL

1. In a bowl, combine rolled oats, whole wheat flour, brown sugar, wheat germ, flax seeds, cinnamon and salt. In a small bowl, whisk egg, oil, honey and vanilla until blended. Pour over oat mixture, mixing until dry ingredients are moistened. Stir in raisins and apricots. Press evenly into prepared pan.

2. Bake in preheated oven until light golden, 20 to 30 minutes. Let cool completely in pan on rack. Cut into bars.

Variations

Replace raisins with dried cranberries.

Replace apricots with more raisins or dried apple.

Shortbread

This section was the most surprising to my tasters, who couldn't believe there are so many versions of shortbread. Shortbread has three basic ingredients — butter, flour and sugar. It's amazing how slight variations in the way they're combined can produce such a wide range of tastes and textures.

Shortbread is actually very easy to make. You can mix it by hand for about 5 minutes, or with a wooden spoon or using an electric mixer on medium speed for about 3 minutes. You can also use a food processor or pastry blender, in which case the butter should be cold and cut into 1-inch (2.5 cm) cubes. Most recipes require a bit of kneading to smooth out the dough after mixing.

To get even edges, plain shortbread bars should be cut when they come out of the oven and are still warm, then cut again when they're cool. They tend to break unevenly if they aren't cut until cold. Another unusual element to making shortbread is that the pan is always ungreased — there's so much butter in the dough, it almost greases the pan, preventing sticking. Use a sharp knife to cut shortbread. Store it in a cool, dry place or in the refrigerator for up to one month. You can freeze shortbread for up to three months, but the texture will change slightly.

You probably have a favorite shortbread recipe – the one you have traditionally enjoyed. But it's fun to try others and compare. I know I changed my "favorite" several times while preparing this chapter. Maybe you will, too.

◄ *Chunky Chocolate Shortbread and Lemon Poppy Seed Shortbread*

Chunky Chocolate Shortbread

This crisp shortbread cookie has lots of crunch from the nuts and a great chocolate flavor from the chopped chocolate.

MAKES 20 TO 54 BARS OR 24 SQUARES
(see Cutting Guide, page 10)

- Preparation: 20 minutes
- Baking: 35 minutes
- Freezing: excellent

- Preheat oven to 350°F (180°C)
- 13- by 9-inch (3 L) cake pan, ungreased

1 cup	butter, softened	250 mL
½ cup	superfine granulated sugar (see Tips, page 196)	125 mL
1¾ cups	all-purpose flour	425 mL
¼ cup	cornstarch	50 mL
4	squares (1 oz/28 g each) bittersweet chocolate, coarsely chopped	4
⅔ cup	coarsely chopped pecans, toasted	150 mL

1. In a bowl, beat butter and sugar until light and creamy. Combine flour and cornstarch. Stir into butter mixture, mixing well. Stir in chocolate and pecans. Press evenly into pan.

2. Bake in preheated oven until lightly browned around edges, 30 to 35 minutes. Let cool completely in pan on rack. Cut into bars or squares.

Lemon Poppy Seed Shortbread

The poppy seeds give an interesting crunch and attractive look to these rich, buttery bars.

MAKES 18 TO 48 BARS
(see Cutting Guide, page 10)

- Preparation: 20 minutes
- Baking: 35 minutes
- Freezing: excellent

- Preheat oven to 300°F (150°C)
- 9-inch (2.5 L) square cake pan, ungreased

1 cup	butter, softened	250 mL
1 cup	confectioner's (icing) sugar, sifted	250 mL
2 cups	all-purpose flour	500 mL
2 tbsp	poppy seeds	25 mL
2 tbsp	grated lemon zest	25 mL
1 tbsp	freshly squeezed lemon juice	15 mL
2 tbsp	granulated sugar	25 mL

1. In a bowl, beat butter and confectioner's sugar until light and creamy. Stir in flour, poppy seeds and lemon zest and juice, mixing well. Knead to form a smooth dough. Press evenly into pan. Sprinkle with granulated sugar.

2. Bake in preheated oven until lightly browned around the edges, 30 to 35 minutes. Cut into bars while warm. Let cool completely in pan on rack. Recut.

Hazelnut Shortbread Bars

Hazelnuts have a unique flavor that really shines in a shortbread dough.

MAKES 18 TO 48 BARS (see Cutting Guide, page 10)

- **Preparation: 15 minutes**
- **Baking: 35 minutes**
- **Freezing: excellent**

TIP

There's no substitute for butter when making shortbread.

- **Preheat oven to 300°F (150°C)**
- **9-inch (2.5 L) square cake pan, ungreased**

1 cup	butter, softened	250 mL
½ cup	superfine granulated sugar (see Tips, page 196)	125 mL
1½ cups	all-purpose flour	375 mL
¾ cup	cornstarch	175 mL
½ cup	finely chopped hazelnuts	125 mL

1. In a bowl, using an electric mixer on medium speed, beat butter and sugar until light and creamy, about 3 minutes. Stir in flour, cornstarch and hazelnuts, mixing well. Using your hands, knead to form a smooth dough. Press evenly into pan. Prick surface all over with a fork.

2. Bake in preheated oven until lightly browned, 30 to 35 minutes. Cut into bars just as the pan comes out of the oven, then let cool completely in pan on rack. Recut.

Chocolate Shortbread Bars

Because there are so many chocolate lovers in the world, I've always believed you should have a chocolate version of every cookie to satisfy them all. These bars are thin, crisp and chocolaty.

MAKES 20 TO 54 BARS (see Cutting Guide, page 10)

- **Preparation: 20 minutes**
- **Baking: 40 minutes**
- **Freezing: excellent**

- **Preheat oven to 300°F (150°C)**
- **13- by 9-inch (3.5 L) cake pan, ungreased**

1 cup	butter, softened	250 mL
½ cup	granulated sugar	125 mL
2 cups	all-purpose flour	500 mL
2	squares (1 oz/28 g each) semi-sweet chocolate, melted and cooled	2

1. In a bowl, using an electric mixer on medium speed, beat butter and sugar until light and creamy, about 3 minutes. Stir in flour, mixing well. Stir in melted chocolate, mixing well. Using your hands, knead to form a smooth dough. Press evenly into pan.

2. Bake in preheated oven until firm and dry, 35 to 40 minutes. Cut into bars just as the pan comes out of the oven, then let cool completely in pan on rack. Recut.

Cornmeal Shortbread

This Italian favorite gets an extra-crunchy texture from cornmeal and almonds. The cornmeal also provides a wonderful yellow color. This is a particularly nice cookie to serve with fresh or stewed fruit.

MAKES 18 TO 48 BARS OR 16 TO 36 SQUARES
(see **Cutting Guide**, page 10)

- **Preparation: 20 minutes**
- **Baking: 30 minutes**
- **Freezing: excellent**

- **Preheat oven to 350°F (180°C)**
- **9-inch (2.5 L) square cake pan, ungreased**

¾ cup	whole unblanched almonds	175 mL
½ cup	yellow cornmeal	125 mL
1¾ cups	all-purpose flour	425 mL
¾ cup	granulated sugar	175 mL
1 cup	cold butter, cubed	250 mL

1. In a food processor, pulse almonds until coarsely chopped. Add cornmeal, flour, sugar and butter. Pulse until mixture resembles coarse crumbs. Press three-quarters of the dough evenly into pan. Using your fingers, scatter remainder on top.

2. Bake in preheated oven until light golden, 25 to 30 minutes. Cut into bars or squares just as the pan comes out of the oven, then let cool completely in pan on rack. Recut.

Rice Flour Shortbread

This thick, melt-in-your-mouth shortbread is similar to the Scottish shortbread usually baked in rounds or shortbread moulds and cut in wedges.

MAKES 18 TO 48 BARS OR 16 TO 36 SQUARES
(see **Cutting Guide**, page 10)

- **Preparation: 15 minutes**
- **Baking: 35 minutes**
- **Freezing: excellent**

- **Preheat oven to 300°F (150°C)**
- **8-inch (2 L) square cake pan, ungreased**

1½ cups	all-purpose flour	375 mL
⅓ cup	superfine granulated sugar	75 mL
⅓ cup	rice flour	75 mL
¼ tsp	salt	1 mL
¾ cup	cold butter, cubed	175 mL

1. In a bowl, combine all-purpose flour, sugar, rice flour and salt. Using a pastry blender, 2 knives or your fingers, work in butter until mixture resembles coarse crumbs. Knead dough on a lightly floured surface until very smooth, about 5 minutes. Press evenly into pan. Prick surface all over with a fork.

2. Bake in preheated oven until lightly browned around edges, 30 to 35 minutes. Cut into bars or squares just as the pan comes out of the oven, then let cool completely in pan on rack. Recut.

Oatmeal Shortbread

The large-flake oats give this shortbread a wonderful nutty flavor and an appealingly rustic appearance. These cookies taste terrific with a glass of cold milk or a mug of hot chocolate.

MAKES 20 TO 54 BARS OR 24 SQUARES
(see Cutting Guide, page 10)

- **Preparation: 15 minutes**
- **Baking: 30 minutes**
- **Freezing: excellent**

- **Preheat oven to 350°F (180°C)**
- **13- by 9-inch (3 L) cake pan, ungreased**

1 cup	butter, softened	250 mL
⅔ cup	packed brown sugar	150 mL
1½ cups	all-purpose flour	375 mL
1 tsp	cinnamon	5 mL
1¼ cups	old-fashioned (large-flake) rolled oats	300 mL

1. In a bowl, using an electric mixer on medium speed, beat butter and brown sugar until light and creamy, about 3 minutes. Stir in flour, cinnamon and oats, mixing well. Using your hands, knead to form a smooth dough. Press evenly into pan. Prick surface all over with a fork.

2. Bake in preheated oven until light golden, 25 to 30 minutes. Cut into bars or squares just as the pan comes out of the oven, then let cool completely in pan on rack. Recut.

Brown Sugar Shortbread

When I was growing up, one of our neighbors made shortbread with brown sugar. I remember especially enjoying its nice butterscotch flavor and wonderful melt-in-your-mouth texture.

MAKES 18 TO 48 BARS OR 16 TO 36 SQUARES
(see Cutting Guide, page 10)

- **Preparation: 20 minutes**
- **Baking: 55 minutes**
- **Freezing: excellent**

- **Preheat oven to 300°F (150°C)**
- **9-inch (2.5 L) square cake pan, ungreased**

2¼ cups	all-purpose flour	550 mL
¾ cup	packed dark brown sugar, divided	175 mL
1 cup	cold butter, cubed, divided	250 mL

1. In a bowl, combine flour and ⅔ cup (150 mL) of the sugar. Using a pastry blender, 2 knives or your fingers, cut in ¾ cup (175 mL) of the butter until mixture resembles coarse crumbs. Melt remaining butter. Work into flour mixture. Using your hands, knead dough on floured surface until smooth, about 2 minutes. Press evenly into pan. Prick surface all over with a fork. Sprinkle remaining brown sugar evenly over top.

2. Bake in preheated oven until light golden, 45 to 55 minutes. Cut into bars or squares just as the pan comes out of the oven, then let cool completely in pan on rack. Recut.

Cherry Pecan Shortbread Squares

Here's another recipe based on a soft shortbread dough. It's enhanced with favorite holiday ingredients — candied cherries and pecans.

MAKES 24 SQUARES (see Cutting Guide, page 10)

- **Preparation: 20 minutes**
- **Baking: 30 minutes**
- **Freezing: excellent**

TIP

When shortbread contains a significant quantity of chunky ingredients, such as the pecans and cherries in this recipe, precutting isn't necessary.

- **Preheat oven to 325°F (160°C)**
- **13- by 9-inch (3 L) cake pan, ungreased**

1 cup	butter, softened	250 mL
⅔ cup	granulated sugar	150 mL
2	egg yolks	2
2 cups	all-purpose flour	500 mL
1 tbsp	grated lemon zest	15 mL
¾ cup	chopped pecans	175 mL
⅔ cup	chopped red candied (glacé) cherries	150 mL

1. In a bowl, using an electric mixer on medium speed, beat butter, sugar and egg yolks until smooth and creamy. Stir in flour and lemon zest, mixing well. Stir in pecans and cherries, mixing well. Using your hands, knead to form a smooth dough. Press evenly into pan.

2. Bake in preheated oven until lightly browned, 25 to 30 minutes. Let cool completely in pan on rack (see Tips, left). Cut into squares.

Variations

Add 4 oz (125 g) chopped bittersweet chocolate to dough.

Replace lemon zest with 1 tsp (5 mL) vanilla.

Cherry Almond Shortbread Bars

The fabulous flavor of almond paste is combined with a crisp crust and the addition of glacé cherries for decoration. All are included in one-step baking, so no last-minute decorating is required.

MAKES 48 BARS (see Cutting Guide, page 10)

- **Preparation: 20 minutes**
- **Baking: 37 minutes**
- **Freezing: excellent**

TIPS

If you prefer, mix the topping in an electric mixer on medium speed for 3 minutes. If using a mixer, ensure the almond paste is soft and cut into small cubes for easy blending. If your almond paste seems hard, soften it in a microwave oven on High power for about 30 seconds.

I like to make these squares with cherries during the holiday season, but if you prefer, you can substitute an equal number of whole blanched almonds, which may be more appropriate at other times of the year.

- **Preheat oven to 350°F (180°C)**
- **13- by 9-inch (3 L) cake pan, ungreased**

CRUST

½ cup	butter, softened	125 mL
½ cup	granulated sugar	125 mL
1¼ cups	all-purpose flour	300 mL

TOPPING

7 oz	almond paste	200 g
¼ cup	granulated sugar	50 mL
¼ cup	butter, softened	50 mL
2	eggs	2
¼ tsp	almond extract	1 mL
48	red candied (glacé) cherries	48
2	squares (1 oz/28 g each) semi-sweet chocolate, melted, optional	2

1. *Crust:* In a bowl, using an electric mixer on medium speed, beat butter and sugar until light and creamy, about 3 minutes. Stir in flour, mixing until thoroughly combined and crumbly. Press evenly into prepared pan. Bake until golden around the edges, 10 to 12 minutes.

2. *Topping:* In a food processor, combine almond paste, sugar, butter, eggs and almond extract. Process until blended and smooth. Spread evenly over crust. Arrange cherries on top in 6 rows of 8, evenly spaced.

3. Bake in preheated oven until set and lightly browned around the edges, 20 to 25 minutes. Cut into bars just as the pan comes out of the oven, then let cool completely in pan on rack. If desired, drizzle with melted chocolate. Let stand until chocolate is set. Recut into bars with a cherry in the centre of each.

Variations

Use a mixture of red and green cherries.

Omit chocolate drizzle and sprinkle lightly with confectioner's (icing) sugar.

Almond Spice Shortbread

A hint of spice in the dough and a crunchy almond topping gives these bars a wonderful flavor and a texture that's quite different from plain shortbread.

**MAKES 20 TO 54 BARS OR 24 SQUARES
(see Cutting Guide, page 10)**

- **Preparation: 20 minutes**
- **Baking: 35 minutes**
- **Freezing: excellent**

TIPS

When creaming butter and sugar, it's important to have the butter at the right temperature. It should be a spreadable consistency. If it's too hard, it won't mix to a creamy light texture, and if it's too soft, the dough will be too soft.

Due to the addition of an egg yolk, this dough is a little softer than regular shortbread dough. That's the advantage of bars — the pan holds the shape. Softer dough in cookies will spread out and flatten, resulting in crisp, potentially overbaked cookies.

- **Preheat oven to 300°F (150°C)**
- **13- by 9-inch (3 L) cake pan, ungreased**

1 cup	butter, softened	250 mL
¾ cup	granulated sugar	175 mL
1	egg, separated	1
½ tsp	almond extract	2 mL
2 cups	all-purpose flour	500 mL
1 tsp	cinnamon	5 mL
¼ tsp	ground nutmeg	1 mL
¾ cup	sliced almonds	175 mL

1. In a bowl, using an electric mixer on medium speed, beat butter, sugar, egg yolk and almond extract until smooth and creamy. Stir in flour, cinnamon and nutmeg, mixing well. Using your hands, knead to form a smooth dough. Press evenly into pan.

2. In a bowl, whisk egg white lightly (you don't want it to be frothy). Brush lightly over dough. Sprinkle almonds evenly over top.

3. Bake in preheated oven until light golden all over, 30 to 35 minutes. Cut into bars or squares just as the pan comes out of the oven, then let cool completely in pan on rack. Recut.

Variations

Omit almond extract. Replace almonds with hazelnuts.

Unblanched sliced almonds look nice on these bars. They're available in some bulk food stores.

Ginger Shortbread

Filled with bits of sweet yet tangy crystallized ginger, these buttery bars are a hit with ginger fans. They're perfect with a cup of tea.

MAKES 20 TO 54 BARS OR 24 SQUARES
(see Cutting Guide, page 10)

- Preparation: 20 minutes
- Baking: 25 minutes
- Freezing: excellent

- **Preheat oven to 350°F (180°C)**
- **13- by 9-inch (3 L) cake pan, ungreased**

2¼ cups	all-purpose flour	550 mL
½ cup	packed brown sugar	125 mL
1 tsp	ground ginger	5 mL
½ tsp	baking powder	2 mL
¼ tsp	salt	1 mL
1 cup	butter, softened	250 mL
⅔ cup	finely chopped crystallized ginger	150 mL

1. In a large bowl, combine flour, brown sugar, ground ginger, baking powder and salt. Add butter and, using an electric mixer on low speed, beat until mixture resembles coarse crumbs, about 3 minutes. Stir in crystallized ginger, mixing well. Using your hands, knead to form a smooth dough. Press evenly into pan.

2. Bake in preheated oven until lightly browned, 20 to 25 minutes. Let cool completely in pan on rack (see Tips, page 196). Cut into bars or squares.

Chocolate Ginger Shortbread

Chocolate and ginger are one of my favorite flavor combinations. They're especially delicious in a buttery shortbread dough.

MAKES 18 TO 48 BARS OR 16 TO 36 SQUARES
(see Cutting Guide, page 10)

- Preparation: 20 minutes
- Baking: 45 minutes
- Freezing: excellent

- **Preheat oven to 300°F (150°C)**
- **9-inch (2.5 L) square cake pan, ungreased**

1 cup	butter, softened	250 mL
½ cup	superfine granulated sugar (see Tips, page 196)	125 mL
2 cups	all-purpose flour	500 mL
½ cup	finely chopped crystallized ginger	125 mL
½ cup	chopped milk chocolate (3 oz/85 g)	125 mL

1. In a bowl, using an electric mixer on medium speed, beat butter and sugar until light and creamy. Stir in flour, ginger and chocolate, mixing well. Using your hands, knead to form a smooth dough. Press evenly into pan.

2. Bake in preheated oven until light golden all over, 40 to 45 minutes. Let cool completely in pan on rack (see Tips, page 196). Cut into bars or squares.

Citrus Shortbread Bars

You can leave these bars plain or finish them by dipping the cooled bars in melted chocolate or drizzling melted chocolate on top. Plain or fancy — the choice is yours.

MAKES 36 TO 48 BARS (see Cutting Guide, page 10)

- **Preparation: 20 minutes**
- **Baking: 45 minutes**
- **Freezing: excellent**

- **Preheat oven to 300°F (150°C)**
- **15- by 10- by 1-inch (2 L) jelly roll pan, ungreased**

1 lb	butter, softened	500 g
1 cup	superfine granulated sugar	250 mL
1½ tbsp	grated lemon zest	22 mL
1½ tbsp	grated orange zest	22 mL
½ tsp	salt	2 mL
3 cups	all-purpose flour	750 mL
1½ cups	cornstarch	375 mL

1. In a bowl, using an electric mixer on medium speed, beat butter, sugar, lemon and orange zests and salt until light and creamy. Combine flour and cornstarch. Stir one-third into butter mixture, mixing well. Repeat twice. Using your hands, knead to form a smooth dough. Press evenly into pan. Prick surface all over with a fork.

2. Bake in preheated oven until lightly browned around edges, 40 to 45 minutes. Cut into bars while warm. Let cool completely in pan on rack. Recut.

Mocha Java Shortbread Sticks

The crushed coffee beans add unique crunch and flavor to this shortbread. They're particularly good with a steamy mug of café au lait or cappuccino.

MAKES 48 BARS (see Cutting Guide, page 10)

- **Preparation: 20 minutes**
- **Baking: 40 minutes**
- **Freezing: excellent**

- **Preheat oven to 325°F (160°C)**
- **9-inch (2.5 L) square cake pan, ungreased**

1 cup	butter, softened	250 mL
½ cup	granulated sugar	125 mL
2 cups	all-purpose flour	500 mL
2 tbsp	cornstarch	25 mL
3 tbsp	coffee beans, crushed	45 mL

1. In a bowl, using an electric mixer on medium speed, beat butter and sugar until light and creamy, about 3 minutes. Stir in flour, cornstarch and crushed coffee beans, mixing well. Using your hands, knead to form a smooth dough. Press evenly into pan.

2. Bake in preheated oven until lightly browned around edges, 35 to 40 minutes. Cut into thin bars while warm. Let cool completely in pan on rack. Recut.

Chocolate-Dipped Peanut Butter Chocolate Shortbread Sticks

The great thing about making shortbread bars is that one large pan makes a large quantity with a minimum amount of work. They taste every bit as good as those you roll out and cut individually.

MAKES 48 BARS
(see Cutting Guide, page 10)

- **Preparation: 20 minutes**
- **Baking: 15 minutes**
- **Freezing: excellent**

TIPS

Coating or moulding chocolate, sold in wafer shapes in bulk stores and cake supply stores, is ideal for dipping. It hardens quickly and, unlike real chocolate, doesn't melt after it's on the product. It tastes great, too.

For an attractive presentation, cut these bars into triangles, dip the base in chocolate and sprinkle finely chopped peanuts on top.

- **Preheat oven to 375°F (190°C)**
- **15- by 10- by 1-inch (2 L) jelly roll pan, ungreased**

SHORTBREAD

¾ cup	butter, softened	175 mL
⅓ cup	creamy peanut butter	75 mL
⅓ cup	granulated sugar	75 mL
⅓ cup	packed brown sugar	75 mL
2 cups	all-purpose flour	500 mL
¾ cup	miniature semi-sweet chocolate chips	175 mL

CHOCOLATE DIP

1⅓ cups	semi-sweet chocolate chips	325 mL
2 tbsp	vegetable oil	25 mL

1. *Shortbread:* In a bowl, using an electric mixer on medium speed, beat butter, peanut butter and granulated and brown sugars until smooth and creamy, about 3 minutes. Stir in flour, mixing well. Using your hands, knead to form a smooth dough. Stir in chocolate chips. Press evenly into pan.

2. Bake in preheated oven until lightly browned around edges, 12 to 15 minutes. Cut into thin bars while warm. Let cool completely in pan on rack. Recut.

3. *Chocolate Dip:* In a small saucepan, combine chocolate chips and oil. Heat over low heat, stirring constantly, until chocolate is melted and mixture is smooth. Dip one or both ends of each bar into chocolate. Place on wire rack over waxed paper. Let stand until chocolate is set, about 1 hour.

Variations

Add ⅓ cup (75 mL) finely chopped peanuts to the dough.

Make half the quantity of chocolate dip and drizzle it over top of the bars.

White Chocolate Cranberry Shortbread Squares

Tart dried cranberries offset the sweet creamy white chocolate in this delicious and easy-to-make shortbread.

MAKES 24 SQUARES
(see Cutting Guide, page 10)

- **Preparation: 20 minutes**
- **Baking: 30 minutes**
- **Freezing: excellent**

TIPS

If you don't have superfine sugar, whirl regular granulated sugar in a blender or food processor until fine.

When shortbread contains a significant quantity of chunky ingredients, precutting isn't necessary.

Unsalted and salted butter are interchangeable in baking. The only difference is the taste. The sweet, delicate flavor of unsalted butter really comes through when butter is the main ingredient.

- **Preheat oven to 350°F (180°C)**
- **13- by 9-inch (3 L) cake pan, ungreased**

SHORTBREAD

1 cup	butter, softened	250 mL
½ cup	superfine granulated sugar (see Tips, left)	125 mL
1½ tsp	vanilla	7 mL
2⅓ cups	all-purpose flour	575 mL
1 cup	chopped dried cranberries	250 mL
¾ cup	white chocolate chips	175 mL

DRIZZLE

½ cup	white chocolate chips	125 mL
2 tsp	vegetable oil	10 mL

1. *Shortbread:* In a bowl, using an electric mixer on medium speed, beat butter, sugar and vanilla until light and creamy. Stir in flour, mixing well. Using your hands, knead to form a smooth dough. Knead in cranberries and white chocolate chips. Press evenly into pan.

2. Bake in preheated oven until lightly browned around the edges, 25 to 30 minutes. Let cool completely in pan on rack (see Tips, left).

3. *Drizzle:* In a small saucepan, heat chocolate and oil over low heat, stirring constantly, until chocolate is melted and mixture is smooth. Drizzle over shortbread. Let stand until chocolate is set. Cut into squares.

Variations

Replace white chocolate with semi-sweet chocolate chips.

Replace dried cranberries with dried cherries.

Try cherry-flavored cranberries for another great taste.

Cranberry Lemon Shortbread

♦

There's nothing better than the combination of cranberries and lemon. The delicate flavor of buttery shortbread really shows off the taste.

MAKES 20 TO 54 BARS OR 24 SQUARES
(see Cutting Guide, page 10)

- **Preparation: 25 minutes**
- **Baking: 35 minutes**
- **Freezing: excellent**

TIPS

Depending on your food processor, you may not be able to mix the cranberries thoroughly into the dough. If so, remove the dough from the food processor and knead gently with hands to distribute cranberries evenly. Most of the cranberries should be chopped, with a few still in large pieces.

Use a small offset spatula to easily spread frosting or glazes on bars. It gets into the corners nicely.

- **Preheat oven to 300°F (150°C)**
- **13- by 9-inch (3 L) cake pan, ungreased**

SHORTBREAD

¾ cup	cold butter, cubed	175 mL
½ cup	confectioner's (icing) sugar, sifted	125 mL
¼ cup	granulated sugar	50 mL
2 tbsp	grated lemon zest	25 mL
1 tbsp	freshly squeezed lemon juice	15 mL
2 cups	all-purpose flour	500 mL
⅔ cup	dried cranberries	150 mL

GLAZE

1 cup	confectioner's (icing) sugar, sifted	250 mL
1 tsp	grated lemon zest	5 mL
1 tbsp	freshly squeezed lemon juice (approx.)	15 mL

1. *Shortbread:* In a food processor, combine butter, confectioner's sugar, granulated sugar, lemon zest and lemon juice. Process until blended. Add flour. Pulse until mixture resembles coarse crumbs. Add cranberries. Pulse until evenly mixed. Press evenly into pan.

2. Bake in preheated oven until lightly browned around the edges, 30 to 35 minutes. Let cool completely in pan on rack.

3. *Glaze:* In a bowl, whisk confectioner's sugar and lemon zest and juice until smooth. Add a little more lemon juice, if necessary, to make a spreadable consistency. Spread over shortbread. Let stand until glaze sets, about 30 minutes. Cut into bars or squares.

Variations

Omit glaze if desired.

Replace cranberries with dried cherries.

Replace lemon zest and juice with orange.

Nutty Shortbread Bars

These bars, which are not too sweet, have a nice nutty flavor and a very "short" texture.

MAKES 18 TO 48 BARS (see Cutting Guide, page 10)

- **Preparation: 20 minutes**
- **Baking: 45 minutes**
- **Freezing: excellent**

- **Preheat oven to 300°F (150°C)**
- **9-inch (2.5 L) square cake pan, ungreased**

1 cup	butter, softened	250 mL
1/3 cup	granulated sugar	75 mL
2 tbsp	cornstarch	25 mL
1 tsp	vanilla	5 mL
2 cups	all-purpose flour	500 mL
1/3 cup	finely chopped walnuts	75 mL
1/3 cup	finely chopped pecans	75 mL

1. In a bowl, using an electric mixer on medium speed, beat butter, sugar, cornstarch and vanilla until light and creamy. Stir in flour, walnuts and pecans, mixing well. Using your hands, knead to form a smooth dough. Press evenly into pan.

2. Bake in preheated oven until light golden around edges, 40 to 45 minutes. Cut into bars just as the pan comes out of the oven, then let cool completely in pan on rack. Recut.

Coconut Shortbread Bars

Funny thing — this shortbread was a favorite of friends who claim to hate coconut. The coconut flavor isn't strong, but the texture is crisp, light and tender.

MAKES 20 TO 54 BARS (see Cutting Guide, page 10)

- **Preparation: 20 minutes**
- **Baking: 40 minutes**
- **Freezing: excellent**

- **Preheat oven to 300°F (150°C)**
- **13- by 9-inch (3 L) cake pan, ungreased**

1 cup	butter, softened	250 mL
1/2 cup	granulated sugar	125 mL
1 tsp	vanilla	5 mL
2 cups	all-purpose flour	500 mL
1/2 cup	rice flour	125 mL
1 cup	sweetened flaked coconut	250 mL

1. In a bowl, using an electric mixer on medium speed, beat butter, sugar and vanilla until smooth and creamy, about 3 minutes. Stir in all-purpose and rice flours and coconut, mixing well. Using your hands, knead to form a smooth dough. Press evenly into pan.

2. Bake in preheated oven until light golden, 35 to 40 minutes. Let cool completely in pan on rack. Cut into bars.

Chocolate Nougat Shortbread

The bars are strong competitors to that all-time favorite, chocolate chip cookies.

MAKES 18 TO 48 BARS
(see Cutting Guide, page 10)

- **Preparation: 20 minutes**
- **Baking: 40 minutes**
- **Freezing: excellent**

- **Preheat oven to 325°F (160°C)**
- **9-inch (2.5 L) square cake pan, ungreased**

1 cup	butter, softened	250 mL
½ cup	superfine granulated sugar (see Tips, page 196)	125 mL
1⅔ cups	all-purpose flour	400 mL
¼ cup	cornstarch	50 mL
¾ cup	coarsely chopped milk chocolate honey almond nougat chocolate bars (6 oz/170 g)	175 mL

1. In a bowl, using an electric mixer on medium speed, beat butter and sugar until light and creamy, about 3 minutes. Stir in flour and cornstarch, mixing well. Using your hands, knead to form a smooth dough. Work in chopped chocolate bars with your hands. Press evenly into pan.

2. Bake in preheated oven until lightly browned around the edges, 35 to 40 minutes. Let cool completely in pan on rack. Cut into bars.

Almond Shortbread Squares

Tender but crisp, the crunchy almonds give these squares an unusual texture for shortbread.

MAKES 24 SQUARES
(see Cutting Guide, page 10)

- **Preparation: 20 minutes**
- **Baking: 35 minutes**
- **Freezing: excellent**

- **Preheat oven to 325°F (160°C)**
- **13- by 9-inch (3 L) cake pan, ungreased**

¾ cup	sliced almonds, toasted	175 mL
2 cups	all-purpose flour	500 mL
1 cup	cold butter, cubed	250 mL
½ cup	granulated sugar	125 mL
½ cup	cornstarch	125 mL
2 tbsp	grated orange zest	25 mL
¾ tsp	almond extract	3 mL

1. In a food processor, pulse almonds until coarsely chopped. Add flour, butter, sugar, cornstarch, orange zest and almond extract and pulse until crumbly. Press evenly into pan.

2. Bake in preheated oven until lightly browned around edges, 30 to 35 minutes. Cut into squares just as the pan comes out of the oven, then let cool completely in pan on rack. Recut.

Not Just for Kids

Kid-friendly ingredients — such as cereal, graham wafers, marshmallows, chocolate chips, peanut butter and caramels — dominate this section, making the recipes favorites for the young as well as the young at heart. These bars are also relatively easy to make, which means that kids can help out in the kitchen because their attention span isn't taxed. Not only does baking provide an opportunity to share quality family time together, but it also helps kids develop practical skills like counting. They'll also learn how to measure, mix and chop, preparing them for the days when they'll be responsible for food preparation themselves. I've tried to keep an eye on cleanup so they won't be daunted by it.

These foolproof recipes guarantee that kids will end up with treats they can be proud to share with their family and friends. Let them choose the recipes and make their own lunch-box treats and after-school snacks. It's fun for everyone.

◄ *Rocky Road Chocolate Bars*

Rocky Road Chocolate Bars

Kids know the ingredients in rocky roads long before they learn to make them, so it won't be hard to get them in the kitchen for these.

MAKES 18 TO 48 BARS, see Cutting Guide, page 10

- **Preparation: 20 minutes**
- **Cooking: 5 minutes**
- **Chilling: 1 hour**
- **Freezing: excellent**

TIPS

Let kids count the marshmallows as they put them in the measuring cup. If you have two helpers, they can each count enough to fill ¾ cup (175 mL) and see if they get the same number.

Use a fine strainer to sift the confectioner's (icing) sugar. Measure it first in a dry measure, then sift it, pushing it through the sieve with the back of a spoon.

- **8-inch (2 L) square cake pan, greased**

CRUMB MIXTURE

1½ cups	graham wafer crumbs	375 mL
1½ cups	miniature marshmallows	375 mL
½ cup	chopped pecans	125 mL
½ cup	confectioner's (icing) sugar, sifted	125 mL
2 tbsp	milk	25 mL

CHOCOLATE MIXTURE

2 cups	semi-sweet chocolate chips	500 mL
½ cup	milk	125 mL
3 tbsp	butter	45 mL
¼ cup	confectioner's (icing) sugar, sifted	50 mL

1. *Crumb Mixture:* In a bowl, combine graham wafer crumbs, marshmallows, pecans, confectioner's sugar and milk. Mix well until all ingredients are moistened. Set aside.

2. *Chocolate Mixture:* In a saucepan, combine chocolate chips, milk and butter. Heat over low heat, stirring constantly, until chocolate is melted and mixture is smooth. Remove from heat. Pour half (about ¾ cup/175 mL) over reserved crumb mixture. Mix well. Spread evenly in prepared pan.

3. Stir confectioner's sugar into remaining chocolate mixture in saucepan, mixing well. Spread evenly over base in pan. Chill until chocolate is set, about 1 hour. Cut into bars.

Variations

Replace pecans with walnuts, almonds or peanuts.
Sprinkle finely chopped nuts over the chocolate topping.
Use colored marshmallows for fun.

Peter Pumpkin Bars

Make these a Halloween tradition. Kids can take them to school for their Halloween party or just enjoy them as a special treat. They're as soft as cheesecake, which is nice for small children.

MAKES 18 TO 48 BARS (see Cutting Guide, page 10)

- **Preparation: 25 minutes**
- **Baking: 25 minutes**
- **Freezing: excellent**

TIPS

If you prefer, use unbleached all-purpose flour in all your baking. It's the same as regular all-purpose flour but has not been chemically bleached.

Be sure to buy pumpkin purée, not pumpkin pie filling, which contains spices and sugar.

This batter doesn't require a mixer, which makes it fun and easy for children to help. They enjoy beating things with a wooden spoon.

It's fun for kids to decorate the frosting with their favorite Halloween candies, such as licorice bats, brooms and witches, candy corn, candy pumpkins, and orange and black M&M's or Smarties.

- **Preheat oven to 350°F (180°C)**
- **9-inch (2.5 L) square cake pan, greased**

BARS

1 cup	all-purpose flour	250 mL
¾ cup	granulated sugar	175 mL
1 tsp	baking powder	5 mL
1 tsp	cinnamon	5 mL
¼ tsp	salt	1 mL
¼ tsp	ground nutmeg	1 mL
2	eggs	2
1 cup	pumpkin purée (not pie filling)	250 mL
½ cup	vegetable oil	125 mL

FROSTING

4 oz	cream cheese, softened	125 g
¼ cup	butter, softened	50 mL
2 cups	confectioner's (icing) sugar, sifted, divided	500 mL
1 tsp	vanilla	5 mL
2 to 3 tsp	milk	10 to 15 mL

1. *Bars:* In a bowl, combine flour, sugar, baking powder, cinnamon, salt and nutmeg. In a separate bowl, whisk together eggs, pumpkin and oil until blended. Stir into dry mixture, mixing until smooth. Spread evenly in prepared pan.

2. Bake in preheated oven until a toothpick inserted in center comes out clean, 20 to 25 minutes. Let cool completely in pan on rack.

3. *Frosting:* In a bowl, using an electric mixer on medium speed, beat cream cheese and butter until creamy, about 3 minutes. Add 1 cup (250 mL) of the confectioner's sugar and vanilla, beating until smooth. Add remaining confectioner's sugar and enough milk to make a soft, spreadable consistency. Spread over cooled bar. Cut into bars.

Variations

Omit the frosting. Dust with confectioner's (icing) sugar or leave plain.

Add ½ cup (125 mL) raisins to the batter.

Chocolate Toffee Cookie Brittle

Kids love to help when they get to enjoy their efforts. The hardest part of the job is waiting for their masterpieces to cool.

**MAKES ABOUT
4 DOZEN PIECES**

- **Preparation: 20 minutes**
- **Baking: 25 minutes**
- **Freezing: excellent**

TIP

The mixture will be crumbly when pressed in the pan, but as it bakes it all comes together.

- **Preheat oven to 325°F (160°C)**
- **15- by 10- by 1-inch (2 L) jelly roll pan, greased**

1 cup	butter, softened	250 mL
1 cup	granulated sugar	250 mL
1 tsp	vanilla	5 mL
2 cups	all-purpose flour	500 mL
¼ tsp	salt	1 mL
1 cup	semi-sweet chocolate chips	250 mL
4	crunchy chocolate-covered toffee bars (1.4 oz/39g each), coarsely chopped, (see Tips, page 147)	4
½ cup	finely chopped almonds	125 mL

1. In a large bowl, using an electric mixer on medium speed, beat butter, sugar and vanilla until light and creamy, about 3 minutes. Stir in flour, salt, chocolate chips, chocolate bars and almonds, mixing well. Press firmly into prepared pan.

2. Bake in preheated oven until top is golden, 20 to 25 minutes. Let cool completely in pan on rack. Break into pieces.

Corn Flake Peanut Squares

Here's an excellent cereal square that kids can easily learn to make for their own lunch box and afternoon snack.

**MAKES 16 TO
36 SQUARES
(see Cutting Guide,
page 10)**

- **Preparation: 15 minutes**
- **Cooking: 5 minutes**
- **Cooling: 30 minutes**
- **Freezing: excellent**

- **9-inch (2.5 L) square cake pan, greased**

¾ cup	packed brown sugar	175 mL
¾ cup	creamy peanut butter	175 mL
¾ cup	corn syrup	175 mL
6 cups	corn flakes cereal, slightly crushed	1.5 L
1 cup	coarsely chopped peanuts	250 mL

1. In a saucepan, heat brown sugar, peanut butter and corn syrup over medium heat, stirring until smooth. In a large bowl, combine cereal and peanuts. Pour syrup mixture over top and, using a large wooden spoon, stir until cereal and nuts are evenly coated. Press evenly into prepared pan. Let cool until set, about 30 minutes. Cut into squares.

Chocolate Candy Cookie Bars

Here's a perfect recipe for children with a short attention span. It's in the oven in a flash so there's no time for them to get bored.

MAKES 20 TO 54 BARS (see Cutting Guide, page 10)

- **Preparation: 15 minutes**
- **Baking: 25 minutes**
- **Freezing: excellent**

- **Preheat oven to 350°F (180°C)**
- **13- by 9-inch (3 L) cake pan, ungreased**

½ cup	butter, melted	125 mL
1⅓ cups	graham wafer crumbs	325 mL
1	can (10 oz/300 mL) sweetened condensed milk	1
2 cups	semi-sweet chocolate chips	500 mL
¾ cup	mini candy-coated chocolate pieces (such as M&M's)	175 mL

1. Pour butter into cake pan and tilt to coat the bottom evenly. Sprinkle graham wafer crumbs evenly over top, moistening all the crumbs. Pour condensed milk evenly over crumbs. Sprinkle chocolate chips, then candies, evenly over top.
2. Bake in preheated oven until golden around the edges, 20 to 25 minutes. Let cool completely in pan on rack. Cut into bars.

S'more Cookie Bars

No kids' section would be complete if it didn't contain some version of the classic s'mores. It goes without saying that this will be on their list of most requested recipes.

MAKES 20 TO 54 BARS (see Cutting Guide, page 10)

- **Preparation: 15 minutes**
- **Baking: 25 minutes**
- **Freezing: excellent**

- **Preheat oven to 350°F (180°C)**
- **13- by 9-inch (3 L) cake pan, ungreased**

½ cup	butter, melted	125 mL
1¼ cups	graham wafer crumbs	300 mL
½ cup	quick-cooking rolled oats	125 mL
1	can (10 oz/300 mL) sweetened condensed milk	1
1¼ cups	miniature marshmallows	300 mL
1 cup	milk chocolate chips	250 mL
1 cup	peanut butter chips	250 mL

1. Pour butter into cake pan and tilt to coat the bottom evenly. Sprinkle graham wafer crumbs and oats evenly over top. Press down lightly with the back of a spoon to moisten crumb mixture. Pour sweetened condensed milk evenly over crumbs. Sprinkle marshmallows, then chips, evenly over top.
2. Bake in preheated oven until golden around the edges, about 25 minutes. Let cool completely in pan on rack. Cut into bars.

Blueberry Cookie Bars

These bars are easy enough for kids to make themselves and so attractive they'll be proud to show them off.

MAKES 18 TO 48 BARS (see Cutting Guide, page 10)

- **Preparation: 20 minutes**
- **Baking: 40 minutes**
- **Freezing: excellent**

TIP

If your jam seems a little sweet, try adding 2 to 3 tsp (10 to 15 mL) lemon juice to it.

- **Preheat oven to 350°F (180°C)**
- **8-inch (2 L) square cake pan, greased**

½ cup	butter, softened	125 mL
½ cup	granulated sugar	125 mL
1	egg	1
1½ cups	all-purpose flour	375 mL
¾ cup	blueberry jam	175 mL
⅓ cup	sliced almonds	75 mL

1. In a bowl, using an electric mixer on medium speed, beat butter, sugar and egg until light and creamy, about 3 minutes. On low speed, gradually beat in flour, until mixture is crumbly. Set aside 1 cup (250 mL) of the mixture for topping. Press remainder evenly into prepared pan. Spread jam evenly over top, leaving a ½-inch (1 cm) border of crust around edges. Stir almonds into reserved mixture and sprinkle evenly over jam.

2. Bake in preheated oven until golden, 35 to 40 minutes. Let cool completely in pan on rack. Cut into bars.

Variations

Try jams such as cherry, apricot and strawberry.

Replace almonds with pecans or omit them for a nut-free bar.

Chocolate Chip Cookie Bars

No kids' section is complete without the ultimate favorite cookie. In this case, it's the same taste in an easy-to-make bar shape.

MAKES 20 TO 54 BARS (see Cutting Guide, page 10)

- **Preparation: 15 minutes**
- **Baking: 20 minutes**
- **Freezing: excellent**

TIPS

When pressing this dough into the pan, lightly flour your fingers to prevent it from sticking.

This dough also makes wonderful cookies, which can be fun for kids to shape. Drop dough by rounded spoonfuls onto a greased baking sheet and bake for 8 to 10 minutes or until light golden but still soft. They'll firm up on cooling.

You don't need an electric mixer for many cookie doughs. A big wooden spoon works well and gives a more homemade look. It's also more kid friendly.

- **Preheat oven to 375°F (190°C)**
- **13- by 9-inch (3 L) cake pan, greased**

1 cup	butter, softened	250 mL
¾ cup	granulated sugar	175 mL
¾ cup	packed brown sugar	175 mL
1	egg	1
1 tsp	vanilla	5 mL
2¼ cups	all-purpose flour	550 mL
1 tsp	baking soda	5 mL
¼ tsp	salt	1 mL
2 cups	semi-sweet chocolate chips	500 mL
1 cup	coarsely chopped pecans	250 mL

1. In a bowl, using a wooden spoon, beat butter, granulated and brown sugars, egg and vanilla until smooth, about 5 minutes. Combine flour, baking soda and salt. Stir into creamed mixture, mixing well. Stir in chocolate chips and pecans. Using floured fingers, press dough evenly into prepared pan.

2. Bake in preheated oven until golden, about 20 minutes. Let cool completely in pan on rack. Cut into bars.

Variations

For a birthday party loot bag treat, replace the chocolate chips with candy-coated chocolate pieces like Smarties or M&M's.

Replace pecans with walnuts or cashews.

Oatmeal Raisin Cookie Bars

Second to chocolate chip cookies in the list of favorites is oatmeal raisin. These take half the time to shape, which means they're ready for eating sooner.

MAKES 20 TO 54 BARS (see Cutting Guide, page 10)

- **Preparation: 20 minutes**
- **Baking: 25 minutes**
- **Freezing: excellent**

TIPS

I like to use some shortening in these bars because it produces a cookie with better texture. Since traditional shortening is loaded with unhealthy trans fats, I recommend purchasing a brand that's trans fat–free. Check the label.

Use old-fashioned (large-flake) rolled oats for a more "oaty" flavor.

To prevent sticking, use floured fingers or the heel of your hand to press the dough into the pan. Don't worry about gooey hands. Kids enjoy this.

These are like a big, thick, chewy cookie. Bake them a little longer to make them crisper.

- **Preheat oven to 375°F (190°C)**
- **13- by 9-inch (3 L) cake pan, greased**

½ cup	butter, softened	125 mL
½ cup	shortening (see Tips, left)	125 mL
⅔ cup	granulated sugar	150 mL
⅔ cup	packed brown sugar	150 mL
2	eggs	2
1 cup	all-purpose flour	250 mL
1 tsp	baking soda	5 mL
1 tsp	cinnamon	5 mL
½ tsp	baking powder	2 mL
¼ tsp	salt	1 mL
3 cups	quick-cooking rolled oats	750 mL
1⅓ cups	raisins	325 mL

1. In a bowl, using a wooden spoon, beat butter, shortening, granulated and brown sugars and eggs until smooth and creamy, about 5 minutes. Combine flour, baking soda, cinnamon, baking powder and salt. Stir into creamed mixture, mixing well. Stir in oats and raisins until thoroughly blended. Using floured fingers, press dough evenly into prepared pan.

2. Bake in preheated oven until light golden, 20 to 25 minutes. Let cool completely in pan on rack. Cut into bars.

Variation

Replace raisins with dried cranberries, chocolate chips or chopped walnuts.

Chocolate-Topped Peanut Butter Oat Bars

◆

It's hard to find a kid who doesn't like the combination of peanut butter and chocolate in any form — bars, cookies, candy, ice cream and cake.

MAKES 20 TO 54 BARS (see Cutting Guide, page 10)

- **Preparation: 15 minutes**
- **Baking: 15 minutes**
- **Chilling: 30 minutes**
- **Freezing: excellent**

TIP

Use a small offset spatula or the back of a soup spoon to spread soft ingredients like peanut butter and melted chocolate.

- **Preheat oven to 350°F (180°C)**
- **13- by 9-inch (3 L) cake pan, greased**

BASE

½ cup	butter, softened	125 mL
1 cup	packed brown sugar	250 mL
½ cup	corn syrup	125 mL
¼ tsp	salt	1 mL
4 cups	quick-cooking rolled oats	1 L
¾ cup	crunchy peanut butter	175 mL

TOPPING

6	squares (1 oz/28 g each) semi-sweet chocolate, chopped	6
¼ cup	butter	50 mL
½ cup	peanut butter chips	125 mL

1. *Base:* In a bowl, using a wooden spoon, beat butter and brown sugar until light and creamy, about 5 minutes. Stir in corn syrup, salt and oats, mixing well. Spread evenly in prepared pan. Bake in preheated oven until top is set and golden, about 15 minutes. Let cool in pan on rack for 15 minutes. Drop peanut butter by spoonfuls over base and spread evenly.

2. *Topping:* In a saucepan over low heat, melt chocolate, butter and peanut butter chips, stirring constantly, until smooth. Drop by spoonfuls over peanut butter and spread evenly. Chill until chocolate is set, about 30 minutes. Cut into bars.

Variations

If you prefer an all-chocolate topping, replace peanut butter chips with 2 additional (1 oz/28 g each) squares of chocolate.

Use creamy peanut butter instead of crunchy, reducing the amount to ½ cup (125 mL).

Sprinkle ⅓ cup (75 mL) finely chopped peanuts evenly over chocolate topping.

Use old-fashioned (large-flake) rolled oats for a more oaty taste and appearance.

Thumbprint Jam Cookie Squares

Thumbprint cookies have been around as long as I can remember. My grandmother and mother always made them at Christmas. It was my job to put the thumbprint into the dough.

MAKES 54 SQUARES (see Cutting Guide page 10)

- **Preparation: 20 minutes**
- **Baking: 20 minutes**
- **Chilling: 15 minutes**
- **Freezing: excellent**

TIPS

Vary the jam to suit your taste or to have a variety of colors. Blackberry and apricot are nice.

If the jam seems skimpy after baking (it will settle when warm), top up with a little more as soon as the squares come out of the oven.

Stir jam to soften before spooning into thumbprint.

- **Preheat oven to 400°F (200°C)**
- **15- by 10- by 1-inch (2 L) jelly roll pan, greased**

3 cups	all-purpose flour	750 mL
1¼ cups	confectioner's (icing) sugar, sifted	300 mL
1¼ cups	butter, softened	300 mL
1½ tsp	vanilla	7 mL
1	egg, beaten	1
1 cup	raspberry jam	250 mL
2	squares (1 oz/28 g each) bittersweet chocolate, melted	2

1. In a bowl, combine flour, confectioner's sugar, butter, vanilla and egg. Using a large wooden spoon, beat until dough comes together, about 5 minutes. Transfer to a lightly floured surface and, using your hands, knead until smooth. Press evenly into prepared pan. Using the tip of a knife, mark dough into 54 squares. With your thumb or the handle of a wooden spoon, press an indentation in the center of each square. Place a scant teaspoon (5 mL) of jam in each thumbprint.

2. Bake in preheated oven until lightly browned around edges, 15 to 20 minutes. Let cool completely in pan on rack.

3. Drizzle melted chocolate randomly over squares. Chill until chocolate is set, about 15 minutes. Cut into squares.

Variations

Omit chocolate drizzle. Leave the squares plain or dust them with confectioner's (icing) sugar before serving.

Sprinkle ¾ cup (175 mL) finely chopped walnuts over dough before making thumbprints.

Chocolate Caramel Peanut Bars

The best part of having little helpers with this recipe is that they can unwrap the caramels. Count the unwrapped caramels to be sure the total matches the wrapped number. Some usually get lost in the unwrapping process.

MAKES 20 TO 54 BARS (see Cutting Guide, page 10)

- **Preparation: 25 minutes**
- **Cooking: 10 minutes**
- **Baking: 35 minutes**
- **Freezing: excellent**

TIPS

Caramels are easier to unwrap if you chill them first.

If you prefer, use a wooden spoon to mix the base. It will take about 5 minutes.

Always assemble your ingredients before starting to bake. That way you'll be sure you have everything and not leave anything out.

Don't keep opened baking soda longer than 6 months. Invest in a new box and retire the old one to the refrigerator as a deodorizer.

- **Preheat oven to 350°F (180°C)**
- **13- by 9-inch (3 L) cake pan, greased**

BASE

2 cups	all-purpose flour	500 mL
2 cups	quick-cooking rolled oats	500 mL
1⅓ cups	packed brown sugar	325 mL
1 tsp	baking soda	5 mL
¼ tsp	salt	1 mL
1 cup	butter, softened	250 mL
1	egg, beaten	1

TOPPING

1 lb	soft caramels, unwrapped (about 60)	500 g
⅓ cup	evaporated milk	75 mL
1¼ cups	semi-sweet chocolate chips	300 mL
1 cup	chopped dry-roasted peanuts	250 mL

1. *Base:* In a large bowl, combine flour, oats, brown sugar, baking soda and salt. Add butter and egg. On low speed, beat until mixture is crumbly, about 2 minutes. Press half of the mixture evenly into prepared pan. Bake in preheated oven until set, about 10 minutes.

2. *Topping:* In a heavy saucepan over low heat, combine caramels and evaporated milk. Heat, stirring, until caramels are melted and mixture is smooth. Remove from heat and set aside. Sprinkle chocolate chips and peanuts evenly over base. Drizzle melted caramel mixture evenly over top. Sprinkle remaining oat mixture over caramel.

3. Return to oven and bake until top is golden brown, 20 to 25 minutes. Let cool in pan on rack for 30 minutes. Loosen edges from sides of pan with a sharp knife. Let cool completely in pan on rack. Cut into bars.

Variations

Replace peanuts with pecans or cashews.

Replace chocolate chips with peanut butter chips.

Frosted Honey Zucchini Bars

Here's a great way to get kids to enjoy vegetables — in a cake-like base with frosting.

MAKES 20 TO 54 BARS
see Cutting Guide, page 10

- **Preparation: 25 minutes**
- **Baking: 30 minutes**
- **Freezing: excellent**

TIPS

I like to leave the zucchini unpeeled because I think the specks of green add interesting detail, but by all means peel it if you prefer.

To dress up these bars, sprinkle the frosting with finely chopped nuts.

Serve larger squares as a dessert.

If you omit the frosting, these bars taste like a moist and delicious breakfast muffin.

Not only does the honey add flavor, it also keeps the bars moist.

These bars are easier to cut if chilled.

- **Preheat oven to 350°F (180°C)**
- **13- by 9-inch (3 L) cake pan, greased**

BASE

1 cup	all-purpose flour	250 mL
1 tsp	baking powder	5 mL
1 tsp	baking soda	5 mL
1 tsp	cinnamon	5 mL
1/4 tsp	salt	1 mL
1/4 tsp	ground nutmeg	1 mL
2	eggs	2
1/3 cup	vegetable oil	75 mL
1/3 cup	liquid honey	75 mL
2 tbsp	milk	25 mL
1 cup	shredded zucchini	250 mL
1/2 cup	well-drained crushed pineapple	125 mL
1/2 cup	raisins	125 mL
1/3 cup	chopped pecans	75 mL

FROSTING

4 oz	cream cheese, softened	125 g
2 tbsp	butter, softened	25 mL
1 1/2 cups	confectioner's (icing) sugar, sifted	375 mL
1 tsp	freshly squeezed lemon juice	5 mL

1. *Base:* In a bowl, combine flour, baking powder, baking soda, cinnamon, salt and nutmeg. In a separate bowl, whisk eggs, oil, honey and milk until smooth. Stir into dry ingredients, mixing well. Stir in zucchini, pineapple, raisins and pecans, mixing until all ingredients are thoroughly combined. Spread batter evenly in prepared pan.

2. Bake in preheated oven until a toothpick inserted in center comes out clean, 25 to 30 minutes. Let cool completely in pan on rack.

3. *Frosting:* In a small bowl, using an electric mixer on low speed, beat cream cheese and butter until smooth. Gradually beat in confectioner's sugar and lemon juice, beating until smooth. Spread evenly over cooled base. Cut into bars. Store in refrigerator for up to 1 week.

Coconut Seeds Cereal Squares

A combination of coconut and seeds adds fiber and flavor to these addictive squares. They make a wonderful snack to pack for long car rides. Luckily, the recipe makes a large pan to satisfy any cravings.

MAKES 24 TO 60 SQUARES
(see Cutting Guide, page 10)

- **Preparation: 10 minutes**
- **Cooking: 2 minutes**
- **Baking: 10 minutes**
- **Freezing: excellent**

TIPS

Sweetened and unsweetened coconut are interchangeable in baking. I have specified unsweetened here with a view to limiting kids' sugar consumption.

Teach kids how to measure brown sugar properly. Unlike granulated sugar, which is simply scooped into a dry measuring cup then leveled off, brown sugar is packed into the cup. To test if they did it right, turn the cup upside down on a piece of waxed paper. When you remove the cup the sugar should hold its shape.

- Preheat oven to 375°F (190°C)
- 15- by 10- by 1-inch (2 L) jelly roll pan, greased

¾ cup	butter	175 mL
1¼ cups	packed brown sugar	300 mL
1 tsp	vanilla	5 mL
2¼ cups	quick-cooking rolled oats	550 mL
¼ cup	sesame seeds	50 mL
¼ cup	flax seeds	50 mL
¼ cup	sunflower seeds	50 mL
¼ cup	unsweetened flaked coconut	50 mL
¾ tsp	baking powder	3 mL
¼ tsp	salt	1 mL

1. In a large saucepan, melt butter over medium heat. Stir in brown sugar and vanilla. Cook, stirring often, until mixture is bubbly, about 2 minutes. Remove from heat. Stir in rolled oats, sesame seeds, flax seeds, sunflower seeds, coconut, baking powder and salt, mixing well until all ingredients are moistened. Press evenly into prepared pan.

2. Bake in preheated oven until light golden, about 10 minutes. Let cool completely in pan on rack. Cut into squares.

Variation
Use other kinds of seeds. Pumpkin seeds add an interesting appearance, texture and flavor.

Double Granola Bars

Two layers of granola bars in one means double the flavor and nutrition in every bite. Kids can help pick some of their favorite ingredients to put in the top layer.

MAKES 18 TO 48 BARS (see Cutting Guide, page 10)

- **Preparation: 30 minutes**
- **Baking: 32 minutes**
- **Freezing: excellent**

TIPS

Sweetened and unsweetened coconut are interchangeable in recipes. I have specified the use of unsweetened in this chapter with a view to limiting kids' sugar consumption.

Granola bars keep very well if they're well wrapped and stored in a cool, dry place — for up to 2 weeks.

These bars aren't too sweet and are easy to eat, which makes them very versatile. They're a good choice for lunches, breakfast on the run, snacks and coffee time.

- **Preheat oven to 325°F (160°C)**
- **8-inch (2 L) square cake pan, greased**

CRUST

½ cup	whole wheat flour	125 mL
⅓ cup	quick-cooking rolled oats	75 mL
¼ cup	ground almonds	50 mL
3 tbsp	packed brown sugar	45 mL
¼ tsp	baking powder	1 mL
3 tbsp	butter, melted	45 mL

TOPPING

¼ cup	butter, melted	50 mL
2 tbsp	packed brown sugar	25 mL
2 tbsp	liquid honey	25 mL
½ cup	quick-cooking rolled oats	125 mL
½ cup	finely chopped almonds	125 mL
½ cup	unsweetened flaked coconut (see Tips, left)	125 mL
⅓ cup	pumpkin seeds	75 mL
¼ cup	chopped dried mango	50 mL
2 tbsp	sesame seeds	25 mL

1. *Crust:* In a bowl, combine flour, oats, ground almonds, brown sugar and baking powder. Stir in melted butter, mixing well. Press evenly into prepared pan. Bake in preheated oven until set and golden around the edges, 10 to 12 minutes.

2. *Topping:* In a bowl, whisk melted butter, brown sugar and honey. Stir in oats, almonds, coconut, pumpkin seeds, dried mango and sesame seeds, mixing well. Spread evenly over crust. Press down gently using the heel of your hand, an offset spatula or the back of a spoon.

3. Return to oven and bake until set and golden, 15 to 20 minutes. Let cool completely in pan on rack. Cut into bars.

Variations

Replace whole wheat flour with all-purpose flour.

Decrease flour to ⅓ cup (75 mL) and add 3 tbsp (45 mL) wheat germ or 2 tbsp (25 mL) ground flax seeds.

Replace pumpkin seeds with sunflower seeds.

Raisin Pecan Tart Squares

A combination of butter tarts and pecan tarts baked into one delicious square, these are great on their own or served with ice cream for a scrumptious dessert.

MAKES 16 TO 36 SQUARES
(see Cutting Guide, page 10)

- **Preparation: 20 minutes**
- **Baking: 40 minutes**
- **Freezing: excellent**

TIPS

The center of the square should be slightly soft when you take it from the oven. It firms up on cooling.

These bars are nice but not too firm, like a butter tart that's almost drippy.

Use real vanilla in baking. No matter how much you use, you'll never get the authentic flavor using artificial vanilla. It may seem expensive but is well worth the cost.

- Preheat oven to 350°F (180°C)
- 9-inch (2.5 L) square cake pan, greased

CRUST

1 cup	all-purpose flour	250 mL
¼ cup	granulated sugar	50 mL
½ cup	cold butter, cubed	125 mL

TOPPING

2	eggs	2
1 cup	packed brown sugar	250 mL
2 tbsp	all-purpose flour	25 mL
½ tsp	baking powder	2 mL
¼ tsp	salt	1 mL
1 tsp	vanilla	5 mL
¾ cup	raisins	175 mL
¾ cup	coarsely chopped pecans	175 mL

1. *Crust:* In a bowl, combine flour and sugar. Using a pastry blender, 2 knives or your fingers, cut in butter until mixture resembles coarse crumbs. Press evenly into prepared pan. Bake in preheated oven until golden around the edges, 10 to 12 minutes.

2. *Topping:* In a bowl, whisk eggs and brown sugar until blended. Whisk in flour, baking powder, salt and vanilla until smooth. Stir in raisins and pecans. Spread evenly over crust.

3. Return to oven and bake just until top is set and golden, 23 to 28 minutes. Let cool completely in pan on rack. Cut into squares.

Variations

Use all raisins or all pecans.

Replace raisins with dried cranberries.

Replace pecans with walnuts.

No-Bake Bars and Squares

In this chapter, I've tried to expand the horizon of no-bake bars beyond the all-time favorite, Rice Krispies Squares. No-bake bars are perfect for hot summer days when it's too hot to turn the oven on. They're also great to make when there's already something in the oven. No-bake bars usually consist of a warm mixture made on top of the stove, mixed with yummy, crunchy ingredients like cereal, nuts, dried fruit and marshmallows. The entire concoction is simply pressed into a pan and left to set for about 30 minutes. All you do is cut to eat.

In most cases, no-bake bars are quick and easy to prepare, with relatively few ingredients, which are readily available. Because they aren't baked and cooking time is short, you get to enjoy them much faster than most bars, which also means they're great to make with kids. And they don't use many dishes, which reduces washing-up time.

No-bake bars are generally cut into larger pieces than baked bars. They are firm and not as delicate or crumbly as baked bars. They usually keep for several weeks without freezing — if they're well hidden.

◄ *Triple-Layer Chocolate Peanut Butter Bars*

Triple-Layer Chocolate Peanut Butter Bars

If you're someone who gets cravings for chocolate and peanut butter, these chewy bars fit the bill. Keep a pan in the refrigerator at all times. Just like peanut butter cookies, they're great with a glass of milk.

MAKES 20 TO 54 BARS (see Cutting Guide, page 10)

- **Preparation: 30 minutes**
- **Cooking: 10 minutes**
- **Chilling: 3 hours**
- **Freezing: excellent**

TIPS

Always sift confectioner's (icing) sugar before using to get rid of any lumps that have formed during storage.

Most no-bake bars keep well for 1 week in the refrigerator or up to 3 months in the freezer. Be sure they are well wrapped and airtight.

- **13- by 9-inch (3 L) cake pan, lined with greased aluminum foil or waxed paper**

BASE

¾ cup	butter	175 mL
⅓ cup	granulated sugar	75 mL
⅓ cup	unsweetened cocoa powder, sifted	75 mL
2	eggs, beaten	2
2½ cups	graham wafer crumbs	625 mL
¾ cup	sweetened fine or medium coconut	175 mL
¾ cup	finely chopped peanuts	175 mL

FILLING

1 cup	creamy peanut butter	250 mL
⅓ cup	butter	75 mL
3 cups	confectioner's (icing) sugar, sifted	750 mL
⅓ cup	half-and-half (10%) cream	75 mL

TOPPING

8	squares (1 oz/28 g each) semi-sweet chocolate, chopped	8
3 tbsp	butter	45 mL
½ cup	finely chopped peanuts	125 mL

1. *Base:* In a large heavy saucepan, melt butter over low heat. Add sugar, cocoa and eggs and cook, stirring constantly, until mixture starts to thicken, about 5 minutes. Remove from heat. Stir in graham wafer crumbs, coconut and peanuts, mixing well. Press evenly into prepared pan. Refrigerate until cold, about 30 minutes.

2. *Filling:* Meanwhile, in a clean saucepan over low heat, melt peanut butter and butter, stirring until smooth. Remove from heat. Add confectioner's sugar alternately with cream, beating until smooth and creamy. Spread evenly over base. Refrigerate until firm, about 2 hours.

3. *Topping:* In a small saucepan over low heat, melt chocolate and butter over, stirring until smooth. Pour over filling and quickly spread to cover evenly. Sprinkle peanuts evenly over top. Refrigerate until chocolate is set, about 30 minutes. Cut into bars. Store bars in refrigerator for up to 3 weeks.

Chocolate Ginger Bars

Two different looks from one bar. You can leave them plain or dust with confectioner's sugar. Both taste great.

MAKES 18 TO 48 BARS
(see Cutting Guide, page 10)

- **Preparation: 15 minutes**
- **Cooking: 5 minutes**
- **Chilling: 2 hours**
- **Freezing: not recommended**

- **8-inch (2 L) square cake pan, lined with greased aluminum foil or waxed paper**

1/3 cup	butter	75 mL
8	squares (1 oz/28 g each) semi-sweet chocolate, chopped	8
3 tbsp	corn syrup	45 mL
8 oz	ginger cookies, crushed	250 g
1/4 cup	chopped crystallized ginger	50 mL
	Confectioner's (icing) sugar, optional	

1. In a heavy saucepan over low heat, combine butter, chocolate and corn syrup. Heat, stirring constantly, until chocolate is melted and mixture is smooth. Remove from heat. Set aside.

2. In a food processor, chop cookies to make coarse crumbs. Measure 2 cups (500 mL). Stir into chocolate mixture along with ginger, mixing well. Spread evenly in prepared pan. Refrigerate until firm, about 2 hours. Cut into bars. Dust with confectioner's sugar, if desired.

Mix 'n' Match Chocolate Bars

I love this combination of sweet chocolate and crunchy, salty pretzels and peanuts.

MAKES 20 TO 54 BARS
(see Cutting Guide, page 10)

- **Preparation: 15 minutes**
- **Cooking: 5 minutes**
- **Chilling: 30 minutes**
- **Freezing: not recommended**

- **13- by 9-inch (3 L) cake pan, lined with greased aluminum foil or waxed paper**

3 cups	semi-sweet chocolate chips	750 mL
2 tbsp	butter	25 mL
4 cups	miniature marshmallows	1 L
1 1/4 cups	candy-coated chocolate pieces (Smarties or M&M's)	300 mL
1 cup	pretzel sticks chopped (1/2-inch/1 cm pieces)	250 mL
1/2 cup	chopped peanuts	125 mL

1. In a saucepan over low heat, melt chocolate chips and butter, stirring constantly, until smooth. Remove from heat. Let cool until just slightly warm.

2. In a large bowl, combine marshmallows, candies, pretzels and peanuts. Stir in chocolate mixture, mixing well. Press evenly into prepared pan. Chill until firm, about 30 minutes. Cut into bars.

Peanut Butter Honey Date Crisps

Besides making wonderful sandwiches, peanut butter is a favorite ingredient for bakers. It gives bars and other treats a rich, nutty flavor.

MAKES 20 TO 54 BARS OR 24 SQUARES
(see Cutting Guide, page 10)

- **Preparation: 10 minutes**
- **Cooking: 5 minutes**
- **Chilling: 1 hour**
- **Freezing: excellent**

- **13- by 9-inch (3 L) cake pan, greased**

½ cup	liquid honey	125 mL
½ cup	creamy peanut butter	125 mL
⅓ cup	packed brown sugar	75 mL
3 cups	crisp rice cereal	750 mL
1 cup	finely chopped dates	250 mL
½ cup	chopped peanuts	125 mL
3 tbsp	sesame seeds, toasted	45 mL

1. In a heavy saucepan over low heat, combine honey, peanut butter and brown sugar. Heat, stirring, until smooth.

2. In a large bowl, combine cereal, dates and peanuts. Stir in honey mixture, mixing well. Press firmly into prepared pan. Sprinkle with sesame seeds. Chill until set, about 1 hour. Cut into bars or squares.

Chocolate Caramel Crisps

These bars save you time because the flavor combination of chocolate and caramel is already in the chocolate bar. You don't need to mix it up.

MAKES 20 TO 54 BARS OR 24 SQUARES
(see Cutting Guide, page 10)

- **Preparation: 10 minutes**
- **Cooking: 5 minutes**
- **Chilling: 1 hour**
- **Freezing: excellent**

- **13- by 9-inch (3 L) cake pan, greased**

1 cup	corn syrup	125 mL
⅓ cup	butter	75 mL
3 cups	crisp rice cereal	750 mL
1 cup	corn flakes cereal, slightly crushed	250 mL
1 cup	chocolate-coated caramel bars, chopped	250 mL
½ cup	chopped cashews	125 mL

1. In a large saucepan over medium heat, combine corn syrup and butter. Heat, stirring, until butter is melted and mixture is smooth. Continue cooking, stirring often, until mixture begins to thicken, about 4 minutes. Remove from heat.

2. Stir in rice and corn flakes cereals, caramel bars and cashews, mixing well. Press firmly into prepared pan. Chill until firm, about 1 hour. Cut into bars or squares.

Chocolate Peanut Butter Bars

These are chewy like a chocolate peanut butter candy bar that's loaded with nuts. Just like peanuts, these bars can quickly become addictive.

MAKES 20 TO 54 BARS (see Cutting Guide, page 10)

- Preparation: 10 minutes
- Cooking: 4 minutes
- Chilling: 1 hour
- Freezing: excellent

> • **13- by 9-inch (3 L) cake pan, greased**

1²⁄₃ cups	milk chocolate chips	400 mL
1 cup	corn syrup	250 mL
²⁄₃ cup	creamy peanut butter	150 mL
2 cups	quick-cooking rolled oats, toasted (see Tip, page 93)	500 mL
2 cups	peanuts	500 mL

1. In a large heavy saucepan over medium heat, combine chocolate chips, corn syrup and peanut butter. Heat, stirring, until mixture comes to a boil. Boil, stirring constantly, until mixture thickens slightly, about 2 minutes. Remove from heat. Stir in toasted oats and peanuts, mixing well. Press firmly into prepared pan. Chill until firm, about 1 hour. Cut into bars.

Date and Almond Crisps

Most no-bake bars fit equally well in the kids' section. Make them together for some family fun. These are a nice backpack or school lunch bar that they can share with friends.

MAKES 18 TO 48 BARS OR 16 TO 36 SQUARES (see Cutting Guide, page 10)

- Preparation: 15 minutes
- Cooking: 10 minutes
- Chilling: 1 hour
- Freezing: excellent

> • **9-inch (2.5 L) square cake pan, greased**

³⁄₄ cup	butter	175 mL
²⁄₃ cup	packed brown sugar	150 mL
1¹⁄₂ cups	chopped dates	375 mL
1	square (1 oz/28 g) semi-sweet chocolate, chopped	1
2³⁄₄ cups	crisp rice cereal	675 mL
³⁄₄ cup	chopped almonds	175 mL

1. In a large heavy saucepan over medium heat, combine butter, brown sugar, dates and chocolate. Cook, stirring often, until thickened, about 10 minutes. Remove from heat. Stir in cereal and almonds, mixing well. Press firmly into prepared pan. Chill until firm, about 1 hour. Cut into bars or squares.

Variations
Replace almonds with walnuts or pecans.

Replace ¹⁄₂ cup (125 mL) dates with dried apricots.

Cool Cranberry Pistachio Squares

The red and green layers on a dark chocolate base make a colorful and tasty square. These look particularly festive on Christmas cookie trays. Cut them into triangles for a different look.

MAKES 16 TO 36 SQUARES (see Cutting Guide, page 10)

- Preparation: 15 minutes
- Cooking: 5 minutes
- Chilling: 2 hours
- Freezing: excellent

TIP

White chocolate must be a good quality or it will be difficult to melt. It never pays to scrimp when it comes to ingredients for baking. One ingredient that's not up to par can ruin your finished product.

- **9-inch (2.5 L) square cake pan, lined with aluminum foil**

1/3 cup	butter	75 mL
7	squares (1 oz/28 g each) semi-sweet chocolate, chopped	7
3 tbsp	corn syrup	45 mL
2 cups	chocolate wafer crumbs	500 mL
1 1/3 cups	white chocolate chips	325 mL
2/3 cup	chopped dried cranberries	150 mL
1/4 cup	chopped pistachios	50 mL

1. In a saucepan over low heat, combine butter, chocolate and corn syrup. Heat, stirring constantly, until chocolate is melted and mixture is smooth. Remove from heat. Stir in chocolate wafer crumbs, mixing well. Spread evenly in prepared pan.

2. In a saucepan over low heat, melt white chocolate chips, stirring constantly, until smooth. Stir in cranberries. Spread evenly over base. Sprinkle pistachios over top. Refrigerate until chocolate is firm, about 2 hours. Cut into squares.

Variations

For an all-chocolate treat, use semi-sweet chocolate chips instead of the white.

Replace dried cranberries with finely chopped candied pineapple.

Chocolate Trail Mix Bars

Each bite tastes like a combination of a chocolate bar mixed with trail mix. How can you go wrong with these two favorites?

MAKES 18 TO 48 BARS (see Cutting Guide, page 10)

- Preparation: 15 minutes
- Cooking: 3 minutes
- Chilling: 1 hour
- Freezing: not recommended

- **9-inch (2.5 L) square cake pan, lined with greased aluminum foil or waxed paper**

2½ cups	quick-cooking rolled oats	625 mL
1 cup	sweetened flaked coconut	250 mL
1 cup	sliced almonds, toasted	250 mL
½ cup	dried cranberries	125 mL
½ cup	chopped dried pineapple or mango	125 mL
½ cup	butter	125 mL
½ cup	milk	125 mL
1⅓ cups	granulated sugar	325 mL
⅓ cup	unsweetened cocoa powder, sifted	75 mL
¾ tsp	vanilla	3 mL

1. In a large bowl, combine oats, coconut, almonds, dried cranberries and dried pineapple Set aside.
2. In a heavy saucepan, combine butter, milk and sugar. Bring to a boil over medium heat, stirring until smooth. Remove from heat. Stir in cocoa and vanilla, mixing well. Stir into dry ingredients, mixing well. Press evenly into prepared pan. Refrigerate until firm, about 1 hour. Cut into bars.

Crispy Nougat Bars

You don't have to spend all day in the kitchen to make fantastic bars. Just don't tell anyone how easy these are.

MAKES 18 TO 48 BARS (see Cutting Guide, page 10)

- Preparation: 5 minutes
- Cooking: 5 minutes
- Freezing: excellent

- **8-inch (2 L) square cake pan, greased**

3	chocolate caramel nougat bars, such as Snickers or Mars (2 oz/58 g each), chopped	3
¼ cup	butter	50 mL
3 cups	crisp rice cereal	750 mL

1. In a large saucepan over low heat, melt chocolate bars and butter, stirring constantly, until smooth. Add cereal and mix until thoroughly coated. Press firmly into prepared pan. Let set for 30 minutes. Cut into bars.

Variation
Add ½ cup (125 mL) chopped peanuts or almonds.

Chocolate Nut Candy Crunch

These crunchy treats make a welcome hostess gift any time of the year.

**MAKES ABOUT
2 DOZEN PIECES OR
1½ LB (750 G) CANDY**

- **Preparation: 15 minutes**
- **Cooking: 6 minutes**
- **Chilling: 2 hours**
- **Freezing: not recommended**

TIP

Try using salted cashews and almonds in this recipe for a pleasantly different taste.

- **9-inch (2.5 L) square cake pan, lined with greased aluminum foil**

2 cups	semi-sweet chocolate chips	500 mL
¾ cup	coarsely chopped cashews	175 mL
¾ cup	slivered almonds	175 mL
½ cup	granulated sugar	125 mL
½ cup	butter	125 mL
2 tbsp	corn syrup	25 mL

1. Sprinkle chocolate chips evenly over bottom of prepared pan. In a large skillet over low heat, combine cashews, almonds, sugar, butter and corn syrup. Cook, stirring, until butter is melted. Increase heat to medium and cook, stirring constantly, until mixture comes together and turns light golden, about 5 minutes. Pour over chocolate chips. Spread evenly in pan.

2. Let stand for 1 hour then chill until chocolate is firm, about 1 hour. Remove from pan. Peel off foil. Break into pieces. Store in a cool, dry place.

Caramel Chews

This tasty combination of crisp cereals, chewy coconut, tart dried cranberries and crunchy cashews is held together with creamy caramel.

**MAKES 18 TO
48 BARS OR 16 TO
36 SQUARES
(see Cutting Guide,
page 10)**

- **Preparation: 5 minutes**
- **Cooking: 10 minutes**
- **Chilling: 1 hour**
- **Freezing: excellent**

- **9-inch (2.5 L) square cake pan, greased**

11 oz	soft caramels, unwrapped (43)	330 g
3 tbsp	half-and-half (10%) cream	45 mL
2 cups	crisp rice cereal	500 mL
1 cup	corn flakes cereal, slightly crushed	250 mL
¾ cup	sweetened flaked coconut	175 mL
½ cup	chopped cashews	125 mL
½ cup	dried cranberries	125 mL

1. In a heavy saucepan over low heat, combine caramels and cream. Heat, stirring constantly, until caramels are melted and mixture is smooth.

2. In a large bowl, combine rice and corn flakes cereals, coconut, cashews and dried cranberries. Stir in caramel mixture, mixing well. Press firmly into prepared pan. Chill until firm, about 1 hour. Cut into bars or squares.

Inside-Out Nanaimo Bars

Reverse the dark and light colors of this popular no-bake bar for a different look and taste.

MAKES 18 TO 48 BARS (see Cutting Guide, page 10)

- **Preparation: 30 minutes**
- **Cooking: 5 minutes**
- **Chilling: 3½ hours**
- **Freezing: excellent**

TIPS

White chocolate can burn quickly, so be sure to use a heavy saucepan, low heat and stir constantly. If the element seems to be too hot, take the pan off the heat and continue to stir until the mixture is smooth.

Custard powder is usually sold in cans or envelopes. Bird's, Horne's and Dr. Oetker are popular brands. If you can't find it, substitute an equal quantity of vanilla pudding powder (the kind that you have to cook, not instant).

- **8-inch (2 L) square cake pan, lined with greased aluminum foil or waxed paper**

BASE

¼ cup	butter	50 mL
2	squares (1 oz/28 g each) white chocolate, chopped	2
1	egg, beaten	1
2 cups	vanilla wafer crumbs	500 mL
½ cup	sweetened fine or medium coconut	125 mL
⅓ cup	finely chopped walnuts	75 mL

FILLING

⅓ cup	butter	75 mL
½ cup	unsweetened cocoa powder, sifted	125 mL
1½ cups	confectioner's (icing) sugar, sifted	375 mL
2 tbsp	custard powder, sifted (see Tips, left)	25 mL
¼ cup	half-and-half (10%) cream	50 mL

TOPPING

4	squares (1 oz/28 g each) white chocolate, chopped	4
1 tbsp	vegetable oil	15 mL

1. *Base:* In a heavy saucepan over low heat, melt butter and white chocolate, stirring until smooth. Stir in beaten egg. Heat, stirring, for 1 minute. Remove from heat. Stir in vanilla wafer crumbs, coconut and walnuts, mixing well. Press evenly into prepared pan. Chill until cold, about 30 minutes.

2. *Filling:* Meanwhile, in saucepan, melt butter over low heat. Add cocoa, stirring until smooth. In a bowl, combine confectioner's sugar and custard powder. Add cocoa mixture and cream. Using an electric mixer on medium speed, beat until smooth and creamy. Spread over chilled base. Refrigerate until firm, about 2 hours.

3. *Topping:* In a small saucepan over low heat, combine white chocolate and oil. Heat, stirring constantly, until smooth. Pour over filling, quickly spreading to cover evenly. Refrigerate until chocolate is set, about 30 minutes. Cut into bars. Store bars in refrigerator for up to 3 weeks.

Cappuccino Nanaimo Bars

Nanaimo bars, which originated in Nanaimo, British Columbia, have become a favorite around the world. Not only do they taste delicious, but they keep extremely well in the refrigerator or freezer.

MAKES 18 TO 48 BARS (see Cutting Guide, page 10)

- Preparation: 30 minutes
- Cooking: 5 minutes
- Chilling: 3 hours
- Freezing: excellent

TIPS

I have specified sweetened coconut because it seems to be more readily available than the unsweetened variety. But sweetened and unsweetened coconut can be used interchangeably in any recipe to suit your preference.

Replace espresso powder with double the amount of instant coffee granules.

Look for finely ground coffee granules so they will dissolve easily, or crush them with the back of a spoon to make them finer.

Lining the pan with foil or waxed paper makes it easier to remove the bars.

- **8-inch (2 L) square cake pan, lined with greased aluminum foil or waxed paper (see Tips, left)**

BASE

⅔ cup	butter	150 mL
⅓ cup	unsweetened cocoa powder, sifted	75 mL
¼ cup	granulated sugar	50 mL
1 tbsp	instant espresso powder	15 mL
1	egg, beaten	1
1½ cups	graham wafer crumbs	375 mL
¾ cup	sweetened flaked coconut	175 mL
¾ cup	finely chopped almonds	175 mL

FILLING

2 cups	confectioner's (icing) sugar	500 mL
¼ cup	butter, softened	50 mL
1 tbsp	instant espresso powder	15 mL
2 tbsp	hot water	25 mL

TOPPING

2 tbsp	butter	25 mL
1 tbsp	instant espresso powder	15 mL
4	squares (1 oz/28 g each) semi-sweet chocolate, chopped	4

1. *Base:* In a saucepan over low heat, combine butter, cocoa, sugar, espresso powder and egg. Cook, stirring constantly, until mixture starts to thicken, about 5 minutes. Remove from heat. Mix in graham wafer crumbs, coconut and almonds. Press evenly into prepared pan. Refrigerate until cold, about 30 minutes.

2. *Filling:* Meanwhile, in a bowl, using an electric mixer on low speed, beat half of the confectioner's sugar and the butter until blended. Mix espresso powder and hot water until dissolved. On medium speed, beat espresso powder into butter mixture along with remaining confectioner's sugar until smooth and creamy. Spread evenly over base. Refrigerate until firm, about 2 hours. Lift out of pan and transfer to a cutting board.

3. *Topping:* In a saucepan over low heat, combine butter, espresso powder and chocolate. Heat, stirring constantly, until smooth. Pour over filling and quickly spread to cover evenly. Refrigerate until chocolate is set, about 30 minutes. Cut into bars. Store bars in refrigerator for up to 3 weeks.

Cake Mix Bars and Squares

The convenience of a cake mix makes it especially quick and easy to bake bars and squares. Not only does it eliminate the need to measure many ingredients, but it also reduces the room for error and saves on washing up. You can use a cake mix to form the base of layered bars or to provide the batter to hold crunchy, chunky ingredients in single-layer bars. And, like other bars, those made with cake mix can be dressed up with a frosting (ready-to-serve for speed and convenience) or a dusting of confectioner's sugar.

I'm sure after you try a few bars made with cake mix, you'll agree they're quick, easy and delicious — a perfect choice for spur-of-the-moment baking. With a chocolate and a white mix on hand, there's no excuse for not baking.

Strawberry Cheesecake Squares

Cut these into large squares for a dessert or into bite-size morsels for a cookie tray.

**MAKES 24 SQUARES
(see Cutting Guide, page 10)**

- **Preparation: 25 minutes**
- **Baking: 45 minutes**
- **Chilling: 3 hours**
- **Freezing: excellent**

TIP

Cooking spray is an easy way to grease baking pans. Don't overdo it though — a fine spray will do the trick.

- **Preheat oven to 350°F (180°C)**
- **13- by 9-inch (3 L) cake pan, greased**

CRUST

1	pkg (18.25 oz/515 g) white cake mix	1
¾ cup	finely chopped almonds	175 mL
¾ cup	cold butter, cubed	175 mL

FILLING

2	pkg (8 oz/250 g each) cream cheese, softened	2
⅔ cup	granulated sugar	150 mL
2	eggs	2
½ tsp	almond extract	2 mL
1 cup	strawberry jam	250 mL
¾ cup	sliced almonds	175 mL

1. *Crust:* In a bowl, combine cake mix and chopped almonds. Using a pastry blender, 2 knives or your fingers, cut in butter until mixture resembles coarse crumbs. Set aside 1 cup (250 mL) for topping. Press remainder evenly into prepared pan. Bake in preheated oven until light golden, about 15 minutes.

2. *Filling:* In a large bowl, using an electric mixer on medium speed, beat cream cheese, sugar, eggs and almond extract until smooth and creamy, about 3 minutes. Spread evenly over hot crust.

3. Return to oven and bake until set, about 15 minutes longer. Let cool in pan on rack for 10 minutes. Stir jam until smooth and spread evenly over filling. Stir sliced almonds into reserved crust mixture. Sprinkle evenly over jam. Bake until top is golden, about 15 minutes. Let cool completely in pan on rack. Chill until set, about 3 hours, or overnight before cutting into squares. Refrigerate leftover cheesecake squares for up to 3 days.

Variations

Replace strawberry jam with raspberry, apricot or cherry.
Replace almond extract with vanilla.

Cherry Cheesecake Bars

Enjoy bite-size cheesecakes for dessert or a snack. Vary the flavor to suit your own family's favorites.

MAKES 20 TO 54 BARS (see Cutting Guide, page 10)

- **Preparation: 20 minutes**
- **Baking: 50 minutes**
- **Freezing: excellent**

TIP

For easy drizzling, melt butter in a glass measuring cup with a spout.

- **Preheat oven to 350°F (180°C)**
- **13- by 9-inch (3 L) cake pan, greased**

CRUST

1	pkg (18.25 oz/515 g) white cake mix, divided	1
½ cup	corn flakes cereal crumbs	125 mL
1	egg, beaten	1
½ cup	butter, melted	125 mL

FILLING

2	pkg (8 oz/250 g each) cream cheese, softened	2
⅓ cup	granulated sugar	75 mL
2	eggs	2
1 tsp	grated lemon zest	5 mL
1 tbsp	freshly squeezed lemon juice	15 mL
1	can (19 oz/540 mL) cherry pie filling	1

TOPPING

½ cup	chopped pecans	125 mL
½ tsp	cinnamon	2 mL
¼ cup	butter, melted	50 mL

1. *Crust:* Set aside ½ cup (125 mL) cake mix for topping. In a large bowl, combine remaining cake mix, corn flakes crumbs, egg and melted butter, mixing until well blended. Press evenly into bottom and slightly up sides of prepared pan. Chill while preparing filling.

2. *Filling:* In a large bowl, using an electric mixer on medium speed, beat cream cheese and sugar until blended, about 3 minutes. Add eggs, one at a time, beating thoroughly after each addition. Beat in lemon zest and juice. Spread evenly over crust. Dollop spoonfuls of cherry pie filling over cheese mixture.

3. *Topping:* In a bowl, combine reserved cake mix, pecans and cinnamon. Sprinkle over filling. Drizzle with melted butter.

4. Bake in preheated oven until topping is just set, 40 to 50 minutes. Let cool completely in pan on rack. Refrigerate until serving. Cut into bars. Refrigerate leftover bars for up to 3 days.

Chocolate Pecan Bars

One pan goes a long way, so this recipe is a good choice for gift giving.

MAKES 36 TO 66 BARS (see **Cutting Guide**, page 10)

- **Preparation: 20 minutes**
- **Baking: 47 minutes**
- **Cooking: 5 minutes**
- **Freezing: excellent**

TIPS

If you don't do much baking, shop at bulk stores for specialty items and smaller quantities. Remember to store nuts in the freezer.

Purchase good-quality shiny metal pans for baking. They bake evenly and don't rust. Dark metal pans can cause overbrowning of edges before the center of the pan is cooked. If using glass dishes, decrease the oven temperature by 25°F (10°C).

These bars will store better if you omit the chocolate drizzle.

- **Preheat oven to 350°F (180°C)**
- **17- by 11- by 1-inch (3 L) jelly roll pan, greased**

CRUST

1	pkg (18.25 oz/515 g) white cake mix	1
2/3 cup	butter, melted	150 mL

TOPPING

5	squares (1 oz/28 g each) semi-sweet chocolate, chopped	5
1 cup	corn syrup	250 mL
1 cup	granulated sugar	250 mL
3	eggs	3
1 tsp	vanilla	5 mL
2½ cups	chopped pecans	625 mL

DRIZZLE, OPTIONAL

2	squares (1 oz/28 g each) semi-sweet chocolate, melted	2

1. *Crust:* In a large bowl, combine cake mix and melted butter, mixing until well blended. Press evenly into prepared pan. Bake in preheated oven until light golden, 10 to 12 minutes.

2. *Topping:* In a saucepan over low heat, combine chocolate and corn syrup. Heat, stirring constantly, until smooth. Remove from heat. Whisk in sugar, eggs and vanilla until blended. Stir in pecans. Spread evenly over warm crust.

3. Return to oven and bake until filling is set around edges and slightly soft in the center, 30 to 35 minutes. Let cool completely in pan on rack.

4. *Drizzle (if using):* Drizzle melted chocolate randomly over bars. Chill until chocolate is set, about 30 minutes. Cut into bars.

Candy Bar Bars

The name says it all. These are just like a candy bar.

MAKES 20 TO 54 BARS (see Cutting Guide, page 10)

- **Preparation: 25 minutes**
- **Baking: 20 minutes**
- **Cooking: 5 minutes**
- **Cooling: 2 hours**
- **Freezing: excellent**

TIP

There are several brands of soft caramels. Choose ones that are easy to unwrap, unless you have kids to do that job for you.

- **Preheat oven to 350°F (180°C)**
- **13- by 9-inch (3 L) cake pan, greased**

CRUST

1	pkg (18.25 oz/515 g) white cake mix	1
¾ cup	butter, melted	175 mL

FILLING

14 oz	soft caramels, unwrapped (about 60)	425 g
⅓ cup	evaporated milk	75 mL
⅓ cup	butter	75 mL
1⅔ cups	confectioner's (icing) sugar, sifted	400 mL
1 cup	chopped pecans	250 mL

GLAZE

1 cup	semi-sweet chocolate chips	250 mL

1. *Crust:* In a large bowl, combine cake mix and melted butter, mixing until well blended. Press evenly into prepared pan. Bake in preheated oven until light golden, 15 to 20 minutes.

2. *Filling:* In a saucepan over low heat, combine caramels and evaporated milk. Heat, stirring constantly, until caramels are melted and mixture is smooth. Stir in butter until melted. Remove from heat. Stir in confectioner's sugar and pecans, mixing well. Spread evenly over crust. Let cool until set, about 1 hour.

3. *Glaze:* In a small saucepan over low heat, melt chocolate chips, stirring constantly, until smooth. Drop by spoonfuls over filling and spread evenly. Chill until chocolate is set, about 1 hour. Cut into bars.

Variation

Peanuts, or a combination of peanuts and pecans, also work well in this bar.

Chewy Coconut Nut Bars

These bars are quick to make and a treat to eat.

MAKES 20 TO 54 BARS (see Cutting Guide, page 10)

- **Preparation: 20 minutes**
- **Baking: 45 minutes**
- **Freezing: excellent**

TIPS

I prefer flaked or shredded coconut. Desiccated coconut is very fine and results in drier baked products.

If you like the topping to be a little less sweet, add 1 tbsp (15 mL) lemon juice.

Pecans or walnuts work well in this recipe.

- **Preheat oven to 350°F (180°C)**
- **13- by 9-inch (3 L) cake pan, greased**

CRUST

1	pkg (18.25 oz/515 g) white cake mix	1
½ cup	butter, melted	125 mL

TOPPING

4	eggs	4
1¾ cups	packed brown sugar	325 mL
¼ cup	all-purpose flour	50 mL
2 tsp	baking powder	10 mL
1 tsp	vanilla	5 mL
1½ cups	chopped nuts (see Tips, left)	375 mL
1 cup	sweetened flaked coconut	250 mL

1. *Crust:* In a large bowl, combine cake mix and melted butter, mixing until well blended. Press evenly into prepared pan. Bake in preheated oven until light golden, about 15 minutes.

2. *Topping:* In a bowl, whisk eggs and brown sugar until blended. Whisk in flour, baking powder and vanilla, mixing well. Stir in nuts and coconut. Spread evenly over warm crust.

3. Return to oven and bake until set and golden, 25 to 30 minutes. Let cool completely in pan on rack. Cut into bars.

Toffee Chocolate Bars

Layers of crunchy toffee bits, creamy caramel and chocolate cover a crisp, cookie-like base, making every bite a sensation.

MAKES 20 TO 54 BARS (see Cutting Guide, page 10)

- **Preparation: 20 minutes**
- **Cooking: 10 minutes**
- **Baking: 30 minutes**
- **Cooling: 1 hour**
- **Freezing: excellent**

TIPS

The toffee bits get softer if you freeze these bars. We love them both ways — frozen and soft or unfrozen and crunchy. Take your pick.

Toffee bits are available in bags. They are broken pieces of the toffee part of Heath or Skor bars (no chocolate).

Don't leave the filling unattended on the stove, even for a minute. It burns very quickly.

- **Preheat oven to 350°F (180°C)**
- **13- by 9-inch (3 L) cake pan, greased**

CRUST

1	pkg (18.25 oz/515 g) white cake mix	1
2 tbsp	packed brown sugar	25 mL
½ cup	butter, melted	125 mL

FILLING

1	can (10 oz/300 mL) sweetened condensed milk	1
2 tbsp	butter	25 mL

TOPPING

1⅔ cups	semi-sweet chocolate chips	400 mL
1 cup	toffee bits (see Tips, left)	250 mL

1. *Crust:* In a bowl, combine cake mix, brown sugar and melted butter, mixing until well blended. Press evenly into prepared pan. Bake in preheated oven until light golden, about 15 minutes. Let cool in pan on rack while preparing filling.

2. *Filling:* In a heavy saucepan over low heat, combine sweetened condensed milk and butter. Heat, stirring constantly, until thickened, 5 to 10 minutes. Spread evenly over crust.

3. Return to oven and bake until top is golden, 10 to 15 minutes. Let cool in pan on rack for 1 hour.

4. *Topping:* In a heavy saucepan over low heat, melt chocolate chips, stirring until smooth. (You can also do this in a microwave on Medium for 2 minutes.) Drop by spoonfuls over filling and spread evenly. Sprinkle toffee bits on top, pressing lightly into chocolate. Let cool completely. If necessary, chill briefly to set chocolate. Cut into bars.

Variation
Use milk chocolate chips in place of semi-sweet.

Cranberry Pecan Bars

You'll love this combination of sweet pecan pie with tart cranberries in an easy-to-eat, bite-size bar.

MAKES 20 TO 54 BARS (see Cutting Guide, page 10)

- **Preparation: 20 minutes**
- **Baking: 50 minutes**
- **Freezing: excellent**

TIP

The crust will puff slightly during baking but settles down again on cooling.

- **Preheat oven to 350°F (180°C)**
- **13- by 9-inch (3 L) cake pan, greased**

CRUST

1	pkg (18.25 oz/515 g) white cake mix	1
½ cup	butter, melted	125 mL

TOPPING

4	eggs	4
1 cup	granulated sugar	250 mL
1 cup	corn syrup	250 mL
3 tbsp	butter, melted	45 mL
1½ cups	coarsely chopped pecans	375 mL
¾ cup	dried cranberries	175 mL

1. *Crust:* In a large bowl, combine cake mix and melted butter. Mix until well blended. Press evenly into prepared pan. Bake in preheated oven until light golden, about 15 minutes. Let cool in pan on rack for 5 minutes before adding topping.

2. *Topping:* In a bowl, whisk eggs, sugar, syrup and melted butter until blended. Stir in pecans and dried cranberries. Pour evenly over crust.

3. Return to oven and bake until set and golden, 30 to 35 minutes. Let cool completely in pan on rack. Cut into bars.

> ### Variation
> Replace dried cranberries with chocolate chips.

Raspberry Meringue Bars

A chewy meringue topping with lots of nuts and coconut covers a layer of jam on a shortbread-like base.

**MAKES 20 TO 54 BARS
(see Cutting Guide, page 10)**

- **Preparation: 20 minutes**
- **Baking: 40 minutes**
- **Freezing: excellent**

TIPS

I have specified sweetened coconut because it seems to be more readily available than the unsweetened variety. But sweetened and unsweetened coconut can be used interchangeably in any recipe to suit your preference.

Before beating egg whites, wipe the bowl with the cut surface of a lemon to make sure it's free of grease.

Cut these bars with a hot, damp knife.

- **Preheat oven to 350°F (180°C)**
- **13- by 9-inch (3 L) cake pan, greased**

CRUST

1	pkg (18.25 oz/515 g) white cake mix	1
½ cup	butter, melted	125 mL
2	egg yolks	2

TOPPING

1 cup	raspberry jam	250 mL
½ cup	sweetened flaked coconut	125 mL
2	egg whites (see Tips, left)	2
½ cup	granulated sugar	125 mL
1 cup	chopped walnuts	250 mL

1. *Crust:* In a large bowl, using an electric mixer on low speed, beat cake mix, melted butter and egg yolks until well blended, about 1 minute. Press evenly into prepared pan. Bake in preheated oven until very light golden, 12 to 15 minutes.

2. *Topping:* Spread jam evenly over warm crust. Sprinkle coconut evenly over top. In a small bowl, using an electric mixer with clean beaters on high speed, beat egg whites until frothy. Gradually beat in sugar, beating until stiff peaks form. Fold in walnuts. Drop by spoonfuls over coconut and spread evenly.

3. Return to oven and bake until topping is light golden, 20 to 25 minutes. Let cool completely in pan on rack. Cut into bars.

Variation
Try other flavors of jam and nuts, such as apricot jam with hazelnuts.

Pecan Toffee Bars

This easy-to-make treat is quite sweet and will be very popular.

MAKES 20 TO 54 BARS (see Cutting Guide, page 10)

- **Preparation: 15 minutes**
- **Baking: 50 minutes**
- **Freezing: excellent**

TIPS

Toffee bits are available in bags. They're broken pieces of the toffee part of Heath or Skor bars (no chocolate).

Cut cooled bars and pack them in a single layer to freeze. If the bars are precut, you can thaw just the number you want to serve.

A drizzle of melted chocolate makes these bars special. If they have been frozen, add the drizzle just before serving.

- **Preheat oven to 350°F (180°C)**
- **13- by 9-inch (3 L) cake pan, greased**

CRUST

1	pkg (18.25 oz/515 g) white cake mix	1
½ cup	butter, melted	125 mL
1	egg, beaten	1

TOPPING

1	can (10 oz/300 mL) sweetened condensed milk	1
1	egg	1
1¼ cups	chopped pecans	300 mL
1⅓ cups	toffee bits (see Tips, left)	325 mL

1. *Crust:* In a large bowl, using an electric mixer on low speed, beat cake mix, melted butter and egg until well blended, about 1 minute. Press evenly into prepared pan. Bake in preheated oven until light golden, 15 to 20 minutes.

2. *Topping:* In a bowl, whisk sweetened condensed milk and egg until smooth. Stir in pecans and toffee bits. Pour evenly over crust.

3. Return to oven and bake until topping is set, 25 to 30 minutes. Let cool completely in pan on rack. Cut into bars.

Variation

Replace toffee bits with chopped crunchy chocolate covered toffee bars, such as Skor or Heath.

Chewy Peanut Candy Bars

These bars are a big hit with kids, young and old.

MAKES 40 TO 48 BARS
(see Cutting Guide, page 10)

- **Preparation: 15 minutes**
- **Baking: 17 minutes**
- **Freezing: excellent**

TIP

To retain the fresh taste in baked goods, buy peanut butter just as you need it.

- **Preheat oven to 350°F (180°C)**
- **15- by 10- by 1-inch (2 L) jelly roll pan, greased**

CRUST

1	pkg (18.25 oz/515 g) white cake mix	1
½ cup	butter, softened	125 mL
1	egg, beaten	1

TOPPING

3½ cups	miniature marshmallows	875 mL
¾ cup	packed brown sugar	175 mL
¾ cup	corn syrup	175 mL
¾ cup	creamy peanut butter	175 mL
2 cups	crisp rice cereal	500 mL
1¾ cups	salted peanuts	425 mL
1¼ cups	miniature candy-coated chocolate pieces (M&M's)	300 mL

1. *Crust:* In a large bowl, using an electric mixer on low speed, beat cake mix, butter and egg until well blended and crumbly, about 1 minute. Press evenly into prepared pan. Bake in preheated oven until light golden, 10 to 15 minutes.

2. *Topping:* Sprinkle marshmallows evenly over hot crust. Return to oven and bake just until marshmallows begin to puff, 1 to 2 minutes. Let cool in pan on rack for 30 minutes.

3. In a large saucepan over low heat, combine brown sugar, syrup and peanut butter. Heat, stirring constantly, until smooth. Let cool for 5 minutes. Stir in cereal and peanuts. Mix well, then stir in candy. Spread evenly over marshmallows. Let cool completely before cutting into bars.

Variation
Colored marshmallows are a fun choice.

Caramel-Filled Brownies

There are many varieties of bars inspired by chocolate caramel candies, but this is one of our favorites (decided on after many taste comparisons!).

MAKES 20 TO 54 BARS OR 24 SQUARES (see Cutting Guide, page 10)

- **Preparation: 20 minutes**
- **Cooking: 5 minutes**
- **Baking: 35 minutes**
- **Freezing: excellent**

TIPS

The brownies may seem soft when you take them out of the oven, but they will firm up on cooling.

Chill caramels for easier unwrapping. It's still a frustrating job but easily forgotten when you taste these squares.

- **Preheat oven to 350°F (180°C)**
- **13- by 9-inch (3 L) cake pan, greased**

FILLING

1 lb	soft caramels, unwrapped (about 60)	500 g
½ cup	evaporated milk	125 mL

BASE & TOPPING

1	pkg (18.25 oz/515 g) devil's food cake mix	1
1 cup	chopped pecans	250 mL
½ cup	cold butter, cubed	125 mL
½ cup	evaporated milk	125 mL
1 cup	semi-sweet chocolate chips	250 mL

1. *Filling:* In a saucepan over low heat, combine caramels and evaporated milk. Heat, stirring constantly, until caramels are melted and mixture is smooth. Set aside. Keep warm while preparing batter.

2. *Base & Topping:* In a bowl, combine cake mix and pecans. Using a pastry blender, 2 knives or your fingers, cut in butter until mixture resembles coarse crumbs. Add evaporated milk and, using a wooden spoon, mix until well blended. (The batter will be thick.) Set half aside. Spread remaining batter in prepared pan. Bake in preheated oven until set, 12 to 15 minutes.

3. Sprinkle chocolate chips evenly over top. Drizzle caramel sauce evenly over chips. Spread carefully to cover base. Drop remaining batter by spoonfuls over caramel.

4. Return to oven and bake just until set, 15 to 20 minutes. Let cool completely in pan on rack. Cut into bars or squares.

Variation

Try using chocolate caramels. It doesn't look as attractive, but real chocoholics won't care.

Butterscotch Nut Bars

This versatile bar is also great cut into larger squares and served warm with ice cream for dessert.

MAKES 20 TO 54 BARS (see Cutting Guide, page 10)

- **Preparation: 20 minutes**
- **Baking: 50 minutes**
- **Freezing: excellent**

TIP

Store nuts in the freezer to keep them fresh.

- **Preheat oven to 350°F (180°C)**
- **13- by 9-inch (3 L) cake pan, greased**

CRUST

1	pkg (18.25 oz/515 g) white cake mix	1
⅔ cup	butter, melted	150 mL

TOPPING

4	eggs	4
1 cup	granulated sugar	250 mL
1 cup	corn syrup	250 mL
¼ cup	butter, melted	50 mL
1⅔ cups	butterscotch chips	400 mL
1½ cups	coarsely chopped pecans	375 mL

1. *Crust:* In a large bowl, combine cake mix and melted butter, mixing until well blended. Press evenly into prepared pan. Bake in preheated oven until light golden, about 15 minutes. Let cool on rack for 5 minutes before adding topping.

2. *Topping:* In a bowl, whisk eggs, sugar, syrup and melted butter until well blended. Stir in butterscotch chips and nuts. Pour evenly over crust.

3. Return to oven and bake until set and golden, 30 to 35 minutes. Let cool completely in pan on rack. Cut into bars.

Variation

Semi-sweet chocolate chips and walnuts are another good combination.

Cranberry White Chocolate Chip Bars

Creamy white chocolate, crunchy nuts and tart cranberries combine in this colorful, festive bar.

MAKES 20 TO 54 BARS (see Cutting Guide, page 10)

- **Preparation: 20 minutes**
- **Baking: 30 minutes**
- **Freezing: excellent**

TIPS

If you prefer, use a wooden spoon to mix the batter. If beating by hand, beat for about 3 minutes.

When baking, check for doneness at the minimum time recommended to avoid being disappointed with an overdone item. You can always bake it longer.

It's a good idea to keep a reliable oven thermometer in your oven to check on the temperature.

- **Preheat oven to 350°F (180°C)**
- **13- by 9-inch (3 L) cake pan, greased**

1	pkg (18.25 oz/515 g) white cake mix	1
¼ cup	packed brown sugar	50 mL
2	eggs	2
¼ cup	butter, softened	50 mL
¼ cup	water	50 mL
1 cup	dried cranberries	250 mL
1 cup	white chocolate chips	250 mL
1 cup	chopped almonds	250 mL
LEMON GLAZE, OPTIONAL		
2 cups	confectioner's (icing) sugar, sifted	500 mL
1 tbsp	butter, softened	15 mL
2 tsp	grated lemon zest	10 mL
2 to 4 tbsp	freshly squeezed lemon juice	25 to 60 mL

1. In a large bowl, using an electric mixer on low speed, beat cake mix, brown sugar, eggs, butter and water until smooth, about 1 minute. Stir in cranberries, chips and almonds. Spread batter evenly in prepared pan.

2. Bake in preheated oven until set and golden, 25 to 30 minutes. Let cool completely in pan on rack.

3. *Lemon Glaze (if using):* In a bowl, combine confectioner's sugar, butter, lemon zest and lemon juice. Using a wooden spoon, mix until blended, adding just enough juice to make a smooth, spreadable consistency. Cut into bars.

Variations

If you prefer, top this bar with Lemon Frosting (see recipe page 110).

Replace the almonds with pecans or walnuts and the cranberries with chopped dried apricots.

Chewy Cherry Bars

These bars make a colorful addition to a holiday cookie tray. You'll never go wrong with extras in the freezer.

MAKES 20 TO 54 BARS (see Cutting Guide, page 10)

- **Preparation: 25 minutes**
- **Baking: 45 minutes**
- **Freezing: excellent**

- **Preheat oven to 350°F (180°C)**
- **13- by 9-inch (3 L) cake pan, greased**

CRUST

1	pkg (18.25 oz/515 g) white cake mix	1
¾ cup	butter, softened	175 mL

FILLING

2	eggs	2
1 cup	packed brown sugar	250 mL
½ tsp	almond extract	2 mL
2 tbsp	all-purpose flour	25 mL
1 tsp	baking powder	5 mL
1 cup	sweetened flaked coconut	250 mL
1 cup	chopped drained maraschino cherries	250 mL
½ cup	chopped pecans or walnuts	125 mL

ALMOND FROSTING

¼ cup	butter, softened	50 mL
½ tsp	almond extract	2 mL
2 cups	confectioner's (icing) sugar, sifted	500 mL
3 to 4 tbsp	half-and-half (10%) cream	45 to 60 mL

1. *Crust:* In a large bowl, using an electric mixer on low speed, beat cake mix and butter until well blended. Press evenly into prepared pan. Bake in preheated oven until light golden, 12 to 15 minutes.

2. *Filling:* In a bowl, whisk eggs, brown sugar and almond extract until well blended. Whisk in flour and baking powder, mixing well. Stir in coconut, cherries and nuts. Spread evenly over warm crust.

3. Return to oven and bake until set and golden, 25 to 30 minutes. Let cool completely in pan on rack.

4. *Almond Frosting:* In a small bowl, using an electric mixer on medium speed, beat butter and almond extract until smooth. Gradually beat in confectioner's sugar and cream until smooth and creamy, adding more cream as necessary. Spread over cooled bars. Chill until frosting is firm, about 1 hour. Cut into bars.

Chocolate Caramel Pecan Crumble Bars

Easy to make and easy to eat! These bars are an excellent choice to keep on hand in the freezer.

MAKES 20 TO 54 BARS (see Cutting Guide, page 10)

- **Preparation: 20 minutes**
- **Cooking: 5 minutes**
- **Baking: 40 minutes**
- **Freezing: excellent**

TIP

Chill caramels to make unwrapping a little easier. Slit wrapper with a small sharp knife to start.

Break up any large lumps in crust mixture with your fingers.

- **Preheat oven to 350°F (180°C)**
- **13- by 9-inch (3 L) cake pan, greased**

CRUST

1	pkg (18.25 oz/515 g) devil's food cake mix	1
1 cup	chopped pecans	250 mL
¾ cup	quick-cooking rolled oats	175 mL
¾ cup	butter, melted	175 mL

TOPPING

1	can (10 oz/300 mL) sweetened condensed milk	1
8 oz	caramels, unwrapped (about 30)	250 g
¼ cup	butter	50 mL

1. *Crust:* In a large bowl, combine cake mix, pecans, oats and melted butter, mixing until well blended. Set aside 1⅓ cups (325 mL) for topping. Press remainder evenly into prepared pan. Bake in preheated oven until set, about 15 minutes.

2. *Topping:* In a heavy saucepan over low heat, combine sweetened condensed milk, caramels and butter. Heat, stirring constantly, until caramels are melted and mixture is smooth. Pour evenly over warm crust. Sprinkle reserved crust mixture evenly over top.

3. Return to oven and bake until topping is golden and bubbly, 20 to 25 minutes. Let cool completely in pan on rack. Cut into bars.

Variation

Use your favorite nut in place of the pecans. Walnuts, hazelnuts, cashews and almonds all work well.

Chocolate Raspberry Almond Oat Bars

The best of both worlds — healthy oats and decadent chocolate chips.

MAKES 20 TO 54 BARS (see Cutting Guide, page 10)

- **Preparation: 20 minutes**
- **Baking: 40 minutes**
- **Freezing: excellent**

TIPS

Stir jam to soften for easy spreading.

Leaving a ½-inch (1 cm) border when spreading jam over crust prevents the jam from sticking to the sides of pan.

Regular raspberry jam works fine, although the seedless has a more intense flavor.

- **Preheat oven to 375°F (190°C)**
- **13- by 9-inch (3 L) cake pan, greased**

1	pkg (18.25 oz/515 g) white cake mix	1
2½ cups	quick-cooking rolled oats	625 mL
1 cup	butter, melted	250 mL
1 cup	seedless raspberry jam	250 mL
1⅓ cups	semi-sweet chocolate chips	325 mL
¾ cup	chopped almonds or pecans	175 mL
	Confectioner's (icing) sugar, optional	

1. In a large bowl, combine cake mix, oats and melted butter. Mix until well blended. Press half (3 cups/750 mL) evenly into prepared pan. Set remainder aside. Spread jam evenly over unbaked crust, leaving a ½-inch (1 cm) border of crust. Sprinkle chocolate chips over jam. Stir almonds into remaining crumble mixture. Sprinkle evenly over chocolate chips.

2. Bake in preheated oven until golden, 35 to 40 minutes. Let cool completely in pan on rack. Cut into bars. Dust with confectioner's sugar before serving, if desired.

Variations

Replace raspberry jam with apricot. It's not as pretty but tastes good. Seedless strawberry jam is also great.

Lots of Lemon Squares

These squares have a hazelnut cookie base with a tart lemony topping. They make a refreshing complement to decadent chocolate delights.

MAKES 24 SQUARES (see Cutting Guide, page 10)

- **Preparation: 20 minutes**
- **Baking: 40 minutes**
- **Freezing: excellent**

TIP

Toast hazelnuts for the best flavor. There's no need to remove the skins. They add a wonderful nutty color and flavor.

- **Preheat oven to 350°F (180°C)**
- **13- by 9-inch (3 L) cake pan, greased**

CRUST

1	pkg (18.25 oz/515 g) lemon cake mix	1
½ cup	finely chopped hazelnuts	125 mL
½ cup	butter, melted	125 mL

TOPPING

4	eggs	4
2 cups	granulated sugar	500 mL
1 tsp	grated lemon zest	5 mL
⅓ cup	freshly squeezed lemon juice	75 mL
¼ cup	all-purpose flour	50 mL
1 tsp	baking powder	5 mL
	Confectioner's (icing) sugar, optional	

1. *Crust:* In a large bowl, combine cake mix, hazelnuts and melted butter. Mix until well blended. Press evenly into prepared pan. Bake in preheated oven until light golden, about 15 minutes.

2. *Topping:* In a bowl, whisk eggs, sugar and lemon zest and juice until blended. Whisk in flour and baking powder, mixing well. Pour evenly over hot crust.

3. Return to oven and bake until set and light golden, 20 to 25 minutes. Let cool completely in pan on rack. Dust with confectioner's sugar before serving, if desired. Cut into squares.

Variation

Replace hazelnuts with unblanched almonds.

Library and Archives Canada Cataloguing in Publication

Snider, Jill, 1947–
    Bars & squares : more than 200 recipes / Jill Snider.

Includes index.
ISBN-13: 978-0-7788-0147-4
ISBN-10: 0-7788-0147-0

1. Bars (Desserts). I. Title. II. Title: Bars and squares.

TX773.S64 2006   641.8'65   C2006-902496-0

Index